*The
Taxation
of Personal
Wealth*

The
Taxation
of Personal
Wealth

Alan A. Tait

HJ2619

 RELEASE

102048

UNIVERSITY OF ILLINOIS PRESS

Urbana · Chicago · London

1967

Preface

I must thank Trinity College, Dublin, for the year's leave of absence during which this book was written, and the University of Illinois which gave me the facilities to complete the work.

Professors J. Due, A. T. Peacock, and W. J. L. Ryan encouraged me to finish the book. The students of Dublin and Illinois, particularly M. Stephens and M. Stevens, helped by their questions and comments. My wife typed many drafts of the manuscript, and by her patience helped me through the many vicissitudes involved.

Alan A. Tait

Contents

Tables

Charts

1

Personal Wealth
and Its Present Distribution

Taxation is never popular. Taxation of wealth is for many the least popular of all taxes. Such a tax alters the very stuff of society: the family, death, and the historical continuity of houses, land, and all personal property. Wealth taxes alter the relations of groups and persons in the social hierarchy. Those who own land, those who have family businesses, those who buy stocks and shares, and those who own nothing, all have their relative positions altered by taxes on wealth. These taxes are a powerful engine for change. Excise taxation seems almost frivolous by comparison. Yet wealth taxes have not attracted as much comment as other forms of government revenue. This book is an attempt to redress part of that neglect.

The present inquiry attempts an appreciation of the criticism of and justification for the inequality of the distribution of personal wealth. It offers a formulation of the relationship between wealth and other taxed items. The questions the inquiry tries to answer are of the sort: Is the distribution of capital likely to be a continuing problem in developed countries? What forms of tax are possible in taxing wealth? Are other forms of government intervention likely to be more "efficient" than wealth taxation? What is the equitable relationship between taxed earned income, gifts, and taxed wealth? What exemptions should be allowed at present and in the future? At what rate should wealth be taxed? What would be the likely economic effects of taxing wealth in different ways? What would be the likely results of not taxing wealth? How can trusts be included in the taxation of wealth? What is the effect of inflation on wealth holders? What is likely to be the effect of automation on wealth holders?

In this first chapter the concept of wealth and its existing distribution in the United States and the United Kingdom is discussed, with some comments on the concept of "property." The reasons for this distribution of wealth and its justification are outlined in Chapter 2. At the beginning of Chapter 3 the main factors (including taxation) affecting the future distribution of wealth are listed, and the rest of the book discusses these in turn. The final chapter is a summary of the conclusions of each chapter and a comment on the problems of the political implementation of the tax proposals.

PERSONAL WEALTH

The word "wealth" is used in the title largely for sentimental reasons. This word has a fine eighteenth-century ring and carries echoes of Adam Smith but it can be a confusing term and our first task is to clear some of the undergrowth.

If we follow the rather rarified discussions in classical terms about wealth as "the material welfare of human beings considered both as a whole, and as individuals, and also in groups,"[1] these provide an unsatisfactory base for our discussion. Such definitions are too diffuse and involve many judgments which are difficult to quantify.

Alternatively, we could use the term "capital." Capital, without making it too difficult, can be considered in real terms as a stock of goods, or in money terms, held in cash or claims on assets which have an exchange money value. Thus, under one of the broader aspects of capital, the ownership by a man of his own physical and mental capabilities can be considered as a form of capital (very unequally distributed), which is quoted in money terms only by the cumulated sales of this asset over a lifetime. It would be possible to put a monetary assessment of the capital an individual owns, locked up in his physical and mental capabilities, at any given moment in his life, by discounting the probable future stream of rewards.

The word "asset," as used above, indicates ownership of capital or a claim on income valued as a credit, as opposed to a capital liability. It

---

[1] E. Cannan, *Wealth,* 2nd ed. (London: P. S. King and Son, 1924), p. 14.

is this concept of "ownership" which has resulted in the term "property." That is, property is wealth assets, the ownership of which is recognized by the legal code of the country.

The legal right to own property is one of those peculiarly unresolved basic questions which have troubled people at all times. The debate splits roughly into those who still look to the natural law concept of property as a revealed, intrinsic right, which man is born with, and the pragmatists who insist that property is a convenient creation of the state hallowed by tradition. The natural right outlook, that a man owned the products of his own labor, predated Locke by some 400 years. "The external goods of laymen . . . are acquired by individuals through their own manufacture, industry, and labour. And individuals as individuals have right, power, and true dominion. . . . And therefore neither prince nor Pope has the dominion or dispensation of such things."[2] Today, a theory of property founded on natural right is accepted only in two countries which, ironically, came to very different conclusions, the United States of America and the Union of Soviet Socialist Republics. The Constitution of the U.S.A. embodies many ideals of natural law, and "In America, the classical theory of natural right is so deeply embedded in popular thought that the spokesmen of big business sometimes repeat the familiar phrases although their manner of doing so often betrays that they are not aware of the contradictions between the classical doctrine and the institutions which they uphold."[3] The Soviet constitution also embodies the right of men to own, *collectively,* that for which they labor as a "natural right."

The alternative framework to the natural law concept of property is also of respectable ancestry. "Whence does each possess what he does possess? . . . By human right, that is, by right of emperors. How so? Because it is through the emperors and princes of this world that God hath distributed human rights to mankind."[4] And so through Hobbes, mixed with the appeals to tradition by Bacon, Montesquieu, and Burke; an outlook that regards property as a creation of the law, upheld by powerful rulers, but presumably open to change by those same rulers; an outlook epitomized by Marshall: "The tendency of careful economic study is to base the rights of property, not on any abstract principles, but on the observations that in the past they have been insepa-

---

[2] John of Paris, *De Potestate Regia et Papali* (ca. 1303), Chap. 7.

[3] R. Schlatter, *Private Property* (New Brunswick, N.J.: Rutgers University Press, 1951), p. 280.

[4] St. Augustine, *Homily VI*, 25, Migne, *Patrologiae Latinae*, Vol. XXXV, translated in *A Library of the Fathers* (Oxford: J. H. & J. Parker, 1848).

rable from solid progress; and therefore it is the part of responsible men
to proceed cautiously and tentatively in abrogating or modifying even
such rights as may seem to be inappropriate to the ideal conditions of
social life."[5] It is the latter concept of personal property that we refer
to in this discussion.

Clearly, in this sense, the ownership of wealth changes through time.
We can no longer claim, under the law, the ownership of other humans
nor, in some countries, the ownership of the air above our plot of
ground, or even sometimes, of the minerals beneath the soil. Also, there
have been extensions to property rights — copyright, patents, corporate
limited liability, and so on. With changing conditions there is a separation between the real capital and the claims recognized by law. It is
difficult to relate the equity shareholder to the steel rolling mill which
is the physical capital producing the income on which he has the claim,
because his claim is not on the capital, but on the income flow. The
valuation of his assets is based on the expectations of that flow continuing or not. Similarly, a beneficiary under a trust has claim to the income only, and here the asset valuation is difficult to determine because
there is no freedom to sell that claim and hence no exchange value.

Our use of the word wealth, defined for our particular convenience,
is taken to mean the ownership of assets (essentially claims) recognized
by the current legal code of the country. It is interchangeable with
property. It includes insurances, debts owed to persons by the government and others, and trust capital. It excludes, unless specified otherwise, the original capital of the human body and talents, and the training of that original human capital. It excludes corporate-held wealth
or state-owned property unless these are discussed specifically. The following is an examination of the distribution of personal wealth.

THE DISTRIBUTION OF PERSONAL WEALTH

We accept the existing estimates of wealth distribution. As is well
known, the system whereby these estimates are derived assumes that
the estates passing at death are a representative sample of the living
both in numbers and the value of the property. "The sampling errors
are largest where the estimates are based on small numbers of estates:
for example in the biggest estates and in the youngest age groups."[6]

---

[5] A. Marshall, *Principles of Economics,* 8th ed. (New York: Macmillan, 1950),
p. 48.
[6] U.K. *Report of Commissioners of Inland Revenue for Year Ended 31 March,
1964, 107th Report,* February, 1965, H.M.S.O., Cmd. 2573, p. 165.

TABLE 1:1
Percentage Share of Personal Wealth Owned by the Top 1 Per Cent of Adults[a]

Year	United Kingdom	United States
1922	—	31.6
1924-30	59.5	—
1929	—	36.3
1936	56.0	—
1939	—	30.6
1951-56	42.0	—
1956	—	26.0
1961	—	28.0

[a] Adults in the United States are defined as age 20 and over, in the United Kingdom as age 25 and over.
Sources: R. J. Lampman, *The Share of Top Wealth Holders in National Wealth 1922-56* (Princeton: National Bureau of Economic Research, 1962), p. 24, and Lydall and Tipping, "The Distribution of Personal Wealth in Britain," p. 92.

The biggest estates are open to error also because they are variable in types of property and in total size. Further, the totals do not represent average prices for the year, as deaths are bunched and favor prices in the first and fourth calendar quarters (i.e., the winter). Some capital is omitted (irrevocably settled property passing when a spouse dies) and some is included twice, if a gift inter vivos is charged to both donor and donee.[7] Apart from the technical limitations, the lack of data, the choice of suitable mortality rates, the guesses of distribution in the lower ranges of wealth ownership, there will be underestimation because of items such as life insurance. However, the deficiencies of techniques do not occur on a scale that discredits the broad validity of the distribution estimates,[8] nor is it likely that the factors leading to the underestimates will be such as to alter radically the distribution pattern — if anything, insurances, trusts, and removal of property abroad will only be used for avoidance on a substantial scale in large estates, thereby emphasizing the inequitable distribution. We take the existing inequality of wealth distribution estimates in Britain and the United States as given, and we do not attempt to amend them.

[7] For a critical explanation of this method see H. F. Lydall and D. G. Tipping, "The Distribution of Personal Wealth in Britain," *Bulletin of the Oxford University Institute of Statistics*, February, 1961, pp. 96-103.

[8] Note that we are talking here about total wealth estimates, not the estimates of different asset holdings, which *are* changed by allowances for age and sex of the owners. This will be discussed later.

Table 1:1 gives the estimates for a rough comparison of the United States and Britain. Clearly the inequality is much more marked in Britain. This comparison is clearest when Lorenz curves are used.

CHART 1:1
Lorenz Curves Showing Capital Distribution Among Adults in the U.S. 1953, and the U.K. 1954

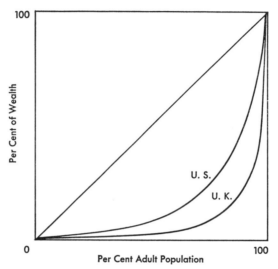

Sources: Lampman, Chap. 6; Lydall and Tipping, "The Distribution of Personal Wealth in Britain," pp. 83-104.

Such inequality in the ownership of wealth that gives to its owners freedom of pattern in consumption and the choice of undertaking unusual "hump" expenditures on education or health, bestows security and power on its possessors, and influences the pattern of saving and risk-taking, which is one of the mainsprings of economic growth, is the concern of everyone. The future of such inequality in our society is of concern to ourselves and our descendants. It is this inequality in the distribution of wealth that is our business in this book.

2

The Basis of the
Existing Distribution of Wealth

The criticisms of, and justifications for, the existing distribution of wealth can be divided into two broad categories: those based on socioeconomic and political grounds, and those which claim that wealth must be taxed to insure equity between taxpayers. I call the first the socioeconomic basis, and the second the equity basis.

THE SOCIOECONOMIC BASIS

Eight points of discussion will be itemized under this heading. These are presented as separate issues but clearly some of them are more minor than others, and not all of them are totally independent of each other. However, they are sufficiently distinct for each to make an individual point. Their common denominator is that each is valid given certain subjective postulates, but that economics cannot prove or disprove their validity. Each of them depends on a value judgment, some more reasonable than others.

1. Some writers will maintain that the laissez-faire market economy of the nineteenth century and the early part of the twentieth threw up great inequalities of income and wealth, and that as society has ceased to accept an unregulated system of laissez-faire as a reasonable way in

which to order the distribution of rewards, so society should cease to accept the inequalities of income and wealth which that now unacceptable system threw up.[1]

One proof that society has ceased to accept the laissez-faire distribution is that much of the historical growth of government activity can be presented as attempts to interfere with the private sector because the free market process was either not producing the goods and services society required, or was producing them inefficiently.

At best this is only a partial criticism. Not all the distributional inequities sprang from the industrial revolution. As is explained below, the roots of distribution run much deeper than that. At worst this argument does not really link the source and result; because society no longer accepts the full untrammeled operation of a laissez-faire society does not necessarily mean that society rejects the residual results of that mechanism. The objections could be to the current evils of the free market, the current poverty and unemployment; these can be ameliorated by altering the operations of the market and redistributing incomes and current flows of income and demand. There is nothing in this that necessarily condemns the inequality of past wealth created by the laissez-faire system.

Between the best and worst interpretations of this criticism of wealth inequality lies a reasonable statement, that much of society's repugnance to the completely uncontrolled operation of the laissez-faire market is attributable not only to the unequal incomes it created but also to the huge disparities in wealth accruing to very few and the provision of even minimum possessions for a comfortable life denied to the many. But not all these social evils resulted from pure laissez-faire.

2. As a gloss to the opinion outlined above it can be held that not only did the theoretical market laissez-faire throw up large inequalities of income and wealth, but the actual system which prevailed was an imperfect laissez-faire structure and one whose imperfections exacerbated the inequalities. Monopolies, imperfect knowledge, and restrictions on entry sometimes put producers in a position where they could earn large "rent" elements, and this increased the inequalities until they were greater than those which would have occurred under the pure laissez-faire structure. So, under this argument, not only did the laissez-faire market produce inequalities, but the fact that in its pure form it never existed made the inequalities worse.

3. With the existing inequality it can be held that relying only on the

---

[1] D. Jay, *Socialism in the New Society* (New York: Longmans, Green & Co., 1962), p. 11.

price mechanism does not adequately "weight" the needs of the poorer members of society. Their dollar has, to the market, the same purchasing power as the rich person's; the only weight attached to it is that of the larger number of poor people in society. Because of this the market mechanism produces goods to satisfy a rich demand when the factors involved in their production could be more "usefully" employed.

This involves a value judgment as to that which is "useful," or possibly, desirable. Most persons would agree with the Victorian approach to some minimum exemptions from income tax which would allow the poorest members of society the necessities of life, without any indulgences. It would be absurd today to accept a society that provided jewels to adorn the rich but no bread to feed the poor — although such societies have flourished in the past.

This is the argument that highly progressive taxation is justified to relieve poverty.[2] But the desirable relief of poverty does not in itself say anything about the payments to the poorer members of the community being financed by transfers of wealth from the rich. In terms of a growing economy, the raising of the lower incomes could be at the expense of reducing the pace of advance of the higher incomes while not reducing the absolute income or wealth of anyone. Although the removal of poverty is a valid base for the taxation of those who have and the transfer to those who have not, it does not necessarily involve any wealth transfer except insofar as additions to wealth may be slowed by the income taxation needed to finance the current transfers.

Once the subsistence base for transfers to the poor is left behind the route is uncharted. Some might claim that when the most glaring inequities are ameliorated a society as wealthy as the United States today, and one growing so quickly, can afford large inequalities in income and wealth. But poverty is essentially a very relative outlook. The poor of North America may be rich by the standards of Jamaica, and those in Jamaica affluent compared to the poor of Calcutta. Even in the richest economy in the world the relative position of the poorer members of society may remain the same, or as will be debated later, worsen. While they may have enough to eat, somewhere to live, and clothes to wear, they still may feel acutely their poverty relative to others in the society in which they happen to live. They are all the more likely to resent that poverty if they feel that the richer members of the society obtained their wealth in a way which is not open to everyone to emulate. Clearly, birth and inheritance are not easily copied. It may be held

---

[2] B. De Jouvenal, *Ethics of Re-distribution* (Cambridge: Cambridge University Press, 1951), p. 14.

that the government can take over the production of those goods and services which are not produced for the poor by the market (housing, sanitation, parks, etc.). But it should not redistribute income and wealth too drastically as this would seriously upset the market for some of the goods and services demanded by the rich, particularly those connected with "art" and "culture" which are of value for society (and posterity). Clive Bell[3] would maintain that it is only possible to have a civilized society where there are persons who have a measure of material security, referring to "the soul destroying dominion of work." Others maintain that work tires the body and blunts the intellect. Civilization requires a leisured class.

The basic position taken by those who maintain the need for a leisured class on grounds of culture (as opposed to saving, etc.) must be that if society is to have such a favored class then it should be chosen by some method other than the wasteful method used today — inheritance. "Inheritance has paved an easy road for those who have no talent and been brought to bear against those who have. With what one might have hoped was the permanent decline of militarism and superstition in the eighteenth century 'Age of Enlightenment,' it became the principal stronghold of privilege and the chief means for the shackling of the disinherited in the interest of a quite irrationally selected elite."[4] We see that society was and is rewarding many persons too lavishly when we compare their contribution to society to that of others. In this way a cost is imposed on society by the inefficient use of resources, indicating that some other method of allocation could be found. The age of the meritocracy creeps up decked with culture as well as efficiency. The exact form of the examination to select the meritocracy would be an interesting speculation; presumably it would have to balance the requirements of enterprise, managerial skills, academic ability, and sensitivity to the arts, qualities not always found together. This boils down to saying that if the richer members of society are to have their needs weighted more heavily than those of the poor then the advantages which wealth bestows — security, leisure, potential spending power (including the influence on art), social position, and income — are accepted more easily by society as a reward for effort rather than as a winnings in a birth lottery. In the past, people seemed to accept birth as sufficient criteria for all the privileges which

---

[3] C. Bell, *Civilization* (London: Chatto and Windus, 1928).

[4] F. D. Graham, *Social Goals and Economic Institutions* (Princeton: Princeton University Press, 1948), p. 134.

wealth confers, but this has been increasingly attacked and other requisites, particular talent or enterprise, are looked for.

4. The other side of the argument maintains that there is a wide degree of acceptance of the existing pattern of inequality. Neither the United States nor Britain is rising in rebellion against the inequities of society. In the United States there is an initial sympathy for the concept of equality, although the extension of this from equal voting rights and equal opportunity to equality of wealth is not readily made. Whereas in Britain, there is not only a widespread acceptance of inequality but even a form of inbred pride in it. The "proletarian snobbery" is exemplified by the English popular newspapers' "society page," which panders to the "tenderly wistful interest in the vacuous doings of the upper ten thousand."[5] Anyone who has lectured to British undergraduates on the public finance aspects of the redistribution of income and wealth will recognize the Tawney taunt that "in England the instinctive feeling [to the concept of economic equality] is one, not of sympathy, but of apprehension and repulsion, as though economic equality were a matter upon which it were not good taste to touch."[6]

But there is an ambivalent quality to this acceptance; resentment is felt by some parts of society, and sometimes unfounded superiority exhibited by other parts, and these consume much time and energy in striking attitudes which would be unnecessary in a society that did not have wide differentials of income and wealth. It would be difficult to deny that there is a real loss to the British economy through the dichotomy of many management-worker relationships, based on different backgrounds and class. The labor unions' feeling that "they or them" are set apart in a closed and unattainable world is continuously emerging as a basic grudge in management-labor relations. How far this is built-in in any capitalist economy is difficult to judge (it is not so evident in the United States[7]), but much of the particular bitterness of British labor problems seems to be based on class distinctions, which in their turn are based on the large inequalities of income and wealth and the educational opportunities that these provide.

---

[5] These quotations are from R. H. Tawney, *Equality* (4th ed.; London: Allen and Unwin, 1964), p. 17, where he comments on the "Religion of Inequality."

[6] *Ibid.*, p. 29.

[7] Although, as long ago as 1915 the Industrial Relations Commission research director maintained that one major cause of unrest among industrial workers in the United States was the unjust distribution of income and wealth. See *U.S. Commission on Industrial Relations Final Report and Testimony*, Senate Doc. 415, 64th Cong., 1st Sess., 1916, 1:30-35.

The balance of inherent acceptance and latent unacceptance of the existing distribution of wealth could be held as reflected in the actual extent of redistributive mechanism operating. The forces cancel each other out, but the more active nature of the protest as compared to the acceptance produces some continuing net gain to those who look for more equality.

This point does not tackle the basic question whether the existing inequality is "unfair" or "undesirable." It answers such questions by saying that society's apparent acceptance of a slow change in the existing distribution is the expression of communal desires and therefore, in the context of this society at this time, the existing distribution is not unfair or desirable.

5. To counteract the approach outlined in point 4 above, some attempt can be made to comment on the inequality of wealth distribution in a more objective sense — although still relying on subjective evaluations of what is "desirable." Equality of incomes and wealth could be justified as a means of insuring a high consumption demand, higher income, and greater employment. A matching policy in inflationary periods would be to encourage greater inequality to restrict consumption. Therefore, the argument to justify permanent equality would have to assume a condition of continuing unemployment, or the very unique condition of demand, saving, and investment at equality of income and wealth being just the amounts necessary to guarantee full employment. If this indicates anything about inequality of wealth at all, it only argues for less inequality in conditions of unemployment; it says nothing about total equality.

6. The older idea used to be that economics pointed towards the equalizing of incomes and wealth because of the declining average and marginal utilities of income and wealth. "The more any society approximates to equality in the distribution of wealth among its members, the greater as the whole is the aggregate of satisfactions which the society in question derives from the wealth that it possesses,"[8] other things (e.g., total GNP and population) remaining equal. This assumes that it is acceptable to extend the concept of diminishing marginal utility to income; indeed, it can be claimed that this presentation of income utility was created to justify equality. "In short, the utility argument is a sophisticated version of the direct demand for equality."[9]

[8] H. Sidgwick, *Principles of Political Economy* (3rd ed.; New York: Macmillan, 1901), p. 1111.
[9] G. J. Stigler, *Five Lectures on Economic Problems* (New York: Macmillan, 1950), p. 6.

Even if the idea of diminishing marginal utility of income were not a convenient justification for equality of incomes, it is still a concept which requires interpersonal comparisons of utility, and does not take account of the intensity of satisfactions. This simple use of the diminishing marginal utility of income is not acceptable as a justification for equality of incomes, or equality of wealth.

Even if meaningful measures of "income" between individuals owning different nonmonetary income–yielding assets, living in different environments with different prices, and producing and consuming different quantities of nonmarketed goods and services, even if all these differing ingredients of income were reconcilable into one glorious, intertemporal income, no modern writer — much less politician — would plump for complete equality of income or wealth as a goal.[10]

Most modern writers accept the need for different remunerations for work and enterprise[11] and even for the accumulation of private fortunes out of current earnings; the mainspring of action is dissatisfaction with the existing distribution of wealth. The question "how far towards equality of incomes do we wish to go?" is neither "sensible" nor "pertinent"; no such ideal society exists and it is a "vulgar fallacy" to imagine that one could.[12]

This should not prevent us from asking whether there is not still some merit in the question "how far towards equality should incomes be brought?" So long as the proponents of the inequality argument cannot reasonably maintain that the total marginal spending of the "rich" provides more satisfaction than would the same marginal spending by the "poor" there would be a case for greater equality of incomes. When this line becomes fuzzy, when the distinction between rich and poor is indistinct, when there is genuine difficulty in maintaining the broad generality of the hedonistic approach, then the remaining inequality might be acceptable. There is a simple criticism that taking all the income and wealth of the richer members of society, and distributing it to the poorer members, would not be worth a farthing in additional income or wealth to the poor, so thinly spread would be the

---

[10] It is interesting to note that if individuals are assumed to have freedom of investment in education, and their rewards to vary directly with the length of training, then even perfect equality of ability and opportunity (in the sense of choice of education) "implies neither income equality or symmetry in the income distribution." J. Mincer, "Investment in Human Capital and Personal Income Distribution," *Journal of Political Economy*, August, 1958, p. 302.

[11] C. A. R. Crosland, *The Future of Socialism* (London: Cape, 1956), p. 210; or Jay, pp. 328-329.

[12] Crosland, pp. 215-216.

flecks of gold over the grains of sand. This, in most countries, is true. It is not a valid base for inaction. On Benthamite grounds it could be held that the satisfaction of the poorer members of the community at the diminution of the differential between rich and poor would amply compensate for the dissatisfaction of the richer members at their reduction of income and wealth. But the proponents of this argument[13] are knocking down straw men of their own creation. The argument is one not about absolute equality of incomes, but about reductions in existing inequalities to some point where there is genuine widespread doubt about further movements towards equality. Such doubts will emerge when the lower income and wealth groups feel that they themselves, or their children, have a real chance to enter the rich class.

In other words, the doubt about further changes in incomes and wealth towards equality will be a *function of the reasonable aspirations of society*. The incentive of income and wealth can only be used as a justification for inequality if all persons feel that there is some not too remote chance of attaining the higher rewards. As long as the differentials are too great such aspirations cannot be sufficiently widespread and society will continue to vote for less equality. The more reasonable such expectations, the more likely it is that society will vote for retaining the existing inequality. Those who start a race with a huge handicap have little incentive to win; the reduction of the handicap increases the smell of the hay of success and what was beyond the dreams of the poorer members of society becomes a possibility.

When we say that the members of society will "vote" for more or less equality of income we are verging on the thin ice of social choice determination. Our presentation is close to saying that voting may be taken as an interpersonal measure of preference intensity. So that it is reasonable to prefer x to y:

$$U(x) - c(v) > U(y)$$

when U is the utility attached to a social state and $c(v)$ is the disutility of voting.[14] This is equivalent to

$$U(x) - U(y) > c(v)$$

and can be criticized by saying that the extent of the utility difference is not stated, only that it is greater than the disutility of voting. On the other hand if we are interested only in political choice translated into

[13] De Jouvenal, Appendix.

[14] K. J. Arrow, *Social Choice and Individual Values* (2nd ed.; New York: Wiley, 1963), p. 113.

action then the extent of the difference is not of primary importance. If the distinctions between the alternative social states are sufficiently discreet then the small change can be implemented and another vote taken on a further move in the same direction from x to w, preferring w to x. These small movements also have the "second best" advantage of insuring that society, by proceeding in small jumps, does not miss the optimal solution.

Another criticism of using voting as an interpersonal measure of preference intensity could be that the disutility of voting between individuals would differ. True, but such differences are probably a small element compared both to the total disutility and the total utility involved in the social choice. The voting process is further complicated with particular reference to decisions to redistribute income and wealth, because these decisions are often of the nature "[Since] I am richer than you, I may find it easy to make the judgment that it is better for you to have the marginal dollar than for me."[15] This "extended sympathy" argument is a difficult base on which to construct a theory of social choice.[16] Nevertheless, such social choices are made. Societies do have progressive taxation and some redistributive aims. The closest approximation to reality is, I think, that which treats voting as a measure of interpersonal intensity, unsatisfactory as this may be. The extent to which this redistribution will be carried is in some way a function of the reasonable aspirations of society.

The redistribution of income (defined in the narrow sense of wages, salaries, and monetary income from assets) by progressive income tax and transfers is in itself partially defeating this goal of reasonable aspirations. As income rises so does income taxation, more than proportionally, and the possibility of achieving the wealth ownership which will confer security and nonmonetary income is made increasingly difficult by the increasingly progressive taxation. A citizen of the United States or Britain who is well endowed mentally, who has a reasonable chance to make a success of his career, will find it difficult to gain the fortune of the Duke of Devonshire or the Rockefellers. High taxation of current money income makes the charmed circle of the already rich that much more charmed, because admittance to the circle becomes increasingly less attainable.

Redistribution by income taxation and transfer is self-defeating in that it fossilizes the existing inequalities of wealth. So we are forced to look to the taxation of wealth itself.

---

[15] *Ibid.*, p. 114.
[16] *Ibid.*, p. 115.

There is one fundamental criticism to all the discussion above: that the effect of heavy progressive taxation on income and/or wealth would have unfortunate effects on the incentives to work, save, and take risks. To introduce the overall far-reaching questions of the effects of taxation at this juncture would unbalance the socioeconomic arguments. This point is considered later and in detail in Chapter 15.

7. Another social-political factor looks to the high taxation of wealth not simply to correct past inequities, but to achieve public ownership of the means of production. "There is no form of socialism more desirable than the ownership of land, factories and houses, and so of rent, by the state. And the enforcement of really effective inheritance taxation, payable in land and real property, as well as securities and cash, is the most practicable and equitable way to achieve it."[17] It has been pointed out that "What matters when we are concerned with public versus private ownership is how the ratio public net saving/public net wealth develops in relation to private net saving/private net wealth."[18] This is certainly the important ratio when considering *new* wealth in society, but the socialists, as mentioned above, are interested primarily in the wealth which resulted from the misallocation of a past system, and it is this *existing* wealth which they wish to change. To that end high property taxes are important rather than just the rate of growth of the ratio of net public and private saving.

8. The socio-political reasons for taxing wealth discussed above cannot be proved or disproved by using economics. They depend on the acceptance of various social attitudes and opinions. There remains one further presentation of the argument for greater equality of wealth and for taxation to achieve that end, which is logical given its premises.

The initial premise is that the title to private property rests in the guarantee that a person can enjoy the rewards of his work and saving. "The essential principle of property being to assure to all persons what they have produced by their labour and accumulated by their abstinence."[19] As all those assets which the economist groups under "land" were not created by either the labor or abstinence of man, the institution of property has, by recognizing ownership of these assets, made a

[17] Jay, p. 181; also his *The Socialist Case* (London: Faber and Faber, 1946), p. 224; or H. Morrison, *Socialization and Transport* (London: Constable, 1933), p. 247.

[18] B. Hansen, "Aspects of Property Taxation," *Travaux de l'Institut International de Finances Publiques,* 1962, p. 21.

[19] J. S. Mill, *Principles of Political Economy* (London: Longmans, Green, Reader, and Dyer, 1875), p. 140.

false start in defining property — an unfortunate beginning from which society has never recovered. "They have made property of things which never ought to be property and absolute property where only a qualified property ought to exist."[20] Not only has this created a property ownership where there should be no property ownership, it has established an inequitable base for the distribution of property on a basis which is no longer acceptable.

Existing distribution is the outcome of historical accident, immured in time and fossilized by law. It is necessary to clear this point, that the original distribution of property, often on some basis no longer socially acceptable (rule of force, exploitation of child labor, etc.), is legalized and transmuted through generations by the power of the law.

The extent of the inequality of distribution and the consequent gravity of the problem depends, in each country, on the historical features of that country's growth. In Britain, where an ordered, legally conscious, ancient system of property holding has continued for many generations, where these wealth holdings are based on an aristocratic structure, itself rewarded for its conquering ability or by kingly dispensations; where superimposed on this base an industrial revolution created vast quantities of wealth which were distributed either on the land-owning basis of the aristocracy (the coal owners), or through the laissez-faire market structure, where capital owners (in the conventional sense, not looking upon working power as a lifetime capital) had large rewards and labor smaller rewards: where all these forces act it is not surprising that the distribution of capital should be so remarkably unequal.

In France, where property ownership was deranged by the revolution at the end of the eighteenth century and where the historical forces have not been able to act uninterrupted for a continuous period of a length approaching the British example, it would not be surprising if the distribution of property ownership were less unequal than in Britain. In a new country like the United States of America, where the allocation of land and minerals has been completed only within the last century, and where an original aristocratic structure is lacking, the distribution of property is not so unequal as that in Britain. This relative equality exists despite a most untrammeled industrial expansion with great inequalities in the rewards to labor and capital.

It is likely that in most developed countries highly unequal capital distribution will exist. The extent of this inequality will depend on the type of historical accidents outlined above. When a country is younger

---

[20] *Ibid.,* Book, II, Chap. 1, Sect. 5, p. 255.

in terms of legally recognized property ownership it does not necessarily mean that the distribution of property will be more equal. The force of arms which won a sheik the right to water in the midst of sandy continents might have been exercised only a hundred years ago, but the oil revenues accrue to him today and result in startling inequalities of income and wealth.

Although the unequal distribution of "land" by now unacceptable actions is the primary inequality following from the initial premise that the title to private property lay in the right of an individual to enjoy the fruits of his labor and abstinence, it is not the only inequity. For as this statement does not say that the title to property also rests in the right to enjoy the fruits of someone else's (the forefathers) labor and saving, the conclusion is that only current earning and saving are the completely justifiable title to property. The law by codifying and guaranteeing the successive rights of generations to inherit the fortunes of previous generations piles inequity on inequity. Yet the difficulty of this state is recognized: "naturally speaking, the instant a man ceases to be, he ceases to have any dominion: else if he had a right to dispose of his acquisitions one moment beyond his life, he would also have a right to direct their disposal for a million of ages after him; which would be highly absurd and inconvenient."[21] Inconvenient it certainly is, and one of the major inconveniences is the highly unequal distribution of wealth which results.

We have come a long way from the original premise that a man's title to property rested in the guarantee to enjoy the rewards of his work and saving. If this is accepted the argument above follows. But, of course, it is perfectly possible to deny this definition of the title to property. It could be held that the right to property lay in possession (finders keepers) and then in bequest. But this appears a more shaky foundation than the previous one. To accept simple possession as a base for the legal right to property is to accept the jungle code of victory to the strong, or possibly the cunning. In some "natural-law" origin it could be argued that the rational apportionment of property (essentially land) would be to compensate those less generously physically endowed by nature with more of the natural provisions; so that the weaker would be compensated with property rather than the strong. The whole present basis of possession seems less convincing in discussion than the rights to the fruits of labor.

In many ways this "natural title" appears the strongest argument for

---

[21] Sir William Blackstone, *Commentaries on the Laws of England* (3rd ed.; Oxford: Clarendon Press, 1768), Book II, Chap. I, pp. 10 and 12.

taxation to intervene in the existing distribution of wealth. Certainly, of the socioeconomic arguments it is the strongest. It implies not equality of income and wealth, but a distribution resting largely on the earnings of each generation. As it is impossible to return to a state of nature and start reapportioning land, the present inequitable distribution of property must be accepted but taxed very heavily until eventually inherited property disappears. The right to own land will then be only temporary, bought by current effort and savings and relinquished at death.

Note that of all the eight arguments presented as socioeconomic bases for taxing wealth and altering its present distribution, none can be *proved* by economics. If you have a preconceived idea of what would be a desirable economic state (full employment, or means of production communally owned) then economics will indicate that redistribution of wealth would help to achieve it. But in itself, none of the economic reasoning *proves* anything about redistribution. It does show that there are a number of situations where contemporary thought indicates that redistribution might be undertaken. We might recognize that wealth and its advantages are more easily accepted as rewards for work and saving; or that redistribution of wealth might reduce the burden of taxation on currently earned income making it more likely that people could aspire, with reason, to the upper brackets of wealth ownership. Or that much of the present distribution of wealth could be considered accidental, and much based on origins no longer socially acceptable. All these can be presented as a reasonable contemporary basis for redistribution. They cannot be proved. Our appreciation of them may change. They are a child of current social feeling, they could be different in a hundred years' time; but what they aim to change is not something that can be easily rectified once changed. Redistribution should not be undertaken lightly. The conviction based on socioeconomic grounds should be widespread before action implements ideas.

EQUITY BASIS

The second broad category of arguments for taxing wealth arises principally as a consequence of taxing any form of income. Because income is derived both from work and wealth the relationship between the two sources and their relative taxes has been confused, particularly in tax legislation. We will argue that to tax only some forms of income and ignore other forms is inequitable; therefore equity forces us to consider the taxation of wealth. It does not require us to redistribute the existing wealth. There are two parts to the problem: the income which wealth yields, and because taxation of this does not always satisfy the equity of the tax structure, the taxation of wealth itself.

We can argue that equity requires individuals in similar circumstances to be treated in the same way (the problem is to define the similar circumstances), and that those in unlike circumstances should be "weighted" and taxed accordingly (the problem is the assessment of the differences). It is then usual to say that personal income provides the best basis for comparison of circumstances (wealth differences are reflected largely in income) and that "costs" or "expenses" are best set off against income to allow for differing circumstances. The result is the recommendation to place primary reliance on income tax.[22] If we accept this system, then, in the extreme form, wealth income is only taxed when it accrues to the individual. This means that corporate income is excluded. But even this drastic simplification does not result in an equitable tax base, for if wealth income does not change but the capital value of wealth does rise, then the wealth-income tax yield is smaller than it would be if capital gains were included in the definition of wealth income. Even if these capital gains were included as income they would only enter the income flow when realized, so that there is the whole problem of irregularity and averaging over time, etc. In any case, this tax base still has the defect of not including all forms of wealth, e.g., non–income-yielding assets. To complete the tax base, an imputed income would have to be included. Insofar as these non–income-yielding assets are not included then the rate of tax, in order to yield a given revenue, must be higher.

Generally it can be held that income, usually narrowly defined, is not the only measure of comparative circumstances. Satisfaction is obtained from both the flow of income and the stock of wealth.[23] The stock of wealth, it is true, yields a current flow of satisfaction, but some of this is difficult to quantify (security, power, etc.), and some, although measurable, is administratively difficult to deal with on an annual basis

[22] H. C. Simons, *Personal Income Taxation* (Chicago: University of Chicago Press, 1938), Chap. 10.

[23] If we rule out any possibilities of interpersonal comparisons, that is we say that society cannot or *should* not make such comparisons, we can say that the balance of income (and wealth) should be struck where "the marginal social rate of income transferability (between individuals) should be equal to the ratio of the marginal utilities." R. H. Strotz, "How Income Ought to be Distributed: A Paradox in Distributive Ethics," *Journal of Political Economy*, June, 1958, p. 203.

(capital gains). The taxation of some forms of incomes, particularly the conventional ones of wages and salaries, makes it desirable to extend the tax base to include all forms of income, and this will include wealth either directly as a stock or converted into a flow of yields or satisfactions.

SUMMARY

If the eight social-political criteria are accepted, then we must consider not only the taxation of wealth, but the redistribution of existing wealth. On the other hand the equity criterion says little about redistribution; it accepts the given distribution of wealth and discusses equitable treatment within that context. It cannot be proved by economics that wealth should be redistributed. It ought to be taxed if incomes are taxed. The difficulties of fixing the appropriate rates would be eased if the distribution were less unequal than it is. Though economics cannot prove that wealth should be redistributed, some of the socioeconomic criteria discussed above made a strong plea for it on current social grounds.

3

The Future Distribution of Wealth:
Factor Payments

The previous chapters have shown that the distribution of wealth in most countries is likely to be very unequal, and that there are some reasonable criticisms of such inequality. The next question is: Should wealth taxes be used to ameliorate some of this inequality? This is not the only, or even the major, reason for having taxes on wealth. As will be shown later, the principal justification for having wealth taxes is to insure equity throughout the tax structure. But as wealth taxation is also an important means of taxing the *stock* of wealth it is interesting to ask whether this unequally distributed stock will grow more unequal or less? If the circumstances of growth are such that this existing inequality will cease to matter in the long run then using wealth taxes to alter this inequality can be held to be unimportant, although inclusion of wealth as part of the tax base will still require the use of taxes on wealth. It is to this future distribution that we turn now.

CHANGES IN PERSONAL WEALTH

The future distribution of wealth is determined by:
(i) the existing distribution of wealth which yields an income to its owner, reinforcing the inequity (see Chapter 1);

 (ii) the future flow of factor payments (see Chapter 3) ;
(iii) differential changes in savings rates (see Chaper 4) ;
 (iv) differential asset price changes (see Chapter 4) ;
  (v) changes in the structure of wealth taxation (see Chapters 5-12) ;
 (vi) changes in the structure of income taxation (see Chapters 12-
       13) ;
(vii) changes in the legal code (see Chapter 14) ; and
(viii) demographic factors (see Chapter 14).

Demographic changes seem almost beyond the bounds of public finance, but like changes in the legal code they affect the distribution of wealth, and will be considered later. Numbers (v), (vi), and (vii) are interrelated in that changes in the legal code could alter the liability to income or wealth taxes. The existing distribution of wealth we have noted already. The future flow of factor payments is the influence which we will consider in this chapter.

FACTOR PAYMENTS: AN AUTOMATIC SOLUTION

It has been maintained that in advanced societies as the nation becomes richer (with full employment) the propensity to save increases, capital accumulates, the marginal efficiency of capital falls to zero, and the rate of interest follows suit; the rentier succumbs to his easy death, the income from capital is eliminated, and with this vanish many, though not all, of the invidious aspects of the inequalities of wealth distribution.[1] So we might look forward to an advanced society solution to inequality. But accumulation does not necessarily lead to a declining rate of interest, for it is likely that new ideas, new outlets, and new inventions continue to offer themselves, thereby creating new wants to be satisfied. Only in a static, noninnovating, advanced society could the above conclusions follow from the accumulation of capital. Or we could assume that capital accumulation takes place more quickly than technical advances increase the return on marginal investment; for this there is no empirical evidence.[2] Moreover, the short run analysis cannot be applied to the likely long run implications of changing incomes on the consumption function. The consumption function can be changed even if innovation does not occur; society can reappraise its desires, or the state may either change the desires of society or lessen the

---

[1] Note many of the assets still have a "rent" element, see below.

[2] H. Smith, "The Economics of Socialism Reconsidered," *Economic Journal,* September, 1955, p. 419.

savings motive (through guaranteeing health insurance, pensions, education, etc.).

Although it is unlikely that interest on capital would decline in an advanced society it is even more improbable that rent would vanish. Even if we accept the decline of the rate of interest, as it moves downwards the value of real, fixed property (e.g., land) rises and hence rent is high.

In fact, the only way in which the social millennium can result following this line of thought is by the marginal productivity of capital falling to zero, *and* the marginal disutility of labor falling to zero.

We must accept that all these contingencies are far removed from our lifetime, and the problems of the distribution and importance of wealth remain.

ALTERNATIVE DISTRIBUTION THEORIES

From Ricardo onwards economists have concerned themselves with the problems of isolating those forces which determine the shares of the factors of production. Originally rent considered as the surplus over marginal yield, and wages determined by the living standard of the working classes, left a residual which was profits. But wages in developed countries have not declined to subsistence levels, indeed the evidence suggests that the share of labor has been, and continues as, a fairly constant share of national income.

The empirical studies suggest[3] that the share of wages has been steady since 1880 in the United Kingdom and since 1909 in the United States (earlier estimates are not available), and that cyclically labor's share has not fluctuated violently.

The possible explanations of this have been divided primarily between the marginalists and the macroeconomic approach. The marginalist viewpoint, best represented by Hicks,[4] indicates that change in the distribution of national income following upon changes in the supply of different factors depends on the elasticity of substitution of that factor which is changing.[5] This "neo-classical" viewpoint has been furthered by the controversial writings of Samuelson, Solow, and Robinson (J.),[6] which, very broadly, try to use marginal productivities or marginal substitution ratios as determinants of wages and profits.

---

[3] A. L. Bowley, *Wages and Income in the United Kingdom Since 1860* (Cambridge: Cambridge University Press, 1937), espec. Table XV, p. 99.

[4] J. R. Hicks, *Theory of Wages* (New York: St. Martins Press, 1963).

[5] *Ibid.*, pp. 115-117.

[6] See particularly a symposium on production functions and economic growth in the *Review of Economic Studies*, Vol. XXIX, No. 80 (3), June, 1962.

Unfortunately, we cannot view the demand and supply functions as separate. Macroeconomics asks us to accept that the demand schedules are not independent of the prices paid to factors: aggregate demand determines employment and incomes; the distribution of these incomes, in turn, influences the level and structure of aggregate demand. Consequently, we have attempts to replace the marginalist analysis by a macroeconomic approach, and the best known of these are those of Kalecki[7] and the more recent, and equally well-known, work of Kaldor.[8] The Kaldor model is contrasted to the Ricardian/Marxian viewpoint in that wages are a residual and profits are determined by the propensity to invest and the capitalist propensity to consume (if savings from wages are zero). The size of workers' savings reduces total profits, but total profits will still change by an amount greater than a change in investment.[9] In the Ricardian model profits would be the residual.

In the Kalecki approach pivotal positions are ascribed to monopoly elements and raw material prices. An increase in monopoly reduces the wages share of the national income because it raises prices relative to wages and hence increases aggregate turnover relative to wages. An increase in raw material costs will also reduce labor's relative share.

Kalecki explains the relative stability of labor's share by those considerations. In 1880-1913, for instance, the relation of wages and raw material prices did not change and hence stability of labor's share can be explained by the lack of change in the degree of monopoly. Of course, as this is difficult to measure, it is convenient to use the "residual" approach; if the solution remains constant and one of the two determinants is constant then the other determinant must also be constant. During the period 1913-35, the rise in the degree of monopoly is countered by a fall in the price of raw materials. The cyclical stability of labor's share is explained by the compensating movements of these forces; the increasing monopoly in the downswing of the cycle is offset by reduced raw material costs. In the upswing monopoly is reduced and raw material costs increase.

This approach can be criticized on a number of grounds. There is no empirical evidence of a basic assumption that short-term marginal costs are constant and that long-term considerations as well as short-

[7] M. Kalecki, *Essays in the Theory of Economic Fluctuations* (London: Allen and Unwin, 1939), Chap. 1, and *The Theory of Dynamic Economics* (New York: Rinehart, 1954), Part I.

[8] See N. Kaldor, "Alternative Theories of Distribution," *Review of Economic Studies,* Vol. XXIII, 1955-56, p. 83.

[9] *Ibid.,* p. 96.

term marginal costs are relevant for pricing policy,[10] but the principal difficulty is in the danger of aggregation. Is it legitimate to "average out" degrees of monopoly for the whole economy? When the individual industries are examined does the analysis continue to hold good?

Dunlop[11] maintains that attention must be paid to the industries which go to make up the aggregate. He argues that two counteracting forces are the rate of return to labor and the changing importance of industries. Those industries which decreased most in importance during a depression (mining, railways, construction) had a high labor share which increased during the depression; thus the decreased importance of industries in which the share of labor increases most rapidly during a depression, tends to make for a relatively stable share in the whole economy.

This leads Dunlop to concentrate on the individual firms and on influences such as:

(i)   the size and direction of technical change;
(ii) the elasticity of demand for the product;
(iii) the shape of the short run labor cost function;
(iv) movements of the relative prices of factors of production and substitutability between them.

Obviously, (ii) and (iv) are similar to the forces of monopoly and raw material price changes that Kalecki isolated.

Still, at the individual firm level it has been suggested that the wage share will decrease as firms increase in size.[12] As a firm grows, value added increases more than proportionally due to the economies of large scale production; wages advance but value per man increases faster due to economies of scale. This assertion is of great importance because, as will be argued later, forces in the growth of national income are of a nature which tends to increase the value added not only proportionately but absolutely, compared to the aggregate reward to labor. Steindel, in support of his thesis, examines eighty industries and finds that in fifty-eight labor's share declines as the size of the firm increases, in fourteen the opposite is true, and in eight there is no clear-cut answer. A rationalization of his argument is that economies of scale enjoyed by the larger firm require large amounts of capital, and as capital, on this

---

[10] W. W. Rostow, *The British Economy of the Nineteenth Century* (Oxford: Clarendon Press, 1948), Appendix.

[11] J. T. Dunlop, *Wage Determination Under Trade Unions* (New York: A. M. Kelly, 1950).

[12] J. Steindel, *Maturity and Stagnation in American Capitalism* (Oxford: Blackwell, 1952), pp. 24-40.

scale, is difficult for the small firm to raise, there is a restriction on freedom of entry and large producers earn a "surplus" above "normal" profits. In other words, the monopoly element enables capital to earn more than wages, an argument similar to that of Kalecki and Dunlop.

Generally, the degree of monopoly in the system is important and, by implication in a growth context, so are the forces making for the increase or decrease of monopoly elements. These forces are:

(i) Economies of scale and consequent difficulty for new entrants, which increase value added and which work against the lessening of inequality. This makes it more likely that the flow of factor incomes will accrue increasingly to capital.

(ii) Straightforward monopoly legislation will tend to curb the power of producers and, if anything, this form of government intervention is likely to increase rather than decrease; and the forms which it takes could become more complex and subtle, e.g., the U.S. government use of stockpiles to prevent industry-wide price increases could be represented as a use of almost monopoly power to combat monopoly power. On the other hand monopoly legislation could be used to curb the power of trade unions and this could diminish the effectiveness of unions in appropriating their "share."

(iii) The efforts of trade unions to "appropriate" or to improve on their share of the cake will obviously affect the future distribution of income and wealth. The success of such maneuvers apart from government legislation mentioned above will depend on the future relative bargaining positions of management and labor, and could be represented in four cases:

(a) if there is an active trade union force and a buyers' market (i.e., it is difficult to sell finished goods) this will tend to squeeze profits and increase the share of wages; this is often represented as the case in very "open" economies that are trying to improve their balance of payments.

(b) an active trade union and a sellers' market will result in management giving in to wage demands fairly easily to retain their labor and maintain production. Whether this increases the wages share depends on the movement of relative prices;[13]

---

[13] In a growing economy this makes a trade union job easier; Walter Reuther said, "We will never question whether we want a big or a little pie of national *wealth* to divide, or deviate from our conviction that the big pie is always the easiest to split." *The Challenge of Automation* (Washington, D.C.: Public Affairs Press, 1955), p. 9.

(c) a weak trade union structure and a sellers' market is likely to reduce the wages share;

(d) a weak union and a buyers' market is certain to reduce the wages share.

A new force, the full implications of which do not seem to have been realized, is the movement toward government-sponsored policies to achieve economic goals. National growth plans tend to "allocate" factor shares. There is a temptation in assessing potential national growth rates for demand and the consequent pressure on resources, for the planning agency to allocate increases in private and government expenditures, and these projections become goals against which the actual performance of the economy is measured. Thus the reasoning behind the allocation can determine the actual division and can lead to government action to insure that the allocated figures are met. To the extent that the government tries to play safe and maintain the existing division this could fossilize the distribution, but to the extent that a government, either from conviction or in an effort to attain trade union compliance with its plans, decides to alter the existing distribution, this could be a considerable force in lessening inequality.

The fact that the market is usurped as the agent for allocating broad factor shares strengthens the position of those who claim that the basis for the distribution of income and wealth should be something other than the accident of history, birth, or family. Planning should replace luck in distributing factor shares if planning is accepted for growth.

The second principal division affecting factor flows is that relating to movements in the relative prices of the factors of production. For growth the important features of this division must be the substitutability of these factors one for the other and the future course of the growth of these factors. The factor of labor if viewed simply as total population looks certain to grow larger; if viewed as trained, available, working labor, the future availability depends on the crude increase in population, the legally required school leaving age, the usual retirement age, the social norms that permit or forbid women to work, and the government-sponsored retraining and resettlement schemes.

The substitutability of capital and labor depends, apart from trade union action, on technology, and the rate of growth of capital, on saving. It is to these influences that we turn now.

4

The Flow of Factor Payments Continued:
Technology, Saving, and Price Changes

In Chapter 3 the main monopoly influences on factor shares were isolated; this left the substitutability of capital and labor to be considered
in this chaper.

TECHNOLOGY

Technology, affecting the substitution of capital for labor, is at once
the hope and fear of the future. The simplest claim is that, as in the
days of the Luddites, the new machines will create unemployment. It is
held that their full impact has yet to be seen or appreciated. We are
only in a gestation period now and when the technical difficulties have
been overcome there will be a competitive forward surge which will
create unemployment (whether it is called structural, frictional, or un-
skilled) as yet undreamt of. "Industrial technique will soon succeed in
completely replacing the effort of the worker,"[1] and this implies reduced wages (absolutely or relatively) compared to profits. The owners of capital, the owners of the new machines, will reap the reward of
the new technology, automation.

Against this simple case a number of arguments can be marshaled.

---

[1] J. Ellul, *The Technological Society* (New York: Knopf, 1964), p. 135.

The history of automation, of machines replacing man, has been one of an increasing, not diminished, demand for labor; different skills are required perhaps, but overall there has been an increased demand for labor. The pessimist answers that this is like comparing the hydrogen bomb with bows and arrows; the new problem is one that far outdistances any relation to historical examples.

Or it can be held that automation produces its own new industries. Obviously those firms that supply the machines and components expand, but in addition, whole new ranges of goods that previously were not feasible, transistor radios, polyethylene, communications equipment, and so on, can come into existence. Like a breeder reactor, automation can produce its own fuel.

Again, the potential labor force may contract, with higher school leaving ages and lower retirement ages fighting against an increasing population and larger numbers of women workers. Unemployment may not be the correct term to use. Increased leisure time may be more accurate. Of course, it would be ironic to refer to an out-of-work man existing on dole payments as having "increased leisure"; but if the work week is shortened, while all remain employed and more leisure is available without a decrease in real earnings, then this is held as a gain. This in its turn provides further ammunition to the automation proponents. As leisure increases it usually becomes a very expensive pastime; cameras, cars, yachts, second houses, and even children (who act as a kind of lagged factor, increasing demand but ultimately increasing the labor force) are required to enjoy the leisure time, thus providing more demand for goods and services and a greater incentive to work and earn income.

However, despite these arguments in favor, the most pervasive opinion is still the fear of unemployment and the consequent reduction in demand. But many writers hold the optimistic viewpoint that intervention at the management and government levels in retraining workers and providing social security at an earlier age should meet the issue.[2] The point which such writers miss is more subtle than the one they raise and debate. It concerns not the employment and unemployment of workers, or the underconsumption theory as such; it is concerned with the *relative* rates of growth of the reward to labor, compared to that of capital.

The optimistic viewpoint can be represented by saying that real out-

---

[2] J. Diebold, *Beyond Automation* (New York: McGraw-Hill, 1964), Chaps. 3, 8, 9, 10; Report to the National Commission on Technology, Automation, and Economic Progress, *Technology and the American Economy*, Vol. I., February, 1966.

put per head will be higher with automation. The value of total output per head determines the amount of total income available to be distributed among the population. But the distribution of this total income is determined by the marginal product of labor (in the absence of trade union minimum wage laws, etc., which push the allocation to a nonefficient position). Thus, if automation does greatly increase the average output per head, and if the average elasticity of substitution is less than unity, then automation could raise the value of real output per head relative to the marginal product of labor without an absolute fall in employment. The efficient allocation of resources might require, simply, that wages do not rise. The accompaniment of this must be an increasing reward to the owners of capital.[3]

The solution proposed by the "automation optimists," that of educating redundant workers and altering school curricula to anticipate future changes in industry's technical demands, could make the situation worse. Better education is likely to raise the workers' productivity and expectations and make it more difficult to reallocate them to jobs when they realize that their wages will not be rising. Workers may find themselves running a very hard educational race just to stay in the same place in real rewards, whereas those who are the rentiers of the system could theoretically opt out of the educational rat race and live on the increased rewards of owning property.

To combat this future there are two possible alternatives which can operate without direct intervention by the government. First, trade unions do exist, and thus the efficient allocation of labor is not determined solely by the marginal product of labor. Within the area of employment covered by the unions, wages might be maintained or might even expand more than the increase in marginal product. This means that the brunt of the adjustment would fall on those not covered by unions; unless some minimum wage legislation guaranteed a low income base there would emerge a nonunionized, very low income class. But this is not a very attractive outlook and "American labour has no illusion that the problems associated with technological change can be solved through collective bargaining alone, without recourse to government action."[4]

Alternatively, if a guaranteed minimum wage existed many firms might not find it profitable to employ labor and a considerable un-

---

[3] J. E. Meade, *Efficiency, Equality and the Ownership of Property* (London: Allen and Unwin, 1965), pp. 25-26.

[4] W. Reuther, "U.S.A. — A Free Society Faces the Age of Automation," *Times Review of Industry and Technology*, March, 1965, p. 18.

employment problem could emerge — part of the present unemployment in the United States is a minor sample of this in action. And again "Collective bargaining cannot bear the full burden of dealing with unemployment and the humane adjustment to technological change."[5] Combined trade union and government action could raise school leaving ages and negotiate longer holidays, shorter work weeks, and earlier retirements, so that "employment" could continue. This is, apparently, the world to which many professional men look.[6] But a world dependent on union battles and on government legislation which still leaves the ownership of wealth undisturbed would be to many a not very attractive promised land. The fear still lurks that there would be some who would not be under the wing of the unions and who would have to rely on the transfer organized by government. This is the likely solution but is there a better one?

The second option without direct government intervention would be to accept that there will be an increasing reward to capital and highly trained workers, and to look forward to a high demand for personal services which would mop up the less skilled members of society. It can be argued that servants have only recently vanished from common usage in advanced society and that there is no real reason to expect that an institution which has existed for thousands of years should disappear permanently. It can be held that our servantless state is only a hiatus in development. With the emergence of very affluent capitalists and technologists and the consequent large number of industrially unemployed there will follow a demand for the personalized services which only a human can provide.

If neither the trade union power state nor the servant state is attractive, then we must look to government intervention to alter the flow of factor payments, either by taxing the flow itself and by transfer payments switching the flow to others, or by taxing the wealth, which gives rise to the factor payment flow, and redistributing this revenue to either the public or private sector. Here we come to two basic splits in government policy. The taxation of wealth as defined in the conventional sense discussed in Chapter 1, excluding the personal trained skills and earning potential of an individual, by itself will not necessarily meet the demands of equity. The transfer payments will have to be linked to such wealth taxation to insure that they provide the opportunity for every member of society to make the greatest use of his skills. That is,

---

[5] *Ibid.,* p. 19.

[6] Diebold, *Beyond Automation;* or the essays in Reuther, *The Challenge of Automation.*

the accompaniment to wealth taxation ought to be large scale encouragement to education. You can tax wealth and/or "earned" income and still not achieve equity if there is not a compensating expenditure on education which gives everyone an equal opportunity to develop the wealth represented by his skills. The nonprovision of educational facilities can be likened to a form of highly regressive wealth tax falling on those who have innate skills but who do not have the opportunity or monetary wealth to develop them. We will return to this question of the desirable form which government expenditure should take, transfer or government purchases of educational goods and services, at a later point in the discussion.

For the time being the important factor is that if we are unwilling to accept the options of a trade union transfer state or a servant state, then we have to turn to government intervention to alter the factor flow. However, before discussing the actual forms of taxes and transfers adopted we must continue to examine further influences on the distribution of wealth and the flow of factor payments, in particular the savings propensities of different wealth-owning groups.

SAVING

The growth of wealth depends on the saving in society. The usual Keynesian model of factor flows adopts a single marginal propensity to save and assumes that the adjustment of savings to a given amount of investment takes place through changes in income. What really causes the principal income shares to be what they are was a question Keynes did not consider. An approach has been suggested by Meade and Pasinetti[7] which indicates that the future course of the marginal propensity to save of pure capitalists (those with no wages or salaries) is the important element determining the profits share. Yet, "One of the most serious gaps in our knowledge of the structural changes in the savings of households is the absence of information extending over long periods about the distribution of saving among saver groups of differ-

---

[7] N. Kaldor, "Alternative Theories of Distribution," *Review of Economic Studies,* Vol. XXIII, 1955-56; Kaldor, "A Model of Economic Growth," *Economic Journal,* December, 1957; Kaldor and Mirrless, "A New Model of Economic Growth," *Review of Economic Studies,* June, 1962; Pasinetti, "Rate of Profit and Income Distribution in Relation to the Rate of Economic Growth," *Review of Economic Studies,* October, 1962; Meade, "The Rate of Profit in a Growing Economy," *Economic Journal,* December, 1963; Pasinetti, "A Comment on Professor Meade's 'Rate of Profit,' " *Economic Journal,* June, 1964; Meade and Hahn, "The Rate of Profit in a Growing Economy," *Economic Journal,* June, 1965.

ent income and wealth levels, different occupations, different ages, and other characteristics."[8] Yet this is precisely the sort of information which is needed. The Pasinetti expression suggests that a change in profits would be equal to the change in investment divided by the marginal propensity to save of pure capitalists. The smaller this marginal propensity the larger will be the increase in profits resulting from a change in investment. Thus, pure capitalists by reducing their marginal propensity to save will increase their profits, but in so doing they will, of course, decrease the rate of growth of their capital stock on which they earn their profits.

The person with the larger amount of wealth is not so worried by the potential income loss through illness. He is not obliged to save for education, retirement, or legacies to leave at death. He has the security of property, and therefore is not obliged to save so much as those who have little property.

The person with the smaller amount of wealth whose aspirations are to have greater security for himself and his family will have a greater impetus to save in order to achieve that security.[9]

Clearly, the pressure is on those with less property to save more.

Consumption is determined by lifetime consuming power anticipations, and these are best expressed in terms of wealth and the wage rate and *not* by disposable income. The superiority of wealth as a consumption determining variable is due to the directness of its effect; the market value of current wealth fully reflects anticipated property income changes, whereas current rates of *property income accruals* indicate anticipated consuming power *only* if expectations of future property income maintain a stable relation to current property income, which is an unlikely situation in the real world of business cycles. . . . The relation of consumption to total disposable income is based upon the implicit assumption that the relative importance of property and labour power, in determining consumption, is the same as their relative importance in disposable income. Empirical estimates . . . indicate that the disposable income approach grossly underrates the importance of (income from) wealth. Over the period studied [1929-50] wealth accounted for over half of consumption, but for less than one third of income, suggesting that the

---

[8] R. W. Goldsmith, *A Study of Saving in the United States* (Princeton: Princeton University Press, 1956), III, 161.

[9] It should be mentioned that in the long run if economic growth takes place through capital accumulation, and there is no change in the ratio of capital stock to "capacity" output (technological change is "neutral") and no change in the rate of interest, then consumer assets and consumer income "will necessarily grow in proportion, and it becomes idle to inquire whether saving depends on income or assets or both." — G. Ackley, "The Wealth-Saving Relationship," *Journal of Political Economy*, April, 1951, p. 156. However, this reasoning assumes that there are no changes in the distribution of assets — or that all groups have identical asset-consumption functions — both of which, in our discussion, appear to be unwarranted assumptions.

marginal and average propensity to consume property income (when wealth varies proportionately with property income) is about three times as high as the propensity to consume labour income.[10]

This effect is enhanced if we consider the other side of the question. The income earner with little wealth holding tends to make his savings contractual, and the smaller his income the more likely he will do so. The health insurance, the unit trust which automatically reinvests current proceeds to provide for educational endowments, life assurance policies, building society mortgages, and hire purchase agreements — none of these give the saver the easy option of spending any current yield on his saving. Very often the forms of saving by lower wealth holders are such that profits are discounted in some asset purchase or insurance premiums, and such agreements do not give the saver the option of consuming or saving the profits yielded on his past savings. Thus his marginal propensity to save *out of profits* is bound to be almost unity and the contractual element in his period payments fixes his marginal propensity to save out of total income in the medium and long run. Discretionary savings increase with income. "When a person is very U [equivalent to a U.S. income above $50,000, in Britain £10,000] he saves a great deal in noncontractual forms. For tax, and other reasons, the U-saver may well own a large share of a private company, and in this case he saves large sums in the form of company retentions out of earnings. From our sample data we are able to place the point of initial appearance of net positive discretionary savings in the income scale at about £3,000 [in 1956]."[11] So that, in the absence of taxation, it can be argued that the lower wealth holder will have a great impetus to save.

Persons with identical incomes could have very different marginal propensities to save, depending on their wealth holding. This could be expressed by saying that the marginal propensity to save increases with rising incomes but that it increases faster for those who have little property than for those who have a large amount.

The graph (Chart 4:1) shows wealth (Z) as a proportion of a given income (fixed). At the initial point in time the individual at B has very little wealth and exactly the same income as the individual at A. Through time the small wealth holder, starting at B, increases his wealth holding by saving a larger proportion of his income until at C

[10] W. Hamburger, "The Relation of Consumption to Wealth and the Wage Rate," *Econometrica,* January, 1955, pp. 10, 11. (Italics mine.)

[11] L. E. Klein, K. H. Straw, and P. Vandome, "Savings and Finance of the Upper Income Classes," *Bulletin of the Oxford University Institute of Statistics,* November, 1956, p. 318.

CHART 4:1

Rates of Saving from Two Identical Incomes When Persons
Own Different Amounts of Wealth

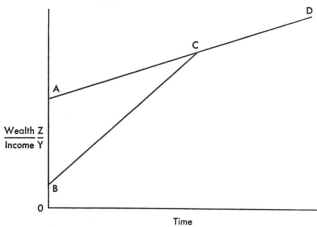

he reaches the same wealth position as the person starting at A and his
security is the same as that person's, so that his saving levels off to the
same rate (the slope of CD). This has connections with the discussion
in Chapter 2 on the "reasonable aspirations" of income earners. In
this case the reasonable aspirations of the first individual encouraged
him to save until he satisfied those goals at C.

Economic units have the notion of a desirable relationship between their income and their wealth which, they are constantly trying to realise. This relationship is such that the faster they grow in terms of income the higher is
their saving-income ratio and the lower is their wealth income ratio. If individuals have what they consider an excess of wealth in relation to income
they will tend to reduce their saving and so allow their income to rise relative
to their wealth. In the opposite case they will tend to increase their saving
and so enable their wealth to rise relative to their income.[12]

These forces of decreasing necessity to save with higher income and
wealth and the contractual element of saving in the lower wealth and
income brackets are likely to reduce the inequality of wealth distribution over time. The question is how long a time? With the existing
unequal distribution of wealth and the high taxation of income, those
(in the vast majority) who start life with little property have a long
way to go to reach those who have the security of large wealth holdings.
Their path is made all the more difficult by the taxation of current
income. Indeed, it is not just the existing unequal distribution of

---

[12] R. Stone, "Private Saving in Britain, Past, Present and Future," *The Manchester School of Economic and Social Studies,* Vol. XXXII, No. 2, May, 1964.

wealth which makes it difficult to equalize opportunity and security, it is the huge difficulty of emulating those who were lucky enough to make their fortunes before the income tax structure was made so progressive. Once more the critical point is that of expectations.

This pattern of large fortune accumulation in the early expansion of a country and the subsequent imposition of a highly progressive personal income tax structure administered with increasing efficiency is likely to be the sequence in most developing countries. In these countries there is the initial difficulty of administering efficiently a highly progressive personal income tax structure, combined with the opportunities for amassing considerable personal fortunes from land speculation and exploitations of natural resources; an inequality of wealth builds up while at the same time with increasing urbanization, increasing public sector expenditure, and rising money incomes, the rates of personal income tax are increased, and probably the tax structure is better organized and more efficiently administered. Thus the new, higher wage earners find it increasingly difficult to emulate the saving of those who were first in the field.

PRICE CHANGES

Following the layout indicated at the beginning of Chapter 3 we turn now to the fourth factor influencing the future distribution of wealth, differential asset price changes. We will then consider some of the aspects of changes in the structure of wealth taxation vis-à-vis government expenditure, before proceeding with an examination of alternative wealth tax structures in Chapter 6 and those following.

How do differential price changes affect the asset holdings of those who hold different amounts of wealth? Are there any advantages in being a top wealth holder, as opposed to a lower wealth holder, in a period of changing prices?

Comparing wage earners and profit receivers the general hypothesis is that wages tend to lag behind prices during an inflation; but this has been questioned in recent studies[13] and the more general commonsense conclusion seems to be that those whose incomes are fixed are the major losers, and are not correlated closely to particular income size groups.

For wealth-owning income groups analysis indicates that inflation is regressive,[14] especially in the lower income groups, as their members are the recipients of highly institutionalized payments.

---

[13] M. Bronfenbrenner and F. D. Holzman, "A Survey of Inflation Theory," *American Economic Review,* September, 1963, p. 649.

[14] *Ibid.,* p. 651.

We are interested in the reactions of wealth owners, who have different amounts of wealth, to differential asset price changes. The impact of price changes will depend not only on their original asset structure, but first, on their ability to anticipate price changes correctly, and second and separately, their ability to adjust their earnings, assets, liabilities, and consumption to the anticipated change. Thus there is a double criterion consisting first of the correct anticipation, and second the ability to use that forecast.

As a check on the capacity of wealth holders to change their asset structure correctly (that is to hedge against the price movements) in inflationary and deflationary situations, a simple test is proposed. The figures for estates passing at death in the United States and Britain are split into three wealth groups and six asset categories. To get total wealth estimates using the estate multiplier method the figures for asset holdings according to age and sex composition would be needed, and these are available for a very limited number of recent years[15] and would not give the required time period. However, the figures for estates passing at death do represent the actual decision of the wealth holders as to the composition of their asset structures compatible with current conditions and foreseeable changes, although the figures will be weighted in favor of the asset structure preferred by the old rather than by the middle aged groups, especially as present tax law provides the "prospect of eventual tax-free transfer of accrued gain with a stepped-up basis equal to the new market value in the hands of the heir . . . distorts investment choice and frequently results in complete immobility of investments of older people."[16] These figures are available over an extended period of time when substantial price changes have occurred. They are taken for 1926-60 for the United States and 1920-60 for Britain, and presented in current and real values. The choice of years and index number is discussed in Appendix I.

What result might be expected? In the light of the double criterion we should look first to the *timing* of asset structure changes (revealing

[15] Lampman, *The Share of Top Wealth Holders*, for the U.S.; J. R. S. Revell, "Assets and Age," *Bulletin of the Oxford University Institute of Statistics*, Vol. XXIV, No. 3, August, 1962, for Britain.

[16] President's 1963 Tax Message, *Hearings Before the Committee on Ways and Means*, rev. ed., House, 88th Cong., 1st Sess., 1963, Part 1, p. 49. The Revell study shows that when age and sex patterns are taken into account there are substantial changes in the total wealth estimates compared to using the simple estate multiplier method. In particular, by ignoring these factors we are likely to overstate the importance of quoted securities and underestimate the significance of household goods, insurance, and unquoted company securities.

anticipation) between different wealth groups, and then to the extent and speed of the change of structure (showing ability to change).

Clearly these changes are not the result of differential price changes alone; changes in relative tax rates, in external conditions (war), in individual liabilities and nonmonetized commitments, and of course, other sources of income, all affect the freedom of the individual to change his asset holding. But the degree of aggregation is large and in periods when price changes are large they are likely to be a dominating influence on asset structures, although we are obliged to consider some of the other influences.

We might expect wealthier persons to have better knowledge, more perfect information, and to hire better advisors than the lower wealth groups; therefore their anticipation of price changes should be ahead of those with less wealth. The "turning points" of the top wealth holders should be ahead of the middle group, and the middle group ahead of the lowest group.

After a turning point the wealthier groups should change their asset structure more quickly, moving boldly into those assets which provide a hedge, and out of those which are relatively less rewarding. Graphically, the slope of their percentage change should be steeper and their "committed" position should be more favorable than that of the lower wealth groups.

So that in an inflation, for example, the wealthier groups would have an advantage through anticipation, and through greater freedom of action in committing their wealth to those assets which they consider will provide a hedge against the inflation. They can do this because they are not obliged to hold such a large proportion of their wealth in assets which are difficult to alter, e.g., houses and personal furnishings, etc.; also they can hold a much smaller proportion of their assets in a highly liquid form (e.g., cash and mortgages). In this way their freedom for action is greater and ought to be reflected in more striking changes in their asset structure, which in turn confers gains on them compared to lower wealth groups. If this reasoning is correct, then among persons who hold differing amounts of wealth differential price changes of assets, either up or down, are regressive.

The selection of the assets to be examined, the years chosen, the grouping of the wealth owners and the price indices used, are given in Appendix 1. Tables 4:1 and 4:2 show the percentage each asset represents of the total for each wealth-owning group. Charts 4:1-8 show selections of this data. We will discuss the United States data first, then the United Kingdom.

TABLE 4:1

Percentage of Assets in Current and Real Terms Held in Six Categories of Assets by Three Wealth Groups

United States (1926–60)

Year	Group $'000	Bonds Current	Bonds Real	Cash Current	Cash Real	Insurance Current	Insurance Real	Stocks Current	Stocks Real	Real Estate Current	Real Estate Real	Other Current	Other Real
1926	60–200	14.8	31.3	14.8	18.0	3.8	4.7	30.9	15.6	21.6	15.3	13.5	15.1
	200–800	15.9	34.5	11.7	14.7	2.8	3.5	40.4	21.1	16.5	12.1	12.2	14.1
	800+	16.3	37.1	6.4	8.4	1.3	1.7	51.8	28.3	10.8	8.3	13.3	16.1
1927	60–200	13.6	29.3	16.0	18.7	4.3	5.1	31.6	19.2	24.0	16.5	10.5	11.2
	200–800	22.9	45.9	11.9	12.9	3.5	3.8	41.5	23.3	16.9	10.8	3.3	3.3
	800+	10.7	25.8	6.8	8.9	1.2	1.6	55.5	37.7	11.5	8.8	14.2	17.1
1928	60–200	12.6	26.3	14.6	16.3	4.1	4.5	37.7	28.6	19.6	13.0	11.0	11.2
	200–800	14.2	29.3	11.0	12.0	3.4	3.8	44.7	33.5	15.2	10.0	11.3	11.3
	800+	13.5	28.7	5.4	6.2	1.9	2.2	62.4	48.5	8.5	5.8	8.3	8.6
1929	60–200	14.2	26.0	14.8	15.0	4.6	4.7	39.3	35.3	19.9	12.6	7.1	6.4
	200–800	13.6	24.7	10.5	10.5	3.2	3.3	47.5	42.5	13.7	8.6	11.5	10.4
	800+	16.4	28.9	5.4	5.3	1.5	1.5	58.4	50.5	7.7	4.7	10.5	9.2
1930	60–200	13.1	30.6	15.3	3.7	4.9	6.0	35.7	32.1	19.5	14.9	11.5	12.6
	200–800	26.6	45.9	9.6	8.6	3.9	3.5	46.2	30.7	13.1	7.4	4.8	3.9
	800+	11.6	24.4	9.0	9.9	1.3	1.4	57.5	46.5	8.0	5.5	12.5	12.3
1931	60–200	14.0	29.0	15.4	17.7	7.2	8.3	34.4	20.8	10.1	13.2	10.4	11.0
	200–800	18.8	37.7	13.2	14.7	4.3	4.8	39.6	23.1	13.4	9.4	10.6	10.4
	800+	22.4	44.7	8.1	8.8	1.8	2.0	45.4	26.0	10.2	7.0	11.9	11.5

1932	60–200	18.9	41.4	19.4	22.2	6.6	7.5	30.5	10.4	18.5	12.6	6.0	5.9
	200–800	22.7	49.6	14.0	15.9	5.4	6.1	37.5	12.7	14.3	9.7	6.1	6.0
	800+	35.6	67.6	9.3	9.2	1.9	1.9	38.0	11.1	10.7	6.4	4.5	3.8
1933	60–200	19.7	44.1	17.2	18.2	4.5	7.2	35.2	15.0	15.6	10.4	5.4	5.1
	200–800	23.7	52.1	11.2	11.5	5.7	5.8	40.6	17.0	13.7	8.9	5.1	4.7
	800+	36.2	68.7	7.6	6.8	1.8	1.6	43.2	15.6	7.3	4.1	4.0	3.2
1934	60–200	23.8	47.3	16.5	17.3	6.5	6.8	36.1	16.4	16.1	11.3	0.9	0.9
	200–800	26.2	51.6	12.5	13.0	5.0	5.2	41.6	18.7	10.8	7.5	3.9	3.9
	800+	32.7	61.1	9.0	8.9	2.4	2.4	45.4	19.4	6.0	4.0	4.5	4.3
1935	60–200	21.1	45.9	14.0	14.2	8.0	8.2	36.8	17.0	14.3	9.2	5.8	5.5
	200–800	23.3	50.9	11.5	11.7	4.6	4.7	44.1	20.3	10.2	6.5	6.2	6.0
	800+	22.3	52.2	5.8	6.4	1.7	1.8	57.8	28.5	5.3	3.6	7.1	7.4
1936	60–200	19.3	40.4	14.7	14.2	6.0	5.8	40.6	25.6	14.4	9.1	5.3	4.9
	200–800	21.9	45.0	11.1	10.5	5.1	4.8	47.3	29.4	9.9	6.0	4.7	4.3
	800+	21.9	46.1	7.7	7.5	1.7	1.6	54.8	34.8	6.0	3.8	7.9	7.3
1937	60–200	15.6	33.3	19.5	20.0	7.6	7.8	35.0	22.5	20.5	14.7	1.7	1.7
	200–800	20.3	41.8	13.3	13.2	4.6	4.5	45.6	28.3	12.2	8.4	3.9	3.9
	800+	28.4	53.8	6.4	5.9	1.4	1.3	52.1	29.8	5.3	3.4	6.5	5.9
1938	60–200	14.9	33.8	19.3	20.4	7.5	8.0	33.1	16.7	19.5	15.1	5.7	6.1
	200–800	20.3	44.8	13.5	13.8	5.4	5.6	43.5	21.2	11.8	8.9	5.5	5.7
	800+	30.6	60.4	8.2	7.5	1.7	1.6	47.5	20.8	5.1	3.4	5.8	6.3

TABLE 4:1 (Continued)

Year	Group $'000	Bonds Current	Bonds Real	Cash Current	Cash Real	Insurance Current	Insurance Real	Stocks Current	Stocks Real	Real Estate Current	Real Estate Real	Other Current	Other Real
1939	60–200	14.1	32.7	19.5	20.2	8.3	8.6	32.9	17.3	19.1	15.0	6.1	6.3
	200–800	19.1	43.5	13.0	13.2	5.0	5.1	45.8	23.7	11.4	8.8	5.6	5.7
	800+	24.9	53.8	8.0	7.7	1.8	1.8	52.6	25.8	5.4	3.9	7.3	7.0
1940	60–200	13.6	32.3	19.7	20.7	8.2	8.7	32.5	15.7	19.5	15.9	6.5	6.7
	200–800	19.0	44.1	14.7	15.1	5.2	5.4	44.1	20.8	11.9	9.5	5.1	5.1
	800+	25.1	55.8	11.3	11.2	1.8	1.7	53.7	24.3	4.3	3.3	3.9	3.7
1941	60–200	13.1	31.5	20.1	21.6	8.3	9.0	31.3	13.1	20.2	17.4	6.9	7.4
	200–800	18.7	43.8	14.9	15.7	5.8	6.1	41.6	17.0	12.2	10.3	6.8	7.1
	800+	25.1	57.0	11.4	11.6	1.5	1.5	51.1	20.2	7.1	5.8	3.9	3.9
1942	60–200	13.3	28.5	19.2	22.6	8.9	10.4	30.9	11.3	20.3	18.2	7.4	9.0
	200–800	19.4	41.5	16.0	18.7	6.0	7.0	40.6	14.8	11.5	10.2	6.5	7.8
	800+	30.3	61.4	10.7	11.8	1.9	2.1	49.0	16.9	4.2	3.5	3.9	4.4
1943	60–200	12.9	25.9	17.6	20.5	9.9	11.5	29.9	13.6	21.2	18.5	8.6	10.0
	200–800	18.3	37.4	13.7	16.3	7.2	8.6	42.7	19.7	11.4	10.2	6.6	7.8
	800+	23.1	48.7	8.9	10.9	2.0	2.5	55.1	26.3	5.3	4.9	5.6	6.8
1944	60–200	12.5	25.3	17.0	20.3	10.2	12.2	29.6	14.7	22.2	21.3	8.4	10.8
	200–800	17.4	35.0	12.0	14.3	6.6	7.9	45.0	22.3	12.2	11.7	7.0	8.8
	800+	28.0	53.3	8.3	9.4	2.4	2.7	51.2	24.0	5.2	4.7	4.9	5.9

1946	60–200	11.6	20.4	17.0	18.8	9.4	10.4	28.2	15.9	25.2	23.8	8.7	10.7
	200–800	15.5	28.6	12.0	13.9	6.5	7.6	43.3	25.6	14.8	14.7	7.5	9.7
	800+	23.2	42.3	9.1	10.4	2.5	2.9	53.1	31.2	7.4	7.3	4.6	5.9
1947	60–200	11.1	17.6	17.0	19.5	9.6	11.0	26.3	12.0	26.6	27.7	9.4	12.2
	200–800	15.4	26.5	13.1	16.3	6.8	8.4	41.7	20.7	15.5	17.5	7.5	10.6
	800+	20.2	36.6	12.3	16.2	2.1	2.8	52.4	27.5	6.9	8.3	5.8	8.6
1948	60–200	11.4	17.0	17.1	20.5	8.7	10.5	28.4	12.9	25.5	28.7	8.8	11.8
	200–800	14.7	24.0	12.6	16.5	6.1	8.0	44.2	22.0	14.6	18.0	7.8	11.5
	800+	23.1	39.3	11.1	15.1	1.9	2.6	52.2	26.9	6.3	8.1	5.2	8.0
1953	60–200	8.8	10.6	16.5	19.2	7.8	9.1	31.1	19.7	27.3	30.9	8.5	10.5
	200–800	11.5	15.3	12.0	15.4	4.7	6.1	49.0	34.1	15.5	19.3	7.3	9.8
	800+	18.1	25.9	7.2	9.9	2.1	2.9	61.7	46.0	5.7	7.7	5.2	7.6
1954	60–200	8.9	11.4	17.6	20.4	7.9	9.1	34.4	25.9	28.7	30.5	2.4	2.8
	200–800	11.0	14.7	12.5	15.2	5.0	6.0	49.4	38.7	14.7	16.3	7.3	9.1
	800+	13.4	18.6	7.6	9.7	2.0	2.5	62.5	51.3	7.1	8.2	7.4	9.7
1958	60–200	6.9	6.9	16.8	16.8	7.0	7.0	33.6	33.6	27.6	27.6	4.4	4.4
	200–800	8.7	8.7	11.8	11.8	4.1	4.1	51.7	51.7	16.1	16.1	7.7	7.7
	800+	14.3	14.3	6.9	6.9	0.9	0.9	62.8	62.8	7.9	7.9	6.9	6.9
1960	60–200	6.5	5.6	17.5	15.9	6.8	6.2	35.5	39.8	26.6	26.0	7.1	6.6
	200–800	8.0	6.6	11.6	10.2	3.7	3.2	54.3	59.1	15.0	14.2	7.5	6.8
	800+	15.2	12.5	5.9	5.1	1.3	1.1	65.5	70.3	6.5	6.0	5.6	5.0

TABLE 4:1 (Continued)

Percentage of Assets in Current and Real Terms Held in Six Categories of Assets by Three Wealth Groups

United Kingdom (1920–60)

Year	Group £'000	Bonds		Cash		Insurance		Stocks		Real Estate		Other	
		Current	Real	Current	Real	Current	Real	Current	Real	Current	Real	Current	Real
1920	5–25	18.0	28.1	15.5	14.1	3.1	2.8	26.3	17.2	22.0	17.8	14.9	20.0
	25–100	18.5	29.4	10.7	9.9	2.6	2.5	35.1	23.4	18.5	15.2	14.6	20.0
	100+	18.5	29.9	7.8	7.2	2.0	1.9	34.6	23.4	25.2	21.0	11.9	16.6
1922	5–25	21.6	46.3	16.3	12.9	3.1	2.5	27.6	16.2	20.1	12.1	11.2	10.0
	25–100	21.8	51.1	11.9	10.3	2.1	1.7	36.5	23.5	16.6	11.1	2.3	2.3
	100+	21.7	46.4	10.5	8.4	2.4	1.9	32.0	18.8	18.1	11.0	15.3	13.6
1923	5–25	22.2	47.2	15.2	11.2	3.1	2.2	29.3	27.1	19.2	10.6	11.0	8.3
	25–100	23.6	48.7	11.6	8.3	2.0	1.4	37.6	25.6	14.7	8.0	10.5	8.0
	100+	24.6	56.3	10.6	8.4	2.7	2.1	35.8	18.1	16.0	6.4	10.4	8.7
1924	5–25	22.8	47.6	15.1	10.9	3.2	2.2	29.6	20.2	19.2	11.0	10.1	8.1
	25–100	23.7	48.9	11.6	8.3	2.6	1.8	37.4	25.1	15.6	8.8	8.9	7.0
	100+	27.8	54.2	8.9	6.0	1.8	1.2	38.2	24.4	14.0	7.5	9.2	6.9
1925	5–25	22.2	45.2	14.8	10.7	3.0	2.2	29.8	22.2	19.0	10.7	11.4	9.0
	25–100	22.4	45.1	10.7	7.7	2.1	1.4	39.3	29.0	14.2	7.8	11.4	9.0
	100+	23.2	43.5	12.6	8.5	2.4	1.6	35.2	24.2	18.1	9.4	8.5	12.8
1926	5–25	22.9	45.6	16.0	11.3	2.9	2.0	30.5	23.9	18.8	10.4	8.9	6.8
	25–100	22.0	43.6	11.9	8.4	2.1	1.4	38.3	30.0	13.9	7.6	11.8	9.0
	100+	23.3	45.2	11.9	8.3	2.8	1.9	43.3	33.1	10.5	5.6	8.1	6.0

1927												
5–25	23.3	45.4	14.4	9.7	3.1	2.1	29.7	24.5	17.1	9.1	12.5	9.1
25–100	22.0	43.0	17.5	11.9	2.3	1.6	39.6	32.6	13.3	7.2	5.3	3.9
100+	20.4	40.4	11.4	7.9	2.6	1.9	35.0	29.4	10.0	5.5	20.3	15.1
1928												
5–25	21.3	41.7	15.5	10.3	2.9	1.9	29.4	27.5	16.1	7.9	14.8	10.7
25–100	23.0	42.7	13.7	8.7	2.3	1.5	41.6	36.9	13.4	6.2	6.0	4.1
100+	22.6	41.5	9.3	5.8	2.1	1.3	44.0	38.5	9.3	4.3	12.5	8.5
1929												
5–25	22.2	42.4	16.7	11.2	3.0	2.0	31.0	28.5	16.7	8.6	10.3	7.4
25–100	22.7	41.4	12.8	8.1	2.5	1.6	44.8	39.4	11.8	5.8	5.5	3.7
100+	22.6	42.6	13.0	8.6	3.1	2.0	39.5	35.9	12.4	6.3	9.6	6.7
1930												
5–25	23.1	47.5	17.4	11.8	3.5	2.4	30.7	23.7	17.3	8.9	8.0	5.7
25–100	24.8	49.1	13.2	8.7	2.2	1.3	39.2	29.4	13.3	6.6	7.3	5.0
100+	23.7	43.0	12.2	7.5	4.1	2.5	38.0	26.0	11.5	5.3	10.5	15.8
1931												
5–25	24.1	40.8	17.2	9.1	3.5	1.8	29.2	14.6	17.4	7.1	8.5	4.7
25–100	25.4	55.8	13.5	9.3	2.7	1.9	38.2	24.7	12.5	6.6	2.4	1.7
100+	23.1	50.7	13.5	9.2	4.0	2.7	35.9	23.1	12.3	6.5	11.1	7.8
1932												
5–25	25.4	59.4	17.0	10.1	3.6	2.2	28.2	15.4	17.2	7.9	8.4	5.0
25–100	27.8	62.3	13.6	7.6	2.8	1.6	37.7	19.7	13.6	5.9	4.4	2.5
100+	23.2	56.4	8.5	5.2	2.2	1.4	41.2	23.4	13.5	6.5	11.4	7.1
1933												
5–25	23.8	58.1	17.5	9.8	3.5	1.9	30.0	18.6	17.0	7.0	8.2	4.6
25–100	24.6	58.7	13.3	7.2	2.5	1.4	38.3	30.5	15.7	6.3	5.6	3.0
100+	27.1	61.4	17.1	8.6	3.2	1.7	34.7	20.0	8.5	3.2	9.3	4.8

TABLE 4:1 (Continued)

Year	Group £'000	Bonds		Cash		Insurance		Stocks		Real Estate		Other	
		Current	Real	Current	Real	Current	Real	Current	Real	Current	Real	Current	Real
1935	5–25	23.5	57.0	17.1	8.2	3.2	1.5	32.4	23.7	16.0	5.8	7.9	3.7
	25–100	25.3	57.6	12.7	5.7	2.1	.9	41.6	28.6	10.7	3.7	7.6	3.4
	100+	20.7	51.5	12.2	6.0	3.4	1.7	41.4	31.2	10.8	4.1	11.4	5.6
1936	5–25	22.5	52.9	17.1	8.0	3.2	1.5	33.4	27.7	15.9	6.0	7.8	3.8
	25–100	21.1	49.4	12.5	5.7	2.2	1.0	44.5	35.9	10.5	3.9	8.6	4.0
	100+	20.7	47.2	9.5	4.4	2.2	1.0	49.1	39.6	7.7	2.8	10.8	5.1
1937	5–25	21.7	49.3	17.2	9.1	3.3	1.8	33.8	28.5	15.7	6.6	8.3	4.7
	25–100	22.2	48.1	12.2	6.1	2.0	1.0	44.5	35.8	10.4	4.2	8.7	4.8
	100+	20.1	45.1	14.7	7.6	4.3	2.3	45.0	37.5	10.0	4.2	6.0	3.4
1938	5–25	22.4	52.2	17.6	10.0	3.5	2.1	32.3	23.6	16.3	7.5	7.8	4.6
	25–100	22.6	51.4	13.1	7.3	2.7	1.5	43.2	30.7	11.1	5.0	7.2	4.2
	100+	22.4	50.5	11.8	6.5	2.4	1.3	47.7	33.7	8.4	3.7	7.2	4.2
1948	5–25	20.5	35.8	22.8	17.7	3.0	20.2	25.0	18.1	21.0	19.7	7.8	6.5
	25–100	20.6	36.8	14.0	11.0	1.9	1.5	40.6	29.9	12.7	12.1	10.2	8.7
	100+	18.6	34.0	7.4	6.0	2.1	1.7	48.3	36.5	11.1	10.9	12.6	11.0
1949	5–25	21.7	36.8	20.5	16.1	2.8	2.2	23.5	15.9	20.8	19.7	10.6	9.3
	25–100	22.2	38.6	14.9	12.0	2.1	1.7	38.4	26.5	13.4	13.0	9.0	8.1
	100+	19.1	34.9	12.8	10.8	1.8	1.5	50.0	34.8	10.3	10.5	8.1	7.6

Year	Category												
1950	5–25	21.5	34.3	21.3	17.4	3.0	2.4	22.6	15.6	21.0	20.6	10.7	9.7
	25–100	22.1	36.3	16.2	13.6	1.9	1.6	38.1	27.1	12.4	12.6	9.3	8.7
	100+	19.3	32.9	11.3	9.8	2.1	1.8	46.4	34.2	11.8	12.4	9.1	8.8
1951	5–25	20.9	29.8	21.5	18.4	2.9	2.6	22.7	17.5	20.6	20.6	11.0	11.1
	25–100	20.1	29.7	15.6	13.8	1.8	1.6	40.0	31.8	12.3	12.7	9.9	10.4
	100+	18.6	27.6	14.7	13.1	2.6	2.4	47.4	37.9	11.2	11.7	7.0	7.3
1952	5–25	19.7	26.0	23.8	22.3	3.2	3.0	17.9	11.8	20.5	21.0	14.8	15.9
	25–100	20.1	28.5	17.1	17.2	2.1	2.2	37.8	26.7	17.7	19.5	5.1	5.9
	100+	17.4	25.7	12.4	13.0	2.6	2.7	47.0	34.6	11.0	12.5	9.6	11.5
1953	5–25	22.1	29.9	26.5	25.0	2.8	2.6	18.4	12.9	21.6	20.8	8.4	8.8
	25–100	19.2	27.7	17.9	18.0	2.1	2.1	38.9	29.0	12.6	13.0	9.1	11.2
	100+	18.3	26.8	15.7	16.0	1.6	1.6	43.0	32.5	11.5	12.0	9.8	11.0
1954	5–25	23.6	32.1	29.4	26.2	3.0	2.8	17.6	15.2	19.8	17.5	6.4	6.2
	25–100	18.5	30.0	16.6	15.3	1.8	1.7	42.4	37.6	12.2	11.1	8.5	8.4
	100+	16.3	23.2	13.7	12.8	1.5	1.4	48.4	43.5	12.7	11.7	7.4	7.4
1955	5–25	22.1	27.0	30.5	28.1	2.9	2.7	17.4	17.4	20.4	18.4	6.6	6.4
	25–100	16.0	19.4	16.7	15.3	1.9	1.7	45.1	44.9	11.8	10.6	8.5	8.1
	100+	15.4	18.6	13.0	11.9	1.4	1.3	48.2	48.1	15.4	13.7	6.7	6.4
1956	5–25	19.4	21.2	31.9	31.1	2.8	2.7	16.2	15.4	22.0	21.8	7.5	7.8
	25–100	15.8	17.5	17.5	17.4	2.0	2.0	44.2	42.4	11.8	11.8	8.5	8.9
	100+	14.7	16.3	13.0	13.0	1.2	1.2	50.3	48.4	9.6	9.5	11.1	11.6

TABLE 4:1 (Concluded)

Year	Group £'000	Bonds		Cash		Insurance		Stocks		Real Estate		Other	
		Current	Real	Current	Real	Current	Real	Current	Real	Current	Real	Current	Real
1957	5–25	17.1	17.4	32.7	32.4	3.2	3.1	17.6	17.7	24.0	23.8	5.4	5.6
	25–100	14.5	14.7	18.7	18.5	1.9	2.0	44.5	44.5	12.4	12.2	8.0	8.2
	100+	14.7	15.0	11.7	11.5	1.3	1.2	49.2	49.0	10.8	10.6	12.4	12.6
1958	5–25	15.4	15.4	32.7	32.7	3.3	3.3	15.6	15.6	24.5	24.5	8.5	8.5
	25–100	12.0	12.0	18.8	18.8	2.3	2.3	44.0	44.0	12.6	12.6	10.4	10.4
	100+	17.2	17.2	13.0	13.0	1.7	1.7	53.4	53.4	11.6	11.6	3.0	3.0
1959	5–25	15.3	14.6	31.7	29.3	2.6	2.4	18.3	24.0	25.0	23.3	7.1	6.4
	25–100	12.8	10.2	17.3	13.3	1.9	1.5	47.6	52.0	12.3	9.6	18.0	13.5
	100+	11.8	10.2	12.5	10.6	1.2	1.0	53.1	60.0	16.0	13.7	5.4	4.5
1960	5–25	13.5	10.5	34.4	29.5	3.2	2.7	20.5	31.5	20.3	19.1	7.9	6.7
	25–100	11.6	7.9	17.3	12.9	1.9	1.4	43.0	57.6	12.1	9.9	14.0	10.3
	100+	10.6	6.6	10.5	7.1	1.0	0.7	59.1	72.2	10.7	8.0	7.9	5.4

TABLE 4:2
United States Price Indices 1926-60 (1958 = 100)

	1	2	3	4	5
Year	Bonds	Consumer Prices	Stocks	Building	House Furnishing
1926	113.5	65.3	27.2	38.3	60.3
1927	118.2	64.1	33.2	37.8	58.8
1928	118.5	63.3	43.1	37.9	57.4
1929	114.6	63.3	56.3	39.6	56.7
1930	118.0	61.7	45.5	38.6	55.3
1931	101.5	56.2	29.5	35.6	49.7
1932	97.2	50.2	15.0	30.1	43.3
1933	101.8	47.8	19.4	30.2	42.7
1934	93.2	49.4	21.3	32.8	47.1
1935	108.8	50.7	22.9	31.9	48.1
1936	110.8	51.2	33.5	33.3	48.9
1937	110.4	53.1	33.3	37.1	52.9
1938	112.1	52.1	24.8	38.1	52.4
1939	115.1	51.3	26.1	38.8	51.4
1940	117.3	51.8	23.8	40.2	51.0
1941	121.4	54.4	21.2	43.3	54.4
1942	110.1	60.2	18.8	45.8	62.0
1943	109.9	63.9	24.9	48.0	63.7
1944	109.7	65.0	27.0	52.3	69.2
1945	111.6	66.4	32.7	55.8	74.0
1946	114.6	72.1	36.9	61.8	80.8
1947	113.5	82.5	32.8	74.9	93.6
1948	110.3	88.8	33.6	83.3	99.3
1949	112.3	88.0	32.9	80.8	95.8
1950	112.1	88.8	39.8	85.3	96.6
1951	108.2	95.9	48.3	91.8	107.1
1952	106.4	98.1	53.0	94.3	104.4
1953	102.7	98.8	53.5	95.8	103.9
1954	108.8	99.2	64.2	90.5	102.1
1955	105.0	98.9	87.6	93.1	100.2
1956	101.7	100.4	100.8	97.3	99.3
1957	99.1	102.7	96.0	99.1	100.7
1958	100	100	100	100	100
1959	90.9	99.2	124.1	103.3	100
1960	91.7	97.7	120.8	105.3	100.3

Sources: U.S. Department of Commerce. Bureau of the Census. *Statistical Abstract of the United States, 1961.*
Col. 1. U.S. government bonds $ yield for $100 bond (Table 609).
Col. 2. Consumer prices (Table 451).
Col. 3. Standard and Poor's Corporation, common stock, total (Table 609).
Col. 4. E. H. Boeckh and Associates, small residential structures: composite (Table 1048).
Col. 5. Consumer price index for house furnishings (Table 451).
Also used: *Historical Statistics, Colonial Times to 1957*, Series F., Washington: U.S. Government Printing Office, 1960.

TABLE 4:2 (Concluded)

United Kingdom Price Indices 1920-60 (1958 = 100)

Year	Index of Consumer Expenditure at Average Value	Bonds[a]	Stocks	Real Estate[b]	Other (Clothing and Household Durables)[c]
1920-21	54	93	39	48	80
1921-22	49	96	27	39	59
1922-23	42	113	31	32	47
1923-24	40	116	38	30	43
1924-25	39	113	37	31	43
1925-26	40	112	41	31	44
1926-27	39	109	43	30	42
1927-28	38	109	46	30	41
1928-29	38	111	53	28	41
1929-30	38	108	52	29	40
1930-31	37	111	42	28	39
1931-32	35	112	33	27	36
1932-33	34	133	31	26	34
1933-34	34	149	38	25	34
1934-35	34	161	47	25	34
1935-36	34	172	52	26	34
1936-37	34	170	60	27	35
1937-38	35	151	56	28	38
1938-39	36	147	46	29	38
1948-49	69	155	64	83	74
1949-50	70	151	60	84	78
1950-51	72	141	61	87	80
1951-52	79	132	71	92	93
1952-53	84	118	59	92	96
1953-54	85	122	63	87	94
1954-55	87	133	84	86	94
1955-56	90	119	98	88	94
1956-57	94	105	91	95	99
1957-58	97	100	98	97	100
1958-59	100	100	100	100	100
1959-60	101	104	143	102	99
1960-61	101	92	181	111	100

[a] Calculated by using the yield of 2½ Consols.
[b] Refers only to prices of existing houses.
[c] Was used to deflate personal effects and residuals.
Source: *The British Economy: Key Statistics, 1900-1964*, published for the London and Cambridge Economic Service by the Times Publishing Co., Ltd., London, 1965, pp. 12 and 16.

CHART 4:2

U.S. Assets Liable to Estate Duty: Stock at Current Values as a Percentage of Total Wealth Held

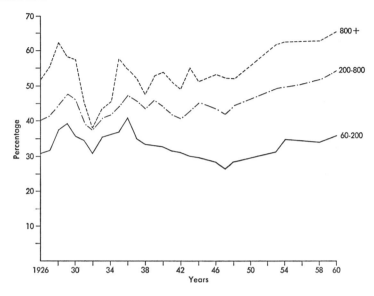

CHART 4:3

U.S. Assets Liable to Estate Duty: Least Squares Fit of Stock at Current Values as a Percentage of Total Wealth Held

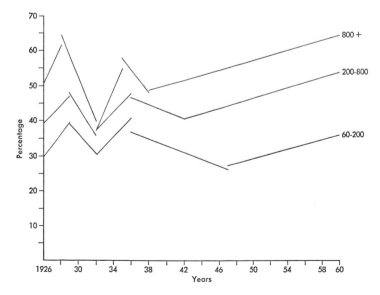

CHART 4:4

U.S. Assets Liable to Estate Duty: Stock at Real Values as a Percentage of Total Wealth Held

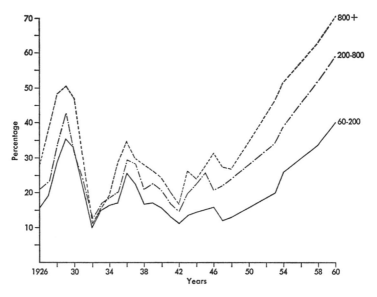

CHART 4:5

U.S. Assets Liable to Estate Duty: Least Squares Fit of Bonds at Current Values as a Percentage of Total Wealth Held

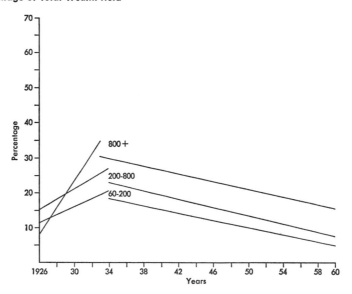

CHART 4:6

U.S. Assets Liable to Estate Duty: Bonds at Real Values as a Percentage of Total Wealth Held

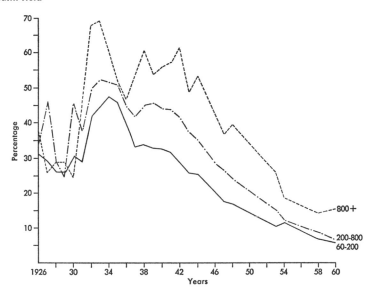

CHART 4:7

U.K. Assets Liable to Estate Duty: Stock at Current Values as a Percentage of Total Wealth Held

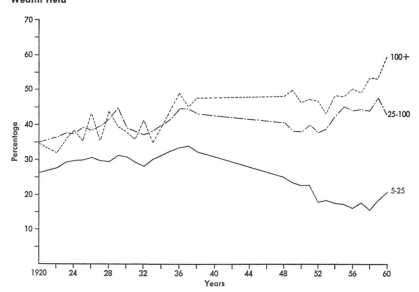

CHART 4:8

U.K. Assets Liable to Estate Duty: Bonds at Current Values as a Percentage of Total Wealth Held

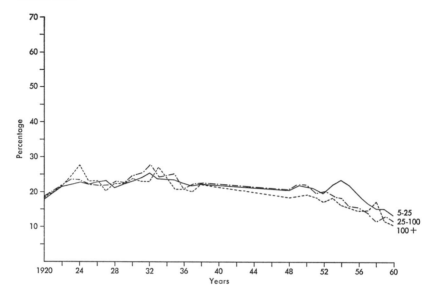

CHART 4:9

U.K. Assets Liable to Estate Duty: Cash and Mortgages at Real Values as a Percentage of Total Wealth Held

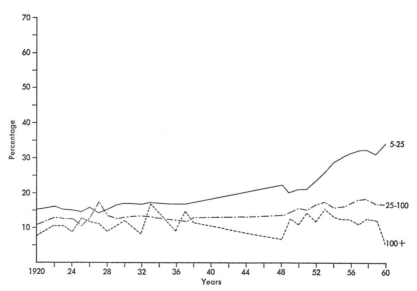

Chart 4:2 shows the percentage change in the U.S. holding of corporate stock in current values. In terms of our double criterion it is quite clear that the "turning points" in the pattern of stock ownership have been made first by the top wealth group, in 1928 instead of 1929 for the other two; all three turned upward in 1932, but the top group turned first in 1935, while the others turned in 1936; the top group turned up again in 1938, the middle group in 1942, and the lowest group delayed until 1947 for their change.

Second, in each case the commitment on the part of the wealthiest group has been the largest, followed by the second wealth group, with the lowest wealth group making the smallest commitment to stocks. Moreover, the rate of change was greater for the upper wealth groups than for the lower ones. All these factors are seen more clearly if a simple "least squares" fit is made between the turning points as shown in Chart 4:3. The earlier turning of the top group is noticeable especially in 1938. Because the series is discontinuous and the changes are all annual the measure of "turning points" is necessarily crude. Chart 4:3 also shows that from 1928-32 the wealthier classes changed their position more rapidly than the lowest group; similarly in 1932-36, the top group expanded its holding the most rapidly.

Whether these were the correct decisions or not (in terms of price hedges) depends on the relative movements of other prices, but as far as stock holdings were concerned the wealthiest group was a leader and committed more funds than the others; this was true also of the middle group compared to the lowest.

In real terms (Chart 4:4) the actual changes in stock prices result in each group having the same turning point, which shows that the highest wealth-owning group *were* correct in their decision, as the actual rise in prices was sufficient to offset the lower proportions of the stock held by the other groups. Chart 4:4 also shows the greater commitment and the faster rate of change of the wealthier groups.

The movement of bonds might be expected to complement that of stocks and Chart 4:5 shows the pattern in current values (least squares). The highest wealth-holding group again had a turning point ahead of the others (1933 compared to 1934). The commitment, and the rate of change, is strikingly shown in the period 1926-34. After 1934, although all holdings declined, their relative position did not. The change in real terms (Chart 4:6) shows the changing commitment more strikingly.

The effects of changing prices are more dramatically shown by the U.K. material. Chart 4:7 shows the percentage of total assets for the three wealth groups held in stocks in current values. The turning point for the wealthiest group could be taken as 1928, and for the other two groups as 1929; after 1937 the wealthiest group started to move increasingly into stocks, the middle group less so, and the lowest group actually reduced their holdings, until a late rally in 1958, and this during a period when the stock price index moved from 46 in 1938 to 181 in 1960.

Bond holdings show (Chart 4:8) the two upper wealth groups with the larger shares of bonds, but the wealthiest class between 1933 and 1935 quickly transferred to the bottom position and thereafter, although the holdings of all three wealth-owning groups declined, the position was reversed from the top turning point so that the change in the highest wealth group was greatest and that of the lowest wealth group the smallest.

Possibly the most stringent test of a hedge against inflation is the quantity of cash persons hold. Obviously those who hold cash during the inflation (in 1936 the U.K. index of consumer expenditure was 36, in 1960, 101) are the losers, and Chart 4:9 shows how in real terms the lowest wealth group greatly increased their cash holdings, from 17.2 per cent in 1937 to 34.4 per cent in 1960, while the middle group increased theirs somewhat, but the wealthiest group reduced their cash holding from 11.8 per cent in 1938 to 6.6 per cent in 1960.

We can say that assuming the upper wealth-holding group was correct in its decisions, the others lagged and made smaller commitments. The question remains: "Was the upper wealth-holding group correct in its judgments?" The choice of asset structure is a complex of motivations for each individual depending on yield, risk, liquidity, and potential capital growth. It is impossible to separate these and obtain a change in asset structure based on some "pure" price change motivation. Generally, we can say that assuming the upper wealth groups were correct, then the evidence above suggests that the wealthier groups have better judgment, or better advice. They start to change their asset structure sooner than lower wealth groups. They change more quickly and their commitment is greater. They appear to take greater advantage of price changes and other relative variables. It seems likely, therefore, that price changes (and differential tax rate changes) are regressive among owners of different amounts of wealth.

SUMMARY

Automation could raise the value of real product per head relative to the marginal product of labor (under efficient allocation) without an absolute fall in employment, but the increased rewards would go to the owners of capital, leaving the wage earners in a relatively worse off position. This situation is unlikely to be corrected by trade union action alone. Even working in conjunction with the government the important question is what kinds of taxes and transfers should be used (e.g., education).

The future course of saving will affect the future distribution of wealth by the possible decline in the marginal propensity to save of those whose wealth holdings grow bigger, and this will increase profits out of a given income and thereby necessarily reduce wages, so that although the rate of growth of large wealth holdings will be slower, the relative rate of growth of small and large holdings is likely to be worsened because the wages share of national income will be reduced. The contractual nature of much of the low wealth and low income groups means that their marginal propensity to save out of wealth money yield is very high but their marginal propensity to save out of total income (wages plus savings/wealth money yield) remains low compared to that of high income and wealth persons.

Income taxation worsens the situation by reducing the reasonable aspirations of the low wealth groups of their ever attaining the security of the high wealth groups. This is likely to be true in most developed countries.

The broad indications are that the lower taxation of wages, the higher taxation of large wealth holdings and their money income, and generous tax-free provisions to savings of a contractual nature would help to offset, in part, these factors.

There is a further form of saving which has grown in importance during this century and will probably continue to be important, saving by corporate businesses. To the extent that this form of saving increases, it diminishes the direct money flow of income to capitalists, but such corporate saving is reflected in an increased asset value. In our discussion of tax policies we can assume either that such capital gains are included in the income tax base, or that they are excluded, thus altering accordingly the efficiency of different wealth tax policies.

When price changes are considered there is a double criterion in assessing their effect on different factor owners; first the extent to which persons anticipate correctly the future price changes, and second their ability to change their asset mix or wage receipt to meet the price change. Those on fixed incomes, regardless of the income size, suffer. Wealth owners suffer inflation as a regressive tax. Both the anticipation of lower wealth groups and their ability to change asset structures are less efficient than those of larger wealth owners. Price changes, particularly inflation, are likely to increase the disparity between large and small wealth holders.

Overall, it appears that government intervention would be required to correct a tendency towards an increased flow of factor rewards to capital which the trade unions could combat only at the risk of considerable industrial unrest and by penalizing the nonunionized labor. If the government cannot stabilize prices then intervention could possibly be justified to correct the imbalances which can result between different factor owners from the differential prices changes.

5

Forms of Wealth Taxes and Considerations of Revenue

Previous chapters examined the influences making for changes in the future distribution of wealth. Although antitrust legislation and trade unions both may prevent increases in inequality there are powerful forces working in the opposite direction — economies of scale, national growth plans, population increase, technological change, savings rates, current income taxes, educational opportunities, and price changes. Perhaps wealth taxation is needed as an additional counterweight. Certainly, without the simple restraint of estate duty it looks as though the distribution of wealth would have become increasingly unequal in the United States and United Kingdom (for a discussion of the redistributive effectiveness of the estate duty, see Chapter 8).

TAXES ON WEALTH

The forms which wealth taxation can take are numerous. The relationships of the various types of wealth taxes to other taxes, particularly income taxation, are complicated and subtle. In general three reasons can be given for taxing wealth:

(i) a socioeconomic justification for redistribution, as discussed in Chapter 2,

(ii) to supplement or complete the existing tax structure,
(iii) for government revenue.

In the next eight chapters various forms of wealth taxation will be discussed in the context of the first two reasons. Consideration of the economic effects of these taxes (on consumption, prices, risk-taking, savings, growth, and factor shares) is left until Chapter 15. This order is adopted because taxes on wealth are necessary primarily in terms of equity, in that they complete the tax structure.

This outlook is strengthened by the discussion below which shows that apart from the justification for taxing, the *structure* of the tax on wealth is dictated not by the economic effects, but by the other taxes existing and the relationship between these existing taxes and any tax on wealth. Thus neither the justification for taxing wealth, nor the structure of a wealth tax, depend on the economic effects. These economic effects have provided some strong arguments for and against wealth taxation (particularly the effects on saving and risk-taking) and as such they will be considered later. But the introduction and form of the tax depend on discussions concerning equity; the tax structure thus evolved can be modified to accommodate economic effects or political expediency, but to put these two considerations in the vanguard of the discussion is to put expediency before equity and carts before horses.

Considerations of equity are usually presented in two parts:

(i) equity between persons in similar circumstances — the problem is to define the circumstances,
(ii) equity between persons in dissimilar circumstances — the problem is to weight the dissimilar circumstances.

But it should be clear that as all taxes are levied through time, changes through time should also be allowed for. This provides two further cases:

(iii) equity between persons in similar circumstances at different points in time,
(iv) equity between persons in dissimilar circumstances at different points in time.

Essentially, 1 and 2 are concerned with equity at a *particular* point in time, whereas 3 and 4 are dealing with equity *through* time.

If government discretionary intervention such as changes in tax rates or structures is extracted then taxes should, as far as possible, satisfy these four equity demands, and especially taxes on stocks (capital) as opposed to flows (income) should be concerned with (iii) and (iv) because they are dealing with an elongated time-tax structure. Each form of wealth tax will be discussed in the context of these four equity requirements.

Before looking at the equity viewpoints we should deal with the third reason for taxing wealth; that is the use of these taxes for revenue.

CONSIDERATIONS OF REVENUE

Until the last years of the nineteenth century taxes were viewed only as sources of revenue. The idea that taxes should perform functions other than the straightforward one of financing government is relatively new. The early taxes on estates and inheritances in the United States and the United Kingdom undoubtedly were fired by the need for more revenue. In the United States the unexpected expenses of dealing with the French attacks on American shipping forced Congress to levy the first type of tax on wealth transfer in 1797 — a stamp duty on receipts for legacies and probates for wills. This tax was removed in 1802, but the war of 1812 revived the financial problems of the Union and in 1815 the Secretary of the Treasury suggested that inheritance and income taxes should be introduced. The end of the war saved the American public, for a time, from these imposts.

The same war had caused deficit financing by the British government. In 1799 the difficulties of revenue persuaded Parliament to introduce the first income tax. The optimistic estimates of its yield were 40 per cent short and other sources of revenue were urgently canvassed. Consequently in 1805 Pitt brought forward a miscellaneous collection of taxes, one of which was 1 per cent on the value of legacies passing to direct descendants and higher rates on shares to more remote relations and strangers. This legacy duty was the first in the long history of British inheritance taxation aimed at revenue raising. There were oddities in the system; it was regressive in that it taxed small estates at 2.5 per cent and top estates at 1 per cent,[1] and it favored the landed proprietor to those who held shares or were in business.

In this way, both America and Britain introduced taxes on the transfer of wealth at death because the government was urgently searching for new sources of revenue. Possibly through this beginning, these taxes became associated in the public's mind with emergency conditions. The justification of wealth taxes because they were equitable came much later.

---

[1] W. Phillips, "How Income Tax Came Home to Roost," *British Tax Review,* September-October, 1959. Also, Leroy Dunn, "A History of British Death Duties," unpublished Ph.D. dissertation, London School of Economics, 1955-56, p. 102.

Immediately after the Napoleonic war ended the British income tax was abolished, but a mild form of death duties was retained because their fairly uncontroversial nature as a revenue sponge had come to be appreciated. The demands of the government for increased revenue and the reluctance of the public to tolerate increased income taxes continually brought death duties into controversy as a reasonable source of relatively unobtrusive finance. In Britain when Gladstone defended the consanguinity clauses in 1853 he made it quite clear that if there was to be any alteration of the existing rates there had to be no alteration of the yield. "Will you retain the tax at the present scale with 10% for strangers or will you reduce it, at the same time raising the tax on direct successions to make up the deficiency of *revenue?*"[2]

It was not until 1894 that death duties were thoroughly overhauled and a simplified estate duty replaced all existing rates. For the first time it was levied on all property, real or personal, on any estate over £1,000. For the first time the principle of progression was accepted in Britain. This was a momentous departure, for although the rates were only from 1-8 per cent the principle was established which was to be paramount in the coming century. No account was taken of the manner in which the estate was distributed between the beneficiaries, but the mild legacy duty still maintained differential rates according to consanguinity. This was the real birth of death duties in Britain as they are known today. In saying that the guiding principle of taxation should be the "ability to bear it of those on whom it is imposed," the Chancellor of the Exchequer, Sir William Harcourt, recognized an equitable principle and a start was made in the use of this form of taxation as an agent of redistribution.

In the United States it was 1916 before the federal government introduced a permanent estate tax. Prior to that, taxes on the transfer of property at death had been as short-lived as the 1797-1802 inheritance tax. In 1862 the Civil War forced the government to introduce an inheritance tax graduated according to consanguinity; the rates were increased in 1864 and in general apathy it was abolished in 1870. As 1894 was a momentous year in British tax history so it might have been in America. The proposal for an income tax with a base defined as "gains, profits, and income," including all property acquired by gift or inheritance,[3] would have been a remarkably modern approach to many tax problems. The Supreme Court declared the income tax, and hence, as part of the income tax, the tax on inheritances, unconstitutional.

---

[2] P. Magnus, *Gladstone, a Biography* (London: Murray, 1954), p. 417.

[3] S. Ratner, *American Taxation* (New York: W. W. Norton, 1942), Chap. 9.

This tax on the transfer of wealth would have been levied for reasons of equity but its defeat in 1894 stopped such a reasoned introduction for another twenty-two years.

Instead, the next time inheritance was used as a tax base in the United States was again primarily for purposes of emergency revenue, to help finance the Spanish-American War. In 1898 a legacy tax graduated according to consanguinity was passed, but as soon as the alarums and excursions of the Spanish-American War, the Philippines insurrection, and the Boxer Rebellion were past, all the war taxes, including the inheritance tax, were repealed in 1902.

It might be thought that the juxtaposition of the 1916 "Preparedness" Revenue Act and the federal estate tax again associated the wealth tax with emergency war finance rather than with equity. The unusual revenue requirements of the period did provide the impetus to introduce the federal estate tax, but by 1916 there was considerable public pressure to limit the huge concentration of wealth in the United States[4] and this supplemented the pure expediency of revenue requirements.

So the origin of both the British and the American estate taxes lies in the need for greater government revenue, but the continuous real and money increase in the yield during the last forty years has resulted from successive increases of the rates of duty, justified, not on grounds of revenue, but on those of equity.

As a revenue raiser, death duties in particular and wealth taxes in general are not as flexible as income or sales taxes. The tax base expands more slowly than either income or consumption (the marginal propensity to save is likely to be under 0.5) with increases in GNP. Revaluation of the tax base is discontinuous, and with death duties changes in rates can cause great inequities between estates which turn over very slowly. The more effective a progressive wealth tax is in redistributing property, the smaller is the yield likely to be. However, net worth taxes have one great advantage over other forms of direct taxation since they permit rates of tax on total resources, which would not be possible under an income tax; clearly a wealth tax of 10 per cent on capital yielding 5 per cent would require an income tax of 200 per cent for an equal yield. This leads to suggestions that it would be reasonable to change from surtax to a net wealth tax.[5] As far as yield goes, a wealth tax does not appear as flexible as the income and consumption taxes, but the low impact rate might offset some of this dis-

---

[4] *Ibid.*, pp. 354-358.

[5] A. T. Peacock, "Economics of a Net Wealth Tax for Britain," *British Tax Review*, November-December, 1963, for a criticism of this approach.

TABLE 5:1

Indices of Estate Tax Yields and GNP of the United States and the United Kingdom
(1950 = 100)

Indices	Year						
	1910	1920	1924	1930	1938	1950	1961
United States							
Estate Tax Yield	–	–	15	8	65	100	335
GNP	–	–	31	32	30	100	182
United Kingdom							
Estate Tax Yield	13	25	–	45	41	100	128
GNP	27	72	–	50	48	100	162

Sources: U.K. Reports of the Commissioners of Inland Revenue; *Statistical Abstract of the United States*.

advantage. It would be an ironic, historic circumstance if taxes on wealth, originally introduced for revenue to supplement other taxes and for a time competitive with income taxes, were resuscitated with improved methods of administration as a new revenue raiser. However, their increased revenue (in absolute terms) in recent years has been justified primarily on the grounds of equity.

An extraordinary form of wealth taxation which has been used sometimes to raise revenue for dramatic or exceptional times is the capital levy. The knightly feudal dues to the king, assessed on rank, which itself was closely correlated to net worth, were a form of capital levy. These levies were common in wartime, requiring the provision of a specific number of armed men, and it is wartime which has often justified capital levies for current revenue. In more recent times, Italy rearmed in 1936 and used a 5 per cent levy on houses and land (valued by capitalizing income). Continued armaments resulted in another Italian levy in 1937 on company capital at 10 per cent, and again in 1938 a levy was assessed on private firms and partnerships at 7.5 per cent.

Similarly the Hungarian "Investment Contribution" of 1938 was partly to finance large public works schemes of a pump priming nature, and partly for rearmament finance. Levied on all property both personal and corporate and payable over a five-year period, the levy appeared successful in providing cash, and the resulting public investment raised production and employment without a significant price rise.[6]

Sometimes the revenue has been required for ends other than war —

---

[6] J. R. Hicks, U. K. Hicks, and L. Rostas, *The Taxation of War Wealth* (2nd ed.; Oxford: Clarendon Press, 1942), p. 251.

to cover a wheat subsidy (Italy, 1921), to meet exceptional postwar expenditures (France, 1945), or to compensate for the ineffectiveness of other direct taxes (Italy, 1947).

The comparative success of such levies[7] is due to their overtly temporary nature; if it is recognized by the public that such taxes are only a passing expedient, then it is easier to gain public acceptance of such measures.

However, the most extensive consideration of wealth taxes levied for revenue have been those connected with the redemption of the national debt. In most advanced countries the idea of redeeming the national debt is enough to make the most conservative boggle. Current budget revenue would never yield a surplus sufficient to make a noticeable dent in the debt pile. Clearly some very exceptional source of revenue is needed, something that embodies a "once and for all" nature and which can be associated on some "quid pro quo" basis with the unusual object of the transaction. Wealth has been suggested as a possible base for a tax designed to reduce national indebtedness.

The British proposals to redeem the debt were the most ambitious,[8] to raise anything up to $84 billion (in 1922). Indeed we will see later that this scale has more of a redistributive character than that of the other national debt redemption levies.[9]

There were eventually six estimates of the scale and probable yield to the British levy; these spread over the years 1922-36 and usually with slightly differing results. (See Table 5:2.) The gross yield envisaged was as high as 71 per cent of GNP at factor cost (the highest continental capital levy yield was 8.2 per cent). The gross yield estimate depended on the scale of rates assumed; this gross yield was then reduced by the revenue lost to the state through the reduced income tax and surtax payments on income derived from the holdings of the national debt; it was further reduced by the lost death duties on the smaller properties, and these two deductions left a "net saving" to the state (column 5).

Problems of valuation must occur, especially where assets are of a highly speculative nature; valuation on a particular date might be extremely unfair if a few days later the expectations upon which the mar-

---

[7] Although the Italian 1921 levy for a wheat subsidy created great resistance and was abandoned after a year.

[8] U. K. *Report of Commission on National Debt and Taxation* (hereafter cited as The Colwyn Report), Vol. XI, 1927.

[9] The Colwyn Commission Minority Report, p. 361, para. 30, and p. 400, para. 181. ". . . we should necessarily consider this [redistribution] an important incidental advantage of a levy."

TABLE 5:2
Estimates of Revenue from a British Capital Levy, 1922-36

1	2	3	4	5	6	7
Authority	Date of Statistics Used	Yield £m	Gross Saving £m	Net Saving £m	Column 5 as Per Cent of GNP	Column 3 as Per Cent of GNP
Dalton	1922	3,000	142	70	1.65	71
Stamp	1922	3,000	142	42–50	0.99–1.18	71
Inland Revenue 1.	1926	2,500	125	48	1.12	58
2.	1926	1,000	50	17	0.25	23
3.	1926	2,000	100	34	0.79	48
Hicks	1936	2,950	97	22	0.22	61

Sources: H. Dalton, *The Capital Levy Explained* (London: The Labour Publishing Company Ltd., 1923), n. D, pp. 80-85.
J. Stamp, *Current Problems of Finance and Government* (London: King and Son, 1924), pp. 250-270.
The Colwyn Report, pp. 250-256 and Appendix XXIX.
Hicks and Rostas, Chap. XXIX.
GNP Estimates: A. T. Peacock and J. Wiseman, *The Growth of Public Expenditure in the United Kingdom* (National Bureau of Economic Research; Princeton: Princeton University Press, 1961).

ket valuation was made were dashed. In such cases some allowance for reassessment would have to be made — perhaps similar to those statements made by the Royal Commission on the Taxation of Profits and Income (1955) which suggested rises and falls of income over 50 per cent as justifying relief through averaging.

The problems of life interests, which can only be solved completely if the holder's actual life span coincides exactly with the actuarial average, could be circumvented by assessing the levy on the whole value of the settled property and making it payable out of the settled fund, the rate fixed by adding the fund to the existing property of the beneficiary. This can lead to inequities — viz., the successor to the life holder who enjoys the property ex the levy date suffers not according to his own wealth position, but relative to that of another, that is, the past life interest. These inequities do not seem so serious as to jeopardize the enactment of the entire levy.

Again, allowance must be made for price changes. The Colwyn Commission did not envisage a lag between the levy and payment sufficient to allow price changes which would significantly alter the "burden" of the levy. Their discussions on price levels are confined to the existing "burden," i.e., interest payments on the debt and the points of time when it was raised.[10] The interesting estimate was made that

[10] The Colwyn Report, paras. 197-202 and 737-743.

"a little over ⅔ of the debt may be regarded as having been raised when prices were above the present level." (This was a very different condition from that existing today when the state must be one of the main beneficiaries from the relief afforded to debtors by inflation.) Obviously, if there are large gaps between assessment and collection serious problems can arise, as they did in the continental levies aimed at reducing debt.

Czechoslovakia imposed a combination of capital levy and capital increment tax during the post–1914-18 war period. Payments, to be made over a three-year period, were accepted in cash, in trustee securities, in kind out of "blocked" real estate, or most significantly, out of deposit certificates which had been issued in exchange for bank notes when 50 per cent of the larger note denominations had been withdrawn in February, 1919. An expected revenue of KC. 12 milliards did not materialize and the fiscal authorities eventually accepted the yield in 1936 to have been about KC. 7 milliards (58.3 per cent of the expected yield).[11] This relatively (to expectations, not compared to similar experiences in other countries, see below) disappointing yield was due to the fluctuating value of money (falling prices greatly increasing the real burden) and to economic and political imponderables.

The Hungarian levy followed the Czechoslovakian pattern with property registered and "blocked" until "redeemed" by levy payment. Inflation allowed the real burden of the levy to be lightened and eventually through the obstruction (lack of cooperation on the part of the taxpaying public so emphasized in the British discussions[12]) of the large property owners the levy was abandoned.

The least successful of these continental levies was that introduced in Austria in 1919 with the registration and "blocking" of various forms of property. Owing to political controversy the imposition of the levy was delayed eighteen months from the valuation, and naturally in this period there was a large flight of capital and the purchasing power of the currency fell; between assessment and imposition the register of property (especially liquid assets) had been completely outdated. The inflation, probably accentuated by the levy, made the assessment ridiculous and the payment farcical. By the end of 1922 the levy had been abandoned.

The following table clearly shows the comparative ineffectiveness of the Austrian levy, and the relatively small yields of all the levies even when expressed as a per cent of national income: of course, the per

---

[11] Hicks and Rostas, p. 216.

[12] The Colwyn Report, p. 247, para. 709, and Appendix XXII.

TABLE 5:3

Yields of Czechoslovakian, Hungarian, and Austrian Capital Levies[a]

Country	Personal Property Rates (Per Cent)	Yield £m	National Income £m	Yield as Per Cent of National Income
Czechoslovakia	1–30	45 (capital levy and increment tax)	550 (1929)	8.2
Hungary	5–20	15	210 (1929)	7.1
Austria	3–65	3	220 (1929)	1.4

[a] In many cases the wildly fluctuating values of the internal currencies, apart from changes in sterling, make assessments very suspect; but the table is presented primarily to indicate comparative effectiveness, not absolute money yields.
Source: Compiled from L. Rostas, "Capital Levies in Central Europe 1919-1924," *Review of Economic Studies*, Vol. VIII, October, 1940, p. 28.

cent they represented of national wealth would be very small indeed and the *net* saving to the government must be extremely small.

The lessons of these levies for revenue lie in their mistakes, e.g., the ineffective control of capital flight, the lapse between valuation and payment, the importance of some minimum degree of cooperation between the levying authorities and the paying public, and the difficulty of maintaining stable purchasing power over the levy period. Finally, it is most important to note that these were all modest levies and their actual "bite" into capital must have been small compared to that envisaged in the British levy discussions.

The principal points of the British survey were the *feasibility* of a really serious levy; enterprise and saving would not be irreparably damaged, but there would have to be some assurance against repetition,[13] and once more the desirability of a degree of public cooperation was emphasized. But for the purpose under consideration — the reduction of the national debt — the large hazard of a capital levy could not be justified. By implication, if some other end were in view, redistribution for example, then such a levy might be more justified.

SUMMARY

Death duties were introduced in the United States and Britain to help finance the expenditures of the Napoleonic War. Not until 1894 in Britain and 1916 in the United States did considerations of equity start to replace those of revenue.

---

[13] The Colwyn Report, paras. 744-748.

Capital levies primarily for revenue have not been very successful in practice and the uncertainties involved in a large levy make it suspect as a means of financing an extraordinary expenditure (e.g., retiring the national debt), or for emergency spending (e.g., on armaments and wartime needs). The uncertainties are those of public cooperation, valuation, maintaining stable purchasing power during the assessment and levy payment, and the control of capital flight. The only levies for revenue which have had any success have been those which established some degree of identity between public and private goals, e.g., Italian rearmament.

Three reasons can be given for taxing wealth: the socioeconomic justification for redistributing wealth, as a supplement to complete existing tax structures, and for revenue. The next eight chapters discuss various taxes on wealth in the context of the first two reasons.

6

Changes in the Structure of Personal Wealth Taxation: Capital Levies

Wealth can be taxed sporadically at regular and irregular intervals by a levy on capital. A recurrent, expected levy on capital is the same as a net wealth tax, and this particular form will be considered in the next chapter. The irregular capital levy will be discussed first.

For the present we will view a capital levy as essentially unexpected, to meet an emergency, or a once and for all need.[1] It can be assessed on capital (company, or personal, or both) owned at a given date.[2]

In the last chapter three reasons were given for taxing wealth. Cap-

---

[1] Note that the emergency is also necessarily once and for all, e.g., to redeem debt created by war expenditure; whereas a once and for all need is not peculiar to an emergency, e.g., the redistribution of wealth in society.

[2] This is the same definition as that used by P. Robson, "Capital Levies in Western Europe After the Second World War," *Review of Economic Studies,* Vol. XXVII, No. 1, October, 1959, p. 23, which contrasts to that used by Hicks, Hicks, and Rostas, p. 180, "A capital levy, as the term seems generally to be understood, is a direct tax of such magnitude as to fall upon the capital of the taxpayer. It need not be assessed on capital, though it usually will be; the important thing is that the levy is too large to be paid out of income." As this latter definition confuses the thing taxed and the means of payment, e.g., an income tax assessment paid by a gift received would not be considered, usually by either the revenue authorities or the public, as either a tax on capital or on gifts, it is probably better to concentrate on the tax assessment rather than on the "ex post" results of payments, which can vary between taxpayers and with tax structures.

ital levies to raise revenue were discussed, but levies have also been suggested for two other roles:

Redistributive levies

(i) from the rich to the poor,

(ii) from the nation to distressed groups.

Levies to supplement the tax base

(i) on extraordinary gains,

(ii) to reduce liquidity.

All capital levies are redistributive in that even if imposed to combat inflation they will most likely result in some redistribution; similarly, a levy to redeem the national debt will likely result in redistribution. The distinctions drawn above are between the major reasons for the levies although each category may overlap with others in some of the side effects.

REDISTRIBUTIVE LEVIES

From the Rich to the Poor

The most debated proposals of this nature have been in Britain. The first capital levy tax rates put forward were those of the Labour Party[3] in 1922, rates which, although slanted to fit in with the then current controversy on the reduction of the national debt, also had the purpose of achieving a substantial redistribution of assets within the community. It is probably not unfair to place these proposals within the context of class redistribution, although the original proposal was not couched in those terms.[4]

The other proposal is that put forward in a *Tribune* 1951 pamphlet which proposed the annihilation of all estates over £100,000 and very high rates on estates under that figure. This again was attached to other ends, i.e., for rearmament (the Korean War) —"Why should we not pay for this war preparation out of the genuine real wealth of the country? . . . a National Defence Contribution starting at £2,000 of capital and working upwards."[5] But the rates proposed (not officially)

---

[3] Dalton, *The Capital Levy Explained.*

[4] J. M. Keynes, The Colwyn Report, p. 539, para. 7611. "The advocate of the capital levy is probably wanting it as the first instalment of a radical redistribution of wealth."

[5] Crossman in *Parliamentary Debates: Official Report* (5th series), Commons, 1950-51, Vol. CDLXXX, col. 372; and see Foot, "The only kind of action which can be taken is some form of capital levy, or rearmament levy," in *ibid.,* col. 231.

TABLE 6:1
The Scale of Levies Proposed in the United Kingdom, 1922 and 1951

Wealth in £'000	1922	1951
0–5	0	0
5–6	5	0
6–8	10	0
8–10	15	0
10–15	20	0
15–20	25	50
20–30	30	50
30–50	35	75
50–100	40	90
100–200	45	95 or 100
200–500	50	95 or 100
500–1,000	55	95 or 100
1,000 +	60	95 or 100

Sources: 1922 — Labour Party, *Labour and the War Debt, a Statement of Policy for the Redemption of War Debt by a Levy on Accumulated Wealth* (London: The Labour Party, 1922).
1951 — *Tribune* Pamphlet, Tribune Publications, London, 1951.

obviously had a more redistributive (some might say confiscatory) ring than that justified by rearmament only.

It is important to distinguish between these two proposals. The 1951 one was explicitly redistributive, so the total yield of the levy would be available to the government to use as it wished (e.g., increased social services, lowered direct or indirect taxation, etc.). On the other hand, the 1920's discussions centered around the reduction of the national debt; the redistributive element here is of a secondary nature, and, of course, the transfers to debt holders would have a very different macroeconomic effect compared to a more general program of government expenditure. A progressive levy must fall with increasing weight upon the owners of wealth. The redemption of debt puts the proceeds of the wealth tax into the hands of the holders of the debt. In this first instance, the capital levy would only be progressively redistributive insofar as the holders of national debt were less wealthy than those who paid in the levy. The evidence of the Colwyn Commission was (although related to another aspect of the tax)[6] that such would be the case. But the second redistributive result of such a levy, apart from that incidental to the redemption of the debt, is that it reduces

[6] The Colwyn Report, p. 264, para. 760, "The percentage of the total estate invested in Government securities remains fairly constant; while the percentage to be taken by the levy rises steeply."

the wealth of those paying the tax and leaves *the former holder of debt no better off* because they have simply exchanged debt (which they viewed as capital) for cash. Their situation is now liquid but it is essentially the same as the one they would have been in had they decided to sell their securities. Thus the taxpayers are worse off, and the tax receivers are no better off; therefore, such a levy must be redistributive.

There is yet a third redistributive element in this national debt levy. With the reduction of the debt, the Inland Revenue no longer has to find so much current revenue to finance the annual interest obligations, resulting in an annual saving to the Exchequer. But this overall saving is reduced by the current income and surtax revenue lost from those who have reduced their estates by paying the levy. This results in a *net* saving usually well under half the original gross reduction in interest payments (see Table 5:2). Depending on how the government spent this money, the first and second redistributive elements can be strengthened. For instance, if social services were expanded or indirect taxes reduced, or family allowances increased, the redistribution could be great.

In his evidence to the Colwyn Commission, J. M. Keynes said,[7] "If this measure [the capital levy] is to be on a scale which would take it out of the category of a mere modification of the incidence of taxation, it ought to be the last, rather than the first, step in any transition from individualistic capitalism to a new order of society."

The easiest way to dismiss such redistributive levies is that adopted by Mr. Chambers[8] commenting on the *Tribune* scheme. "If the main purpose of a capital levy is the redistribution of wealth, all arguments based upon normal principles of taxation and finance miss their mark. The direct redistribution or confiscation of property is a practice wholly alien to any country in which there is a genuine respect for individual liberty."

But without resorting to such claims it is possible to question the practicability of schemes on the scale envisaged by the most recent proposal (1951). If such high rates are levied, are the proceeds to go directly to the state, or are they to be redistributed via the state to, for instance, the holder of the national debt, or to some other arbitrarily selected group, e.g., spent on education, health, etc.? With rates of 100 per cent on estates over $280,000 the state would be obliged to accept payment in kind, and this mass of properties would undoubtedly

---

[7] The Colwyn Report, Minutes of Evidence, Vol. II (3), p. 534.

[8] S. P. Chambers, "The Capital Levy," *Lloyds Bank Review*, January, 1951, p. 3.

be a most heterogenous collection. If the state were to sell these in an attempt to redeem debt in cash or to provide current finance for public works, the effect on the property markets must be to force down the prices, and it is likely that much property would pass into the hands of speculators. On the other hand, if the state decided to administer the properties itself, the dislocation during the transfer process would be great and there would probably be a long time between the handing over of property and its efficient conduct by the state, e.g., farming land, managing miscellaneous businesses, owning real estate, etc. Even if mortgages and shares on industrial concerns were issued to holders of the debt, this would result in a rather odd redistribution to insurance companies, trustees, and private individuals more interested in income than in the risk associated with capital gain. This sort of redistribution is not desirable and certainly not planned.

Overall, "a society like ours is an organic society, a going concern . . . so highly organised and inter-dependent between its various parts, resting as it does on a balance of tensions, thrusts, and strains, that intervention at one point will have effects at numerous and often unexpected other points."[9] It seems doubtful whether the social disruption would justify the gain and it is even more doubtful whether it would be electorally acceptable in present-day conditions, and although the statement of Chambers quoted earlier may be extreme it is nevertheless probable that such taxation would at least require the sanction of a general election or referendum.

From the Nation to Distressed Groups

The three classic cases of this are levies imposed in Finland to compensate the devastated area of Karelia in 1941, and again in 1945, and the German 1952 levy to provide war compensation.

Losses suffered in Finland were assessed on a diminishing scale so that larger property owners received proportionately less. The remarkable feature of this levy was the manner in which payment was facilitated in kind. Land owners received bonds in exchange for their land and paid the levy with bonds. Similarly, companies paid the levy by shares issued to a government company which then used these titles as a form of compensation payment.

The drastic currency reform of 1948 in Germany, including the repudiation of the public debt, was followed by a capital levy of 50 per cent in 1952, to be used to compensate those who had suffered losses in the war, and also those who had suffered a loss through the monetary

---

[9] Crosland, p. 314.

reform (especially through losing savings). As the payment is over the very long period of thirty years, and as part of the liability can be offset against other taxes, it is difficult to forecast the effectiveness of this tax. The sharp rate of growth of Germany since 1952 even with little inflation considerably eases the burden of the debt, and the creation of a vast new property structure since 1952 also makes the base of the tax very small compared to current values.

This type of levy is justified only by exceptional circumstances; consequently the public, who pays, often has little resistance and also has suffered, in some part, similar deprivations to those who are to be compensated; thus the exercise can be conducted without obstruction, but often is unrealistic because values are as extraordinary as the situation.

LEVIES TO SUPPLEMENT THE TAX BASE

All the taxes on wealth which are to be discussed are, in part, justified because they do things which other taxes cannot. Capital levies have been proposed as a method of tackling extraordinary gains which the normal tax forms missed; alternatively, they could be used to reduce potential spending power more swiftly than usual taxation.

Extraordinary Gains

There have been recurrent phases of public feeling against extraordinary income, whether by capital gains,[10] wartime profits, or as in the last few years, rising land values. In this instance the capital levy is perhaps better described as a property increment levy because the yardstick is not only total wealth held but the increased value of this property over a specified period. It is often convenient to combine this with a straightforward capital levy as did Czechoslovakia in 1919, because the latest valuation for the increment levy forms a useful base for the current levy assessment.

In a Hungarian example the progression was double, increasing with both the size of the property and the extent of the increment, with final rates from 5 to 40 per cent.[11]

Germany imposed personal increment levies in 1916, 1917, and 1919, the most ambitious of which was the last. Rates on personal property rose from 10 per cent to 65 per cent (the levy of 1916 had rates rising

---

[10] For the most recent see: 1951-59 minority report of *Royal Commission on Taxation of Profits and Income*, H.M.S.O., 2nd rep., Cmd. 9474, 1954, p. 358, para. 12. Or A. R. Ilersic, *The Taxation of Capital Gains* (London: Staples Press, 1962), pp. 29-30.

[11] Hicks and Rostas, p. 214, espec. n. 1.

to 50 per cent), with a special 10 per cent addition on luxuries[12] and corporate bodies. But payment (as in the later post-1945 German levy) was spread over a thirty-year, or even in the case of land, fifty-year period. With a rapidly depreciating currency the public's disbelief in such a form of taxation increased, and despite attempts to accelerate payment the levy had to be abandoned by the end of 1921.

A more recent example is the capital profits tax of 1940-45 levied in the Netherlands,[13] which attempted to estimate the difference in capital between the beginning and the end of the war; this was a most difficult procedure, partly due to the inadequate nature of the records, and partly because of the influence of price controls in different fields, and finally because even the valuation of company shares was rather arbitrary as there was no stock exchange in 1945. The difficulties of administration were great and there was an element of arbitrariness,[14] which probably would only be tolerated in the exceptional conditions prevailing in postwar Holland.

Another form of increment levy on gains which were considered socially undesirable is the "Compensation and Betterment Act, 1947" in the United Kingdom. This act was designed to insure that profits on land developed for largely urban or industrial use accrued to the state and not the individual owner. Such a policy is obviously connected with classical discussions on the unique qualities of land and the dubious authority of private ownership of land. Basically, the act tried to tax at 100 per cent the increase in value of land that was developed or was granted planning permission. This taxation entailed assessing the original existing use value (at market prices, and to understand the ramifications of assessing market value when a sale does not take place, see Chapter XIV), ". . . the estimation of an existing use value was extremely difficult, since land very rarely changes hands at existing use value where it has any development potential."[15] In addition to this difficulty, sales of land and development of property were peculiarly altered to fit the legislation. Agricultural improvements boomed because they were exempt. Small alterations were oddly constrained by a tax-free development allowance of 10 per cent enlargement, so that

---

[12] Objets d'art and "luxuries" which had been purchased during the war.
[13] D. B. J. Schouten, "Theory and Practice of Capital Levies in the Netherlands," *Bulletin of the Oxford University Institute of Statistics,* Vol. X, No. 4, p. 119.
[14] *Ibid.,* p. 120.
[15] R. Turvey, *The Economics of Real Property* (London: Allen and Unwin, 1957), p. 135.

large houses were knocked into flats (without altering the cubic capacity). A tax levied only on a specified type of property, and not as a general tax, leaves a choice for the taxpayer between assets which are taxed and some which are not; on buying the taxed asset the buyer will be prepared to offer only the price (net of tax) less the grossed up (capitalized) value of the tax. That is, he anticipates his tax liability and compensates for this by paying a lower price for the taxed asset, thus balancing the choice between the taxed and untaxed assets. An even more advantageous alternative was open in this case. Due to the essentially uncertain nature of political power, many persons were skeptical of the continued application of this tax and delayed land sales, and hence development, awaiting (correctly) a change in party power and policy. This was possible because the taxpayer was allowed to decide when he would incur the tax (i.e., when he developed or sold the land), and this always gives considerable latitude to the timing of tax payment, which means, as circumstances change, that there is greater likelihood of inequity.

The principal difficulty of all increment levies is that of assessing the capital held several years previous to the decision to tax by levy; because such decisions are usually *ex post* no steps have been taken to estimate capital at earlier dates and as a result the assessments often must be arbitrary.

Anti-inflationary Levies

Levies of this type were imposed after 1945 in Holland, Denmark, Belgium, and Austria. This type of levy is usually combined with a reform of the currency system whereby funds are blocked and rigid exchange controls prevent capital flight.

In Belgium and Holland the proceeds of the capital levy were used to liquidate the accounts of cash and government securities which had been permanently blocked. To avoid frustrating the whole effort (by allowing new borrowing to meet the levy payments), in both countries the authorities allowed persons whose levy obligations were less than their blocked assets to sell these (directly in the Netherlands, indirectly in Belgium through government-forced loans) to those whose obligations were larger than their holdings of blocked assets. In this manner a redistribution of blocked assets allowed the government to mop up liquidity without the private sector having to resort to new borrowing.

In Austria and Denmark compulsory loans at interest rates of 50 per cent of the prevailing long-term rates, assessed on total wealth, were used to reduce the government account and hence liquidity.[16]

The success of these post-1945 levies is due mainly to the increased efficiency of the financial authorities in stopping capital movements from the country; once capital flight is stopped, then the issue of government securities against the compulsory withdrawal of cash can be carried out even if the public realizes that this is only a prelude to the capital levy.

CONCLUSIONS

To insure equity with a capital levy, as with a successful international devaluation, surprise is essential. The successful capital levy has the element of a trap, and it could be held that this is not the sort of basis on which equitable taxation is based. But the greatest inequity resulting from a levy is that which occurs through time. One generation bears the levy, and unless it is highly confiscatory or levied repeatedly (in which case it loses the element of surprise and should become a net worth tax) people are hit differently according to the age structure of families. Of course, levies on particular forms of property (development land) are inequitable between holders of different types of property and a true capital levy should be assessed on all forms of property.

This is an extraordinary form of taxation; by its nature it is unlikely to form a part of a stable tax structure, even at a low impact rate for revenue; it is tolerated only because it is known to be temporary. In modern conditions where capital flight could be blocked (if surprise were maintained), as shown by the post-1945 levies, then a levy seems practical. The minimum conditions for such a tax seem to be a minimizing of the time lag between valuation and payment, the maintenance of a stable purchasing power over the levy period, a degree of acceptance by the public, control of capital flight, and some guarantee against repetition.

In general, I side with the statement "the relief . . . which it offers, would be insufficient to justify an experiment so large, difficult and full of hazard."[17] There must be better ways of taxing wealth.

---

[16] The actual procedure in Austria was more complicated as the capital levy was used to redeem a forced bond which itself had been used to cancel the money supply. See P. Robson, "Capital Levies in Europe After the Second World War," p. 29.

[17] The Colwyn Report, p. 296, para. 876.

7

Changes in the Structure
of Personal Wealth Taxation:
Net Worth Taxation

NET WORTH TAXATION

Ideally, perhaps net worth taxation should apply to the "national wealth," but often it is taken to be only the net worth of individuals, including the value of stocks and bonds of private and public companies and of government held by individuals. If both individuals and companies were taxed on their assets then this would result in considerable double taxation. "This feature of United States property taxation in the last century proved to be unworkable, and ultimately was for the most part discontinued by practice or law."[1] Privately held companies must have their shares valued, presumably on an asset basis. If no allowance is made for goodwill this means that often they will be undervalued compared to quoted securities, so presumably valuation for such businesses will be on present estate duty lines where goodwill is normally reckoned at x years' purchase of the net profits of the business averaged over a period (usually 3 years). It could be maintained that where a company's assets valuation exceeds the quoted share value, then, if only the value of shares as held by individuals is taken as a base for the wealth tax, some part of national wealth has been left

---

[1] J. Due, "Net Worth Taxation," *Impôts sur la fortune y inclus droits de succession,* Institute de Finances Publiques, Zurich, September, 1960.

out[2] (e.g., shipping companies, rubber companies, etc.). A simple amendment to the usual tax base would be to allow companies full offset of the total share market value against their total assets. So long as the market valuation was larger than the assets no tax would be incurred by the companies. If a residual remained where assets were higher than the shares' market valuation then companies would incur the wealth tax on that residual. This might encourage the more efficient use of assets, as companies with a poor performance and a consequent low distribution and low share valuation will have a high tax liability. However, this is a rather tortuous problem and it is probably easier to argue that companies should be left entirely outside the net wealth tax base — except insofar as private companies must be included, otherwise there would be a temptation for everyone to turn himself into a private company.

Another form of wealth which would be omitted from the tax base would be that owned by government; on the other hand that owed by government would be included. There is no point in the government taxing itself. There again, there is no justification for the government's favoring its own stock issues.[3] The "national wealth" taxed would include all personal property, including government stock, and might include company assets where these exceeded aggregate stock valuation, but the base would exclude government-held property.

Under the personal net worth tax, all tangible personal property would be included, although in some countries special exemptions are made, e.g., Holland, where household effects, articles of art and science are exempted.

It is convenient to exclude many forms of miscellaneous consumer durables. These are in common usage, widely held throughout the community and their valuation for each individual tax unit would be tedious and probably unrewarding. Similar considerations point toward the exemption of houses. But if the argument is that these are widely spread and common to most, then the tax base could be expanded easily by simply assuming that most persons possessed these goods; unfortunately this would lead to inequities, as those who in fact did not possess these properties would be taxed on the unfair assumption that they did. It would disrupt many markets as such goods would have some premium over other goods, i.e., if you are to be taxed as

---

[2] In Sweden, under the net wealth tax "the market quotation of a share is not always accepted if it is considered that its current value does not reflect the true worth of the net assets," Ilersic, p. 47.

[3] Presumably some justification could be made for treating government issues more favorably on some welfare criteria for weighting social expenditure more heavily than the market does.

though you possessed them in any case, then you might as well have them. On the other hand, if such goods are excluded from the valuation, then this discriminates between those who choose to hold some of their wealth in such forms, and those who do not, i.e., those who decide not to own a car or a washing machine, but use public transport and laundries, are penalized under a tax base which excludes cars and washing machines. Similarly, the 1965 U.K. capital gains tax, which excludes a single-owner occupied home, discriminates according to the size of house owned, between different forms of capital, and between those who rent and those who buy accommodation.

The tax base, then, should include consumer durables, land and buildings (at insurance valuations), and intangibles such as stocks and shares, mortgages, bank deposits, cash, etc.

It is normally suggested that there should be some exemption limit;[4] thus the net worth tax would only hit the larger estates and be used as an upper addition to the income tax structure. As with most tax exemptions there must be an element of arbitrariness about this, but in this case we do not have even the simple criteria of the Victorian "subsistence element." If the tax is levied at low levels of wealth, then very large numbers of persons are likely to be involved. The exemption limit is set by what is administratively feasible. Administration costs rise as the numbers in the tax base expand, yet as the increasing number of lower wealth holders are included, the money tax base reduces its rate of growth. These considerations could decide not only the exemption limits but many of the valuation problems as well.

To give an idea of the scale of the exemption problem for the United States and United Kingdom we show the estimated numbers of persons in each range of wealth holding. (See Table 7:11.)

The table gives some idea of the *scale* of administration and exemption. A tax on those with wealth over £100,000 would involve some 40,000 persons in the United Kingdom, and on a similar amount in the United States ($280,000) about 170,000 persons. A tax on those with wealth over £50,000 in the United Kingdom would involve 126,000 persons, and wealth over £25,000 (a reasonable limit) about 343,000 persons in the United Kingdom and 1,433,000 in the United States (over $70,000). Various exemption limits can be proposed, but $70,000 is a usual figure.[5]

---

[4] *The Economist,* 4 April, 1964, and *The Statist,* 1 March, 1963, p. 613, and 10 April, 1964, p. 81. W. Vickrey, *Agenda for Progressive Taxation* (New York: Ronald Press, 1947), pp. 362-363.

[5] Peacock, "Economics of a Net Wealth Tax for Britain," p. 392, and G. S. A. Wheatcroft, "The Administration Problems of a Wealth Tax," *British Tax Review,* 1963, p. 417.

TABLE 7:1
Estimated Total Net Wealth by Size in the United Kingdom in 1963 and in the United States in 1953

United Kingdom				United States			
Range of Net Wealth in £		Number of Wealth Holders in '000	Amount £m	Range of Net Wealth in $'000		Number of Wealth Holders in $'000	Amount $m
Over	Not Over			Over	Not Over		
–	1,000	9,200	4,349	–	–	–	–
1,000	3,000	5,058	9,502	–	–	–	–
3,000	4,000	1,199	4,202	–	–	–	–
4,000	5,000	689	3,097	–	–	–	–
5,000	10,000	1,290	9,008	–	–	–	–
10,000	15,000	397	5,120	–	–	–	–
15,000	20,000	205	3,607	–	–	–	–
20,000	25,000	116	2,573	60	70	176	9,795
25,000	50,000	217	7,658	70	150	915	75,527
50,000	100,000	86	6,212	150	200	181	24,831
100,000	200,000	28	3,854	200	300	163	30,878
200,000	–	12	4,531	300	–	174	125,650

Source: *U.K. Report of Commissioners of Inland Revenue for Year Ended 31 March, 1964*, Cmd. 2573, p. 172; Lampman, Table 24, p. 52.

To administer an annual net worth tax on 1,433,000 persons would require a considerable full-time staff. An attractive alternative is to levy the tax at more infrequent intervals, say, every five years. This amendment introduces the problem of assets whose value changes quickly. But presumably half a wealth tax would be better than none. An alternative might be to tax only some assets whose current valuation is easy, but this leads down the dismal path that the U.S. property tax has followed, until it becomes largely a tax on "real property" and has all the disadvantages of the specific property tax mentioned above. There is, of course, one significant form of property which is exempt under our definition of net personal wealth, and that is the investment in education. There is no intrinsic difficulty in including this invest-ment under a net worth tax, but the taxation, in this way, of personal decisions to invest in education could be held to have invidious over-tones socially, and unfortunate consequences for national economic growth. In any case, as we hope to show later, this problem can be overcome by government expenditure rather than by government taxation.

The statistical details provided by the administration of such a tax could be of interest and use to economics, but the problems and expense of administration are the biggest obstacles to the widespread use of the net worth tax and make it probable that the introduction would be best conducted in stages. A tax on those with wealth holdings over $300,000 would involve some 30,000 persons in the United Kingdom and 174,000 in the United States. If combined with some reduction in the high brackets of income tax, it would probably meet little resistance. As the system is perfected the range of wealth included could be ex-tended gradually without overburdening the administrative system. The costs and administrative difficulties of this simple version raise the question whether the improvement in equity is worth the effort and cost of administration.

Clearly, a net worth tax provides a much broader and more com-prehensive definition of that which comprises "similar circumstances" than an income tax alone, or a capital gains tax alone, or a combination of income and capital gains taxes. As the security and prestige aspects of holding nonmonetary income–yielding assets including cash and near cash deposits are within the tax base, the tax is more equitable.

The comprehensive nature of the tax base also insures that more facets of the circumstances by which persons differ are taken into ac-count in determining the taxes on persons of dissimilar circumstances at a particular point in time. Moreover, if the weighting of the tax structure is progressive then the wealth tax allows a much more rigorous progressive scale than does the usual type of income tax. An income tax of 50 per cent on a 10 per cent money-income yield would need a wealth tax of only 5 per cent; it is relatively easy to have wealth tax rates which result in revenue exceeding 100 per cent of the assets' money yield. If redistribution were desired in the upper wealth strata which would not only destroy the income flow but bite into the capital sum, then a wealth tax would be an admirable agent.

The wealth tax also insures equity between persons in similar circumstances at different points of time, as their similar assets would have corresponding price changes. But between persons in differing circumstances through time the wealth tax would be difficult to administer perfectly. It would be necessary to value all the wealth falling into the tax base on a single date, otherwise differences in stock valuation, interest rates, and profit declarations will cause inequities. Yet it is clear that some valuations will be extremely difficult on this basis unless it is obligatory that all trades, including partnerships, incorporated or unincorporated enterprises, and professions, complete their annual accounts on a particular day — a sort of final Napoleonic Code carried to the point where accountants swing dizzily between feast and famine.

Any spread of valuation dates could cause inequities in valuations. Moreover, any tax whose tax liability is determined by the arbitrary imposition of a date, annual, biannual, quinquennial, etc., is bound to result in inequity between those whose capital has accrued just before the current tax date, and those whose capital accrued just following the previous tax date; their tax liabilities will be the same but one will have had (for five years?) nonmonetary income untaxed. It might be possible to cover this by building in a general interest mark-up on property, varying according to the length of time the property was held between tax assessments. But clearly, even a year's lapse allows for this type of inequity. What is needed is some type of P.A.Y.A. (Pay As You Accumulate) which might cover such an inequity. This would need to link the liability to tax not to some arbitrary date chosen by the Inland Revenue, but rather to a date unique for each person, that is, the date on which he added to his capital. Thus attention on the tax base swings away from only the stock of net worth to the transfer of net worth, which we will examine next.

8

Wealth Transfer Taxation:
The Estate Duty

ESTATE DUTY

Estate duty is levied on the entire estate left by the testator without any reference to the inheritors. It has the great value of simplicity. Since the estate duty is practiced in its most rigorous form in the United Kingdom, it is to that system we will look for examples of its effectiveness.[1]

First introduced in 1889, at 1 per cent to supplement "Probate and Succession Duties" on estates over £10,000, it was justified because "those whose fortunes are considerable, are those who pay least in proportion to their aggregate income and property"[2] and, like any new tax, it was temporary, estimated to be levied for a period of seven years. The progressive principle of estate duty was established in Harcourt's famous budget of 1894, in which a simplified estate duty replaced all existing rates (except consanguinity) and was applied to all property real or personal on any estate over £100, with rates from 1-8 per cent.[3]

---

[1] Similarly, we shall use the U.S. gift tax as our example when we consider gifts taxation.

[2] 335 *Parliamentary Debates* (3rd series), 1889, Vol. CCCXXXV, col. 527.

[3] See the remarks of M. P. Leroy-Beaulieu, a French commentator, on the 1894 budget: "un odieux system de spoliation successorale . . . une insulte au bon sens." In A. W. Soward and W. E. Willan, *The Taxation of Capital* (London: Waterlow and Sons, 1919), p. 142.

By levying the estate duty on the total amount of property changing hands this tax avoids the difficulties of succession duties where not only relationship, but circumstances ought to be considered. It suffers from only one difficulty in application. Strictly, each rate in the progressive scale should be applied only to its appropriate part of the estate; in fact, the aggregate is taken and a rate applied to that. Thus it can happen that when an estate is just sufficiently large to move into the next higher rate the additional duty is more than the excess property above that particular threshold. This difficulty is usually compromised by taking in tax only that amount of property over the tax threshold. This sometimes leads to peculiar sales of houses and other property where the money received for the assets is largely immaterial because it will all go to the Revenue.

The problems of estate duty, which require some further investigation before estate duty is rejected or accepted as a means of taxing personal wealth, will be dealt with under three headings:

(i) Effectiveness,
(ii) "Dynamic" forces,
(iii) Avenues of avoidance.

EFFECTIVENESS

The need for equity has been used as a means of justifying some redistribution of wealth and it is interesting to ask how efficient the estate duty has been in achieving this redistribution.

Chart 8:1 shows three Lorenz curves for 1911-13, 1936-38, and 1950, showing the distribution of wealth in the hands of capital owners with more than £2,000. This limit has been chosen because of the unreliability of figures available for lower capital groups.

It is obvious that the redistribution which had taken place up to 1936 was slight, and any there had been was in favor of the upper middle classes. By 1950 the position was better, but clearly the action of estate duty in redistributing wealth is slow, and this pace will certainly not satisfy the more radical members of society. In 1956, a British Labour Party member wrote about death duties "it is clear that these are not now high enough. Contrary to original expectations they have not effected any large alteration in the pattern of property distribution."[4]

If redistribution is one of the major concerns of the British death duty policy, then the amount of redistribution actually achieved must

---

[4] Crosland, p. 301.

CHART 8:1

Lorenz Curves Showing the Distribution of U.K. Capital Owners with More Than £2,000 Wealth, for 1911-13, 1936-38, and 1950

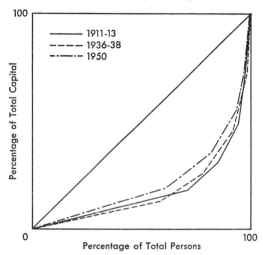

Sources: K. M. Langley, "Distribution of Capital in Private Hands 1936-39 and 1946-47," *Bulletin of the Oxford University Institute of Statistics,* December, 1950; Langley, "An Analysis of the Asset Structure of Estates 1900-1949," *Bulletin of the Oxford University Institute of Statistics,* October, 1951; Langley, "The Distribution of Private Capital 1950-51," *Bulletin of the Oxford University Institute of Statistics,* January, 1954; H. Campion, *Public and Private Property in Great Britain* (Oxford: Oxford University Press, 1939); J. Campion and O. Daniels, *The Distribution of National Capital* (Manchester: Manchester University Press, 1936).

be disappointing. The decline in the share of top groups of wealth holders in the United States can be held to be similarly disappointing, especially when it is remembered that the figures must be underestimates, as are the English figures, because trusts and insurances have been used increasingly over the period, especially by the higher wealth holders, as avoidance avenues.

TABLE 8:1

Changes in the Percentages of Wealth Owned by Percentages of the Population in England, Wales, and the United States, 1922-56

Per Cent of Population (Top)	1922	1924-30	1936	1939	1951-56	Country
0.5	29.8	32.4	–	28.0	25.0	United States
1.0	–	59.5	56.0	–	42.0	England and Wales
5.0	–	82.5	81.0	–	67.5	England and Wales

Sources: Lampman, p. 202, and Lydall and Tipping, "The Distribution of Personal Wealth in Great Britain," p. 92.

DYNAMIC FORCES

It is, at first, surprising how little redistribution there has been. The forces which must be counterbalancing estate taxation are:

1. *The growth of capital:* The pace of growth of wealth in an advanced community today, with the efforts of the government bent to guarantee full employment and claim credit for a rising standard of living, is likely to be high. A 1956 estimate of the probable future rate of growth of profits in Britian was 3-5 per cent per year, and 1-2 per cent for real property.[5] Taking the lower figure of 3 per cent for profits, which assumes that the inflationary trend in prices since the war will be completely eliminated, and allowing the average holding of an inheritance to be thirty years, then the capital value of an average estate (that is, one held in assets which are neither particularly profitable nor remarkably stagnant), can be increased by 2.4 over the period. Simply allowing the passage of time gives a good chance of more than doubling an estate. Thus any estate which is taxed at, or below, 50 per cent stands a very good chance of maintaining or even increasing, its size (in real terms). As estate value increases the proportion of the estate held in industrial shares increases, therefore it is not unreasonable to maintain that with a national growth rate of 3 per cent, if the factor shares remain relatively constant, then estate duties will not provide a strikingly effective form of redistributive agent.

Thus, if we draw a graph (see Chart 8:2) assuming capital accumulation at 2.5 per cent per year for three estates of £250,000, £50,000, and £10,000 in 1897, and apply the appropriate British death duty liability for a transfer of estate in 1924 (27 years) and in 1960 (36 years), we gain some impression of the "bite" of the duties. Twenty-seven and 36 years are taken to give an average of 31.5 years, approximately the average length of a generation. With a growth of only 2.5 per cent it is clear that the growth of capital is offsetting the "cut" of the taxes. Moreover, it is only the much more severe post-1949 rates which are really cutting into the capital. As it is likely that the growth rate of capital in the postwar era has been increased compared to that in 1900-1945, these higher rates may only be offsetting the higher rates of growth.

If it is assumed that there is no consumption out of capital, just accumulation of capital, and there is no change in prices, the argument is conducted in terms of real changes in capital values. If there is only

---

[5] *Royal Commission on the Taxation of Profits and Income,* final report, Cmd. 9474, June, 1955, p. 380.

CHART 8:2
The Tax "Bite" of Estate Duties in the U.K., 1880-1960,
Assuming Capital Accumulation at 2.5 Per Cent per Annum

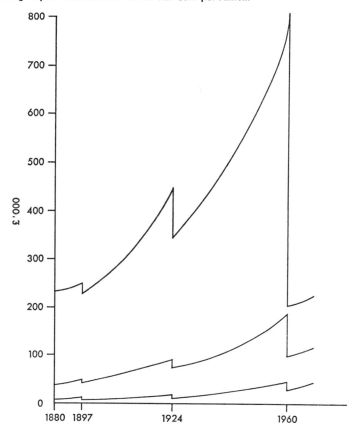

an estate duty in operation then the tax on capital must equal the
change in capital over the period in order to maintain capital at its
original real value.

$$(1-t)\,(K_1 + \Delta K) = K_1$$

$$t = \frac{\Delta K}{K_1 + \Delta K} = \frac{\Delta K}{K_2}$$

Where K_1 is capital at the beginning of the period and K_2 capital at
the end, ΔK is the change in capital value during the period $1-2$;
then the tax rate (t) must be equal to the change in capital value
divided by the capital at the end of the period.

If the above is accepted it is clear that, in theory, the rate of tax must be a changing phenomenon to take account of capital growth.

2. A second offsetting feature to estate taxation redistributing wealth is the "freezing" of ownership. Although the growth of assets helps existing estates to remain large, the high rates of taxation at death and on current income help to insure that new estates are difficult to create; thus while large wealth-holding continues, the addition of more large estates is slow. So redistribution is restrained.

3. The time lag makes redistribution by estate taxes slow. As the impact of this form of taxation is only once every generation, the effectiveness of it must be slow to show.

4. The estimates of wealth are themselves skewed by the death duty receipts. If there is considerable avoidance especially through trusts, insurance, or property moved abroad, then, particularly in the estimates of more recent years, the total wealth shown will be smaller than it really is; also, when compared with estimates for earlier years when avoidance was less and which are likely to be more accurate, the redistribution revealed will be misleading. It is reasonable to believe that avoidance only becomes important in the higher wealth groupings; it is there that the gains from not paying the duties become very striking. In Britain up to £50,000 the rate of tax is below 30 per cent, and not until £100,000 does the rate become 50 per cent, and by £500,000 it is 65 per cent. With these rates the rewards of successful avoidance are great and the advice of experts is amply recompensed; indeed, the cost of some of the more complicated methods of avoidance may only be justified where large sums are involved. Consequently the wealth estimates of recent years are likely to underestimate the amount of wealth held in higher groupings. Therefore, looking at the Lorenz curves, the amount of redistribution shown there is probably misleading and the actual redistribution less than even the small amount calculated (see Appendix II for an estimate of avoidance).

5. High rates are a relatively recent phenomenon. It is only in the last twenty years that the tax rates have become very high and, presumably, greatly encouraged avoidance. In 1939 the maximum rate was 50 per cent and at £50,000 the rate was only 14 per cent.

It is obvious from this discussion that any tax on wealth with a specific policy aim must be of a "dynamic" nature. It must change through time if it is to take account of the changing rates of growth of its base. But the dynamic nature of the tax base is not the only reason for the disappointing performance of the estate duties. Avoidance is another effect on equity.

AVENUES OF AVOIDANCE

Methods of avoidance can be grouped in five categories:

(i) generation skipping,

(ii) conversion into assets which bear lower rates,

(iii) gifts inter vivos,

(iv) the creation of trusts,

(v) overseas domicile.

As gifts, trusts, and overseas domicile are problems common to all transfer taxation and not unique to estate duties, these three methods of avoidance will be dealt with later (in Chapters 12 and 14). But the first two problems mentioned have aspects which affect the equity of estate taxes taxes in particular.

Generation Skipping

The greatest criticism of estate duty is that it is open to a simple evasion. By reducing the number of times an estate changes hands a taxpayer likewise reduces the number of times the estate pays tax and hence (whether rates are proportional or progressive) reduces the total amount paid in tax. An estate passing from A to B to C where A, B, and C are grandparent, parent, and son, respectively, is taxed twice; the same estate passing directly from A to C pays tax once. There is a built-in incentive to jump generations, to hold wealth as long as possible, to transfer it to the youngest acceptable member of the family. The short lived are penalized as their property dwindles at each death while the Abrahams prosper.[6]

As with most taxes, estate duties suffer from erosion of the tax base. Claims are made by interested persons to obtain special treatment for particular assets. If granted, these concessions may give other potential taxpayers the opportunity of transferring their assets into a form which bears a lower rate. The British estate tax has a number of exemptions, e.g., charities and trusts, "Indian Pensions," and the Crown (which is *not* liable). Three examples of this will show the inequity involved.

Assets Bearing Lower Rates

The rate of duty on agricultural property in Britain is reduced by 45 per cent. This favored treatment meted to land stems from the Victorian principle that land carried, in some peculiar manner, responsi-

---

[6] It is estimated, in the United States, that roughly half the property inherited is transferred in a manner that is aimed to skip a generation. See H. M. Groves, *Postwar Taxation and Economic Progress* (New York: McGraw-Hill, 1946), p. 275.

bilities and "burdens" which other property did not. The justification
for treating land differently than other forms of property was best put
by Gladstone, "Real estate deserves to be handled with care and tender-
ness on the grounds that it has more of a presumptive connection with
the discharge of duty than that which is ranked as personal." When
Harcourt introduced his 1894 budget, Queen Victoria wrote:

> The Queen is much concerned about the provisions made in the Budget re-
> garding the death duties which, in her opinion, cannot fail to cripple all
> landowners. Many properties are now only kept afloat at considerable loss
> to the proprietors who, if the Budget becomes law, may be driven to still
> further curtail their expenditure. This must inevitably affect the poorer
> classes, especially the agricultural community, numbers of whom will be
> thrown out of work altogether. . . . Where again will be the inducements to
> owners of property to effect improvements, when by so doing they know they
> are only encumbering their successors.[7]

This feeling persists today and agricultural land and buildings still
have a 45 per cent reduction in duty, and the payment of the duty can
be spread over eight years. But these sentiments appear no longer so
unquestionable as they did to Queen Victoria. To maintain the estates
and the squirachal structure of those who live on the land is it necessary
to reduce their liability to taxation by almost one-half? If the full rates
were to apply to this property from tomorrow on, undoubtedly the
main result would be a reduction in the prices paid for agricultural
property and a loss (tax) would be sustained by those at present owning agricultural land. On the other hand, the prices at which such
property is sold today reflect not only the possible return of that land
plus the "attractions" of a country life, but include a premium paid
for the relief of death duties, and this premium accrues not to the government but to the seller of the property. Those who own agricultural
property do so in the knowledge that some of their estates' value depends on government policy decisions regarding subsidies, which affect
their values to an extent far greater than the relief from death duties.
It is therefore reasonable to argue that owners of agricultural property,
and indeed owners of all property, stand open to changes in fortune
from the decisions of government; it is part of the risk of living in that
country.

---

[7] Queen Victoria to Sir William Harcourt, 1894, *Queen Victoria's Letters* (London: Murray, 1907-30). See also James R. Rhodes, *Roseberry* (New York:
Macmillan, 1965), pp. 340-346. "Property in this country is an enormous and
insidious force . . . it subscribes the election funds. . . . I think it is difficult to
overestimate the resources of property as a political engine. [The proposals] will
raise a most formidable engine against us, perhaps the most formidable. Will it
give us any compensating friends?" Private memorandum for the Chancellor of
the Exchequer, by Lord Roseberry.

It should be possible in future tax systems to abolish the distinction between the business of farming and the business of manufacturing other goods. The Victorian tax schedules which distinguish between the income from land and that from other forms of capital were partially based on the preconception that the business of farming was of an inherently different nature to that of other forms of business. This attitude still prevails. Farming is often referred to as the sort of life to which a gentleman might aspire who wanted something to do, the military officer retired early, the businessman with a country retreat. But as farming is recognized as a multi-product business which requires the complicated allocation of numerous inputs, and which demands an enterprise akin to that of the successful businessman, then it is reasonable to expect farming to be treated for all purposes, including taxation, as a business.

But because a lower rate of tax was granted to agriculture this led to claims for an extension of the reduced rates to small businesses.

Under the Finance Act 1954, Sect. 28,[8] "any estate duty chargeable on the death in respect of industrial hereditaments used in and occupied for the purpose of the business, or in respect of machinery or plant so used" should be taxed at the normal rate reduced by 45 per cent — the same as agricultural property.[9] By this legislation the family firm was placed on the same footing as the family farm.

The forced liquidation of a large portion of an estate, when it consists principally of a family business, can mean the end of the business. Naturally owners of such businesses who find themselves in a position where they are likely to bequeath such a regrettable choice to their legatees, adopt measures to avoid the break-up of the assets. Sometimes, an insurance policy is run to supply the eventual payment of death duties without having to realize many assets. Or large liquid reserves can be built up to avoid the forced sale of the property. A survey in the United States[10] shows that the structure of inheritance taxation encourages the owners of closely held businesses to sell or merge with other firms to avoid forced liquidation. Similarly, it can be argued that the large number of small liquid businesses which were available for "divided stripping" in Britain in the 1950's was, in part, due to the same argument.

---

[8] *Finance Act,* 1954 (2 & 3 Eliz. II) c. 44.

[9] Note this does not include professions or vocations. *Finance Act,* 1954, *ibid.,* Sect. 28. (9).

[10] J. K. Butters, J. Linter, and W. L. Carey, *Effects of Taxation: Corporate Mergers* (Cambridge, Mass.: Harvard University Graduate School of Business Administration, 1951).

In addition to these "structural" changes in companies which take place only because of death duties, an argument maintains that the duties discriminate against the shareholder in a private company compared to a person who holds quoted shares, because the valuation of a private company for estate duty liability is based upon balance sheet net asset values. Sometimes leading industrial shares can have a quoted value (which is the shareholders' base for estate duty liability) much lower than net assets at balance sheet amounts. Such comparisons depend on the state of the market and cannot be used as a basis for a reformed rate of duty; on the other hand, they do indicate that in some states of the market the present valuations could be unfair.

In 1951, the Command Paper[11] on this question of death duties and private companies showed that from their sample no business had actually been closed down or broken up as a result of the action of the duties. But as has been pointed out[12] it is not necessarily the breaking up which is important, but the harm which has been done in insuring that such breaking up has been avoided. The inquiry maintained that in most cases, non-trade assets were enough to meet the duties without touching the business assets. This assumes that selling non-trade assets (car, furniture, house) could leave a man with a business but no home, as an alternative to a home and half a business.

However, the reduction of duty on the value of private companies was based largely on some similarity between these enterprises and farming. But if no special amelioration of taxation is granted to agricultural property, then none would be granted to other businesses. It is the special treatment granted to one particular cause (agriculture) which evades the tax base and lets in the next wave (businesses) which leads to the next and so on.

Finally a provision which appears reasonable but which leads to inequity exempts entirely from duty interesting and/or valuable objects which yield only an income in kind,[13] providing that the owner keeps the objects in the country, takes reasonable care of them, and allows interested persons access to them. The conditions are not very tedious and are certainly worthwhile assuming in order to enjoy the possession and use of beautiful objects while incurring no death duties. Of course, they must not be sold, otherwise they are liable to duty as parts of the

---

[11] *Estate Duty and Family Business:* Report on Statistical Investigation by the Board of Inland Revenue, Cmd. 8295, 1950-51.

[12] A. R. Ilersic, "Estate Duty and Private Companies," *Accounting Research,* 1954, V, 183.

[13] *Finance Acts,* 1930, Sect. 40 (1), (3) (; and 1950, Sect. 48 (1).

previous owner's estate at the actual sale value; their value at time of actual death is ignored.

There appear to be two inequities in this exemption. Why should a person who chooses to put his assets into a form which he knows the government will acknowledge to be of national, scientific, or historic interest escape tax entirely, compared to another who happens to put his assets into objects which he may consider of national interest (avant garde painting which the Treasury deems valueless but which in fifty years' time emerges as undoubtedly of historic and national interest) but which the government ignores? More usually, why should the man with valuable paintings escape tax whilst the man with valuable equities is taxed? The reason can only be that this tax remission is used as a cheap way to encourage wealthy persons to buy and maintain works of art in the country. The public purse is reduced to give private persons the pleasure of private enjoyment of public possessions.

If this is not sufficient to argue for the removal of this exemption, account should be taken of the potential tax relief over a period of time, even if eventually the property is realized. The statute allows payment of one duty only (the sale value aggregated with estate valuation), that appropriate to the last death. Clearly, if the object of national interest has been held for a number of generations, and would have entered into a series of estate valuations and consequently into a number of duty liabilities, the single tax payment is a considerable saving.

Another loophole which this particular exemption creates is through the provision that even if the works of art are sold after death and become dutiable their value does not come into the calculation of the rate of duty which is the rate of the rest of the estate. Hence, a wealthy man who dies owning say, works of art worth £1 million, other estate worth half a million, and a loan at the bank of half a million (i.e., a millionaire who has sold half his assets and borrowed half a million to pay for the works of art) will pay no duty at all even though the works of art are sold immediately after his death.[14]

However, even without the evasive aspect of the exemption, the straightforward equity of the public purse paying for public possessions in private hands is an expensive way to keep valuables in the country. Far better for the state to purchase and display publicly that which it wants to keep so urgently.

None of these exemptions appears justified today. They erode the

---

[14] I am indebted to Professor Wheatcroft for this particular example.

tax base. They encourage transfer of property on grounds of tax avoidance which would not occur in the absence of the exemption. If all possible means of avoidance are included, the amount of revenue lost in Britain this way might be about 34 per cent of the 1960-61 total receipts — over £80 million (see Appendix II for the assumptions behind this estimate).

SUMMARY

The estate duty is an attractively simple tax to administer. It is inefficient in achieving a substantial redistribution of wealth quickly. The infrequently levied estate duty is continually offset by the increase in national wealth. It is a simple tax because it ignores the issues of both horizontal and vertical equity. Horizontal equity might be achieved if it were not for the wide exemptions. Vertical equity, if it is the person receiving the inheritance that is considered, is ignored completely. Equity through time is so little recognized that it provides the major loophole. The problems of exemptions and valuation are not unique to estate taxation, but the simple avoidance is, and this may reduce the tax revenue by over 30 per cent. It is this last criticism which must make those interested in equity reject estate taxes as a form of personal wealth taxation. They can be regarded, as administered today, "as a device for rescuing some revenue potentialities from the sentimentality of legislatures."[15]

---

[15] Although this was written in 1938 it remains true today. Simons, p. 131.

9

Wealth Transfer Taxation: Legacy Duty, Consanguinity Duties, and the Circumstances of the Legatee

LEGACY DUTY

A legacy duty is a transfer tax levied on the amount the legatee inherits. It can be levied as a straight duty, or according to the consanguinity of the legatee to the testator, or it can take account of the circumstances of the legatee.

All legacy duties suffer from disadvantages compared to estate duties. They are administratively more awkward, requiring not only the probate valuations on the total estate but the application of the tax rates to each individual legacy, not simply to one estate. If the rates are progressive, then by increasing the number of portions he leaves a testator lightens his tax burden and the tax yield is reduced. It can be argued that in encouraging this splitting of estates, the legacy duty is, in fact, succeeding in the motive of redistribution.

CONSANGUINITY

Although no longer applied in Britain, most other European countries and some U.S. states do have rates which vary according to consanguinity.[1] Five reasons exist in favor of transfer duties on inheritance varying according to the relationship between the testator and the legatee. First, that inheritance is a "windfall" to strangers, or a slight variant on the same idea, second, that the ability to pay of more distant inheritors is greater. Third, that the tax system must complement the legal system. Fourth, that work and savings motives are encouraged by such allowances. Finally, that the special circumstances of widows and children should be recognized. We shall look at each in turn.[2]

If we do not count upon inheriting a particular estate, and we are surprised when we do, then is it legitimate for the state to levy a higher rate of tax upon such "windfalls" than they would on expected legacies? This is one of the oldest justifications for rates varying according to consanguinity. It is also one of the thinnest. It assumes that expectations have a direct correlation to relationships; regrettably they can sometimes vary inversely, and Palmerston as early as 1853 criticized consanguinity scales on the grounds that relationship in law does not necessarily govern expectancy. Indeed, in some families it can be a positive disadvantage.

The second reason is akin to the first in that the natural expectation of the closer relatives means that they order their way of life differently than they would have if there had been no expectations. This means that when they do inherit the money, they *need* this estate in order to maintain that standard of living which they have enjoyed in expectation of the inheritance; they cannot therefore *afford* to pay the same duties as those to whom the legacy was a surprise.[3] This is a most extraordinary piece of reasoning.

In the first place it is legitimate to argue that if a person is living in expectation of his inheritance he is also presumably living in expectation of his *net* inheritance, and would be foolish to do otherwise. In other words, expectations take account of whatever tax rates are in

[1] E. B. Northcliffe, "European Fiscal Systems," *British Tax Review,* November-December, 1959, p. 447. The 1862 U.S. inheritance tax included consanguinity rates, from 0.75 per cent on direct heirs to 5 per cent on unrelated legatees, but J. A. Bingham "saw no reason for applying different rates to different persons and moved unsuccessfully to amend the provision by making a uniform rate of 3.5%." Ratner, p. 70.

[2] For a more detailed treatment of this subject see A. A. Tait, "A Comment on Rates of Taxation Varied According to Consanguinity," *Finanzarchiv N.S.,* Band 25, Heft 2, July, 1966, pp. 263-267.

[3] In 1795, J. Bentham wrote "Supply Without Burden," an essay in which he proposed taxation according to consanguinity because anyone who expected to inherit a property "could not but excite something of a sensation of loss," if any part of his legacy was taxed. Also see Gladstone's comments: 127 *Parlimentary Debates,* 3rd series, Col. 272.

force. The above argument favoring consanguinity would only be valid in the case of new rates, unsuspected by the potential inheritors, which would leave them with an unforeseen and unforeseeably low amount. But even if it were accepted that this argument was valid in the case of new rates, to embody it in the tax code would mean that the state agrees to take cognizance of the standard of living of the taxpayer and that it levies a *lower* rate as the standard of living rises; this annihilates progressive and even proportional taxation. This argument in favor of consanguinity rates is ludicrous.

Another, more substantial case for rates varied according to relationship is the requirement that the tax code should uphold the civil law. If the law of a country does not allow a person to dispose of his property entirely as he wishes then it is desirable that the tax code should not work in the opposite direction. This is reasonable. But if the legal code already favors particular relationships, further emphasis by special tax rates would overweight the balance of rights previously established. Certainly the legal and tax systems should not work against each other; one or other attitutde should be accepted as correct by current social standards. The civil law should not need to be "upheld" by the tax code.

Some people maintain that both work and savings motives are helped in the knowledge that by leaving your estate to closer relatives you can avoid the higher rates of taxation and at the same time leave more to your family. If any estate transfer taxation discourages work and saving (see Chapter 15) the question is whether the differential rates would discourage these motives more or less than rates applied equally to the whole estate. In the case of a person *wanting* to leave his estate outside his family they could equally be held to discourage saving. On the other hand if a rate of tax is applied to all estates irrespective of to whom they are left, and then under another system the *same* rate is applied to the near relations as before, but a higher rate is placed on strangers, the position of the man who is leaving his estate to the near relations is exactly the same in the two circumstances and his saving will not be affected. It is only the *diversion* of those estates which would have been left to strangers which is affected and, presuming that there is a 100 per cent swing of these estates to the near relations, then the tax yield remains the same and there is no increase in saving. The only way in which there would be an increase in saving between these two systems is if the higher rate on strangers persuaded those who were *determined* to leave their estates outside the consanguinity range to save even more and offset the increased tax, leaving the same net estate to the beneficiary as previously — but this is perverse reasoning and is certainly not the basis on which those supporting consanguinity rates base their claim.

It could be assumed that, in aggregate, the higher rates on strangers enabled the state to levy lower rates on the near relatives, thereby encouraging saving compared to the previously higher rates yet maintaining the total tax yield unchanged; of course if this were successful in encouraging saving and, as a consequence, more estates were left to near relatives, the total yield would be bound to fall and to maintain the yield the rates would have to be raised.[4] In any case the motive is difficult to assess: it is not the effect of transfer wealth taxes on total saving (this is dealt with later), but the extra saving and work effort resulting from the differential rates. Overall it seems unlikely that lower rates on the inheritances of relatives encourages more saving than that which results from an overall estate duty. Any effect is probably small, and if successful, is likely to be vitiated by tax increases to maintain yield.

The final point to be looked at is the demand for a limited range of consanguinity rates applying only to widows and children. This is the strongest case of all for the differential legacy taxes. In all other circumstances the acquisition of a legacy can be held to improve the individual's circumstances, but the death of the head of the family could involve the surviving members in a decreased income. Because of this it can be held that widows and dependent children should have special treatment. Note that there would be only two classes and that the relief would be very limited, e.g., only to widows and, say, children who are still being educated. The category "children" will be of little use, as the average age of inheritance in many advanced countries is forty, by which time the advantages of wealthy parents should have been well utilized and independence gained. There are other difficulties. Should widowers also be put into this special category? At first sight it seems they ought, but it is unlikely that the death of a wife involves the husband in a loss of income, except imputed, which is not taxed in any case, and a replacement in the form of a housekeeper is usually

---

[4] It should be mentioned that if yield is to be maintained compared to a flat estate duty then some rates would have to be very high indeed. When the consanguinity rates were in operation in nineteenth-century Britain with much smaller rates than those in use for death duties at present, 65 per cent of estates went to widows and children, 25 per cent to brothers and sisters, and 10 per cent to strangers; the more you encourage such distribution the lower will be the yield of the tax and rates will have to be raised to maintain the yield. This problem was also realized in the last century; see Magnus, p. 417.

valid for generous allowances against tax liability. Again there is not so much need for this amelioration of the duties at the top end of the scale where earned income is often a smaller item and life assurances offset against surtax usually yield a sum at death. The definition of a dependent child would probably have to include those who are ill or malformed (how ill or badly malformed?), and those at school and university. Again is any widow to be allowed these special rates? A very young widow has a considerable earning power herself. Should these rates be varied according to the age of the widow, or the age of the marriage? What happens if the widow marries again? The areas for discretion are wide and it might be neater to treat this whole problem under the heading of the circumstances of the legatee. This, after all, is the point at issue here; the valid claim for special treatment of widows and children cannot be based on sheer sentiment, or because of the legal system; it essentially depends on their circumstances, on their ability to pay. If the rates could be varied so that widows and children who were already well provided for still paid full rates of tax, while those who were left indigent as a result of their breadwinner's death and heavily taxed estate were lightly taxed instead, this might be a better framework to cope with the problem.[5]

THE CIRCUMSTANCES OF THE LEGATEE

The writers on this topic have all criticized the crudity of the existing systems.[6] "Death duties . . . are levies upon things or upon acts of transfer; they are essentially ad rem charges which take no account of the total circumstances of the recipient."[7] Or much earlier

It is indefensible to charge A., who takes a legacy of 100,000 francs, with a higher duty than B., who takes a legacy of 10,000 francs [both being in the same degree of relationship to the testator], without any investigation into their respective financial positions, for A. might well be the possessor of no other property beyond his 100,000 francs legacy, whereas B. might be a millionaire. To be equitable in progressively graduating succession duty on amount, the individual fortunes of each successor should . . . be looked at."[8]

---

[5] From the standpoint of redistribution, these consanguinity rates are undesirable because they encourage the retention of property in fewer hands; this is contrasted to duties levied according to the circumstances of the legatees which encourage the dispersion of estates amongst the poorer members of society.

[6] L. Robbins, "Notes on Public Finance," *Lloyds Bank Review*, October, 1955; N. Kaldor, *Expenditure Tax* (London: Allen and Unwin, 1958), Chap. 2; Simons, espec. Chap. 7.

[7] Simons, *ibid.,* p. 128.

[8] Cerenville, P., *Les Impôts en Suisse* (Lausanne: Corbaz and Lie, 1898), p. 220.

The discussion can be divided into three subsections, the "Obliterative System," the "Inheritance as Part of Income," and the "Bypassing the State" justification.

The Obliterative System

Robbins maintains that the estate tax "tends to the obliteration of property," and he would prefer to see one that encouraged the wider dissemination of property instead of concentrating capital in the hands of the state, which "uses the proceeds for current expenditure,"[9] and, he implies, carries out in a centralized, impersonalized, uncertain manner the functions once undertaken by property. No doubt it would be preferable to have these things done by the private sector, but it is because these functions were previously inadequately executed by the private sector that the state was obliged to extend its powers. These are the problems of "merit wants"[10] which the market mechanism could provide but which, because of an unsatisfactory past and present social importance, are increasingly the responsibility of the state. It is certain that the allocation of resources by the state will differ from that which the private sector would have chosen (otherwise why have the intervention of the state at all?) ; probably if the two similar ends were possible by either public or private decision most of us would prefer to see the allocation take place in the private sector. But it is unfair to introduce the ends of *expenditure* into a discussion of *revenue,* especially as the tax under consideration is not one levied primarily for revenue, but either for distributional ends or to insure equity in the whole tax structure.

The real merit of Professor Robbins' criticism lies in his distinction between the obliterative character of estate duty and the desired "distributivist" society which could be achieved if inheritance taxes were levied according to the circumstances of the legatee.

Inheritance as a Part of Income

Both Kaldor and Simons justify taxing the legacy instead of the estate on grounds of equity between legatees. For Simons it follows naturally from his definition of income as the algebraic sum of consumption and accumulation.[11] The difference between wealth at the

---

[9] Robbins, p. 14.

[10] R. A. Musgrave, *The Pure Theory of Public Finance* (New York: McGraw-Hill, 1959), p. 13.

[11] $Y = C_{1-2} + (Z_2 - Z_1)$, where C and Z are consumption and wealth respectively, and the period is $1 - 2$. Simons, p. 50.

end and at the beginning of the tax period would include all gifts, bequests, and legacies. This suggestion has been presented in the United States as an "accretions tax."[12]

The reform need not be so drastic as the complete redefinition of the tax base; it would be possible to amend existing estate and gift taxation to include all gifts, and to levy a progressive tax on the receiver, assessed on a scale which was a function of the amount of capital already possessed. This would "make the [existing] system more equitable and ensure its efficiency as a device for re-distributing wealth without providing the same inducements as the present [U.K.] death duties for anticipating the dissipation of capital."[13] The gifts tax would be defined by law with some minimum exemption unit and taxed on a cumulative basis. The principal complaint here is that this tax would have to be complemented by a whole gamut of other taxes (as at present), e.g., progressive personal income taxes on wages and salaries, on ground rents and interest, on dividends, profits, and capital gains. This, as Simons points out,[14] is very cumbersome, and therefore he recommends his treatment of all receipts as income. They would then bear the progressive income tax, with special exemptions for small gifts and family allowances. This would produce a more unified personal tax structure.

Regrettably, having outlined this unified personal tax structure without the numerous "empirical" supernumerary taxes, Simons is forced to conclude that this form of inheritance taxation suffers from a fundamental weakness in that it is not cumulative. That is, it does not relate the rate of tax to gifts and legacies already held, as it is levied at the current income tax rate. Any large transfer made over a long period would be taxed more lightly than if it fell in a single year (this would only be true under a progressive scale, of course). To cover this, Simons has to introduce a second layer of taxation,[15] or supplementary levy. This is a high rate of tax on cumulative receipts having an offset credit for all amounts "paid as personal income tax by virtue of the inclusion of such receipts." This credit would be for the difference between actual tax payments and what they would have been if no such receipts had occurred. This supplementary levy and the basic

---

[12] H. J. Rudick, "A Proposal for an Accessions Tax," *Tax Law Review*, Vol. XXV, 1945; and "What Alternative to the Estate and Gift Taxes?" *California Law Review*, Vol. XXXVIII, 1950, p. 167.

[13] Kaldor, *An Expenditure Tax,* p. 101.

[14] Simons, p. 133.

[15] *Ibid.,* p. 144.

income tax would, for Simons, come close to the ideal of personal income taxation.

There are still critical points to be made about this suggestion. It does not achieve equity between persons through time, i.e., it still penalizes short-lived families, unless it is assumed that a very long time period — several hundred years — means that randomness annihilates significant long or short generation families. If the estate passed through numerous intermediaries there would be a "bonus" for those who reduced the number of intermediaries by "skipping" a generation; indeed, as it is unlikely that minors would already have large fortunes, their supplementary rate of tax would be low, their income tax small, and in addition the transferred estate would escape the intermediary generation.

The attraction of taxing inheritances as part of income lies principally in the increasing marginal rates of income tax reflecting the greater ability to pay of the individual. There is also the theoretical satisfaction of knowing that such a tax would be a satisfactory "whole" forming part of a unified personal tax structure. But this satisfaction is severely reduced by the necessity of imposing a supplementary levy. The reasons for having to apply this extra rate reveal the underlying weakness of treating inheritance as part of income. The two reasons are first, the high marginal rate of progressive tax levied on an increment of wealth in a particular year and the consequent difficulties of averaging, etc.; and second, the difficulty of allowing for the different time spans of generations. The first is a problem generated by progression and could be bypassed if a proportional tax were levied (without exemption limits), but the second is a problem peculiar to inheritance taxation and it is difficult to see a simple adaptation of the personal income tax structure that would adequately cover it, although we will return to this problem later.

Bypassing the State as Agent

One method of levying inheritance taxation is to use the natural desire of people to leave money to persons other than the state. Most people, if put to the test, would prefer to favor the least popular relative with a legacy rather than have the state take a larger portion in tax. The state is, if you like, the least popular of anyone's relatives.

Generally, bypassing the state as a redistributive agency complies with both liberal principles and expediency. As far as possible the structure of the public sector should be angled to leave the individual discretion over the allocation of his resources and the payment of his taxes.[16] All taxes interfere with this liberty, but if the taxpayer is given an option of redistributing his wealth voluntarily, or using the state as an agent, then the field of choice is much wider than the present situation where the government appropriates a portion of the estate. Such an encouragement to "automatic distribution" would achieve Robbins' desired "distributive society." Additionally, although revenue would probably drop under a system such as levying death duties according to the circumstances of the legatee as people take advantage of the legislation to leave estates to their poorer relatives, it fits in better with our accepted tax structure. In our taxation of income an increment of $1,000 is considered "worth" more to the man earning $5,000 than to the man earning $50,000; then, in like manner, a legacy of $1,000 is worth more to the poor than to the rich. This, of course, depends on our acceptance of the declining marginal utility of income and the equal capacity of persons for the enjoyment of given incomes; but these are already accepted in our personal tax structure and it is to this that we are looking as a "norm" for equity. So if we are to be consistent in our overall tax structure it would be in accordance with the principles already adopted in our income taxation to tax more lightly those legacies which accrue to people in poor circumstances than those which go to the already rich; again this will reemerge later in the discussion of a general transfer tax.

As none of the taxes on the transfer of wealth reviewed above (estate duty, legacy duty, consanguinity rates, and the circumstances of the legatee), are satisfactory, more especially none meet the double criteria of equity through time and equity at a particular time, we must now consider those taxes which do attempt to remove inequalities stemming from different generation time spans. First follows a criticism of the Rignano proposals, and then a discussion of the system formulated by William Vickrey.

---

[16] Adam Smith's third tax rule of "Convenience," in *The Wealth of Nations* (5th ed.; London: Methuen, 1904), Book V, Chap. 2, Part II, S. 3.

10

Wealth Transfer Taxation:
The Rignano Proposals

THE RIGNANO PROPOSALS

The basic (or maximum) plan[1] is to distinguish between inherited and currently saved wealth, taxing the inherited wealth more heavily, thereby encouraging saving out of current income and work; this also involves the elimination of inherited property after three generations. The proposal is to tax a person at, say, 20 per cent on an estate inherited from his father, but at 50 per cent on that part of the estate which had come through from his grandfather. When this same man died his son would have to pay only 20 per cent on that part of the estate which had been earned during *his* father's life, 50 per cent on the rest from *his* grandfather, any residual being wiped out. Naturally the estates are not obliged to pass from father to son as in the above example, more generally it would be expressed as from generation to generation.

The social and political atmosphere during the original controversy over this proposal (Italy 1902, France 1904, Britain 1926) perhaps prejudiced influential thinking against such avowedly socialistic sug-

---

[1] E. Rignano and J. C. Stamp, *The Social Significance of Death Duties* (London: Noel Douglas, 1926), pp. 38-39, 114-125.

gestions as "an effective and gradual nationalisation of private capital,"[2] which results from the eventual 100 per cent taxation of estates inherited from grandparents. There is the alternative of Rignano's "minimum" project, distinguishing only two transfers and never taxing at a rate sufficiently high to annihilate property. This would leave considerable scope for alterations in the rates of duty.

Rignano's proposals can be watered down[3] by simply spreading the time period of the duties over a greater span and thus ameliorating the socialistic impact of the scheme, e.g., 20 per cent at the first transfer, 40 per cent at the second, then 60 per cent, 80 per cent, and finally, at the fifth transfer, 100 per cent.

On the other hand, there are two amendments proposed which tend to emphasize the state acquisition of property:

(i) That all inheritances (and gifts), should pass to the state (with certain low exemption limits), and that a reasonable rate of interest should be paid to the inheritor during his lifetime; the inheritor would then have the right to leave this income — reduced by the tax on the next generation — to whomsoever he pleased.[4]

(ii) A modification of (1) whereby a levy, supplemental to the existing death duty rates, would be made on the net inherited estates and in return terminable securities would be issued; the inheritors would then instead of having an estate of X after death duties, would receive X minus the levy and hold a waning asset.[5]

Another modification, similar to those above, is proposed by Henderson[6] where a "re-inheritance" duty extra to death duties already paid is to be levied on the death of the legatee; to prevent the state's losing this revenue through spending or absconding, the money is deducted from the original inheritance and an annuity paid in lieu of interest by the state. It is suggested that this reinheritance duty be made variable according to the legacy left to each individual.[7]

---

[2] *Ibid.*, p. 50.

[3] H. Clay, *Property and Inheritance*, The New Way Series, No. 5 (London: The Daily News Ltd., 1926), p. 33.

[4] H. Dalton, *Some Aspects of the Inequality of Incomes in Modern Communities* (London: Routledge and Sons, 1925), Part IV, Chaps. 9 and 10.

[5] The Colwyn Report, Cmd. 2800, 1927, "Evidence in Chief," paras. 19-20 and questions 554, 505, 553.

[6] H. D. Henderson, "Inheritance and Inequality," *Daily News* pamphlet; New Ways Series, 1926.

[7] *Ibid.*, pp. 17-26.

A final gloss to the Rignano proposal is suggested by Wedgewood,[8] who maintains that where the progressive tax rates of death duties become very high and are thought to discourage work and saving, a proportion of the tax should be optionally payable after a number of years have elapsed from the date of inheritance. The final tax liability would be the original amount due plus a compound interest mark-up for the years the tax was deferred. This would spread the tax burden (two bites at the cherry) and give the inheritor the option of enjoying a larger estate for a period of time with the penalty of a greater eventual tax burden, or of reducing his estate immediately and having a smaller aggregate tax liability. Implicit is the assumption that this would encourage prudent operations with the retained capital to offset both the compound interest and the eventual tax payment.

DISCUSSION OF THE RIGNANO GENRE PROPOSALS

The principal point in favor of the proposal is the encouragement it should give to savings and investment. If we accept the idea that on the whole men care less about the fortunes left to their remote heirs than they do about their present life and that of their children, then it is likely that they will care even less about the legatees of their children's heirs. Once taxation is removed two generations, circumstances change so quickly in the modern age that conjecture about the fortunes needed by those in 2050 is probably not going to galvanize today's businessman to work and save much more than he already does. If this is accepted then the taxation of distant inheritances should be less of a disincentive to saving than the taxing of present inheritances; therefore, it is reasonable to raise the rate of inheritance taxation on "older" legacies. Additionally, if we accept the idea that people do not normally so plan the distribution of their assets to achieve a maximum return, then the more favored position given to currently saved wealth will be an incentive to place wealth in the most "useful" place for the community; this tends to equate usefulness with risk and gambling as much as with blue chips and sound finance.

Both of these "advantages" are questionable (after all, it is a peculiar assumption that people do not use their wealth to the best advantage), but the whole role of saving is considered later. The criticisms more uniquely connected with the Rignano suggestion fall into five categories:

---

[8] J. Wedgewood, *The Economics of Inheritance Taxation* (London: Routledge, 1929), p. 268.

(i)   The Quantitative Solution,
(ii) Changing Money Values,
(iii) Quick Successions,
(iv) Administration,
(v)   The Various Amendments.

The Quantitative Solution

The original Rignano proposal assumes that the portions of estates belonging to different parts of history ("that's Grandfather's estate"), can always be identified. This is the most striking weakness of the scheme. On what grounds can the estate be divided in order that the differential taxes be applied? If the solution is made purely quantitative and a person pays the appropriate rates of tax on the money amounts inherited (i.e., on £100,000 inherited and taxed at 20 per cent leaving £80,000; then a further £100,000 is saved and the subsequent inheritor of the £180,000 estate pays, say, 50 per cent on the first £80,000 and 20 per cent on the remainder), what happens if through ill luck, bad management, etc., the legatee loses his entire original net fortune, and then through hard work and application succeeds in saving an amount which proves to be just sufficient to pay the taxes due on the original estate at second transfer? The quantitative solution, although easy to state and apply, takes no account of the history of the case, and there is always the insecurity of knowing that a deferred tax is hanging over the family which could wipe out the whole estate even if not levied at 100 per cent, but at a lower rate on the money amount of estate which *ought* to pass for the second time. The incentive is then obviously great to squander what remains to avoid giving it to the state.

Likewise, if an inheritor decides to speculate and achieve an increase in wealth through the efforts of horses rather than his own energies, the Rignano proposal does not distinguish between useful production of wealth and an increment due to gambling. Whether any death duty ought to do so is questionable, but the original proposal did claim to encourage the useful allocation of wealth, and yet it can be argued that in some circumstances it could lead to a spendthrift outlook.

Changing Money Values

Apart from the absolute straightforward money valuations of estates and the difficulties ensuing if the family fortune is shrinking, there is the overlay of changing money values. In periods of inflation the tax assessment on the historical money value of the estate will be the lighter the greater the fall in money values; similarly the burden of taxation will be increased in deflationary times. One could maintain that over long periods the swings and roundabouts cancel (as is argued in debt controversy where losses and gains through changes in the rate of interest are held to be self-canceling). Empirically the evidence points to the greater likelihood of a prevailing inflation over the centuries so that over a long enough period families are going to be relieved of some tax burden — unless they are permanently unlucky and always die at the trough of a deflationary period. Nevertheless, there might be some periods when people would be severely hit by falling money values, leading Rignano to suggest:

(i) that the government must reduce to the minimum "the artificial variations in the value of property resulting from excessive emissions of paper money";

(ii) "this difficulty could always be obviated by a carefully devised system of index numbers."[9]

It can be argued that even the provision of an index number correction would not remove inequities resulting from changes in property values from many other sorts of causes and that some might still be unfairly taxed, especially if escheat remained.[10]

For example, if thirty years ago one son inherited a mansion valued at $300,000, and the other a collection of paintings of the same value, it is probable that the first is now much worse off and the second much better, yet their Rignano tax assessment on their inheritance remains the same. Whether this can justifiably be represented as inequitable is questionable. The manner in which estates are held and the ingenuity with which they are juggled to achieve capital gain is one of individual expertise, ineptitude, or whim; should provision be made for the unimaginative, should the prudent and ingenious be penalized? For the government to undertake the responsibility of underwriting changes in all capital values would produce extraordinary results, all property becomes equally liquid, the money supply slips further from central control, and presumably many market forces are suspended.

Quick Succession

Another problem common to all death duties but one which Rignano exacerbates, is the harsh treatment of families where there are quick successions due to close age groupings, accidents, or early deaths.

---

[9] Rignano and Stamp, p. 82.
[10] Wedgewood, p. 262; The Colwyn Report, p. 315.

Under the Rignano proposal not only would the estate be progressively taxed at each transfer, but that part inherited — and enjoyed for only a short time — would be taxed at a higher rate and the saved portion out of current earnings would be small due to the short time available for accumulation. Any relief similar to that at present granted on quick successions would have to be differentially angled to give greater relief to the saved portion than to the inherited portion. However, this objection is in no way unique to Rignano's proposals.

Administration

The Colwyn Commission received a memorandum from the Board of Inland Revenue on the administrative feasibility of the scheme.[11] The board agreed that it was practicable but had three objections to it:

(a) Elaborate and costly records would be necessary. The board maintained[12] that to ascertain the various portions of the estate and the number of times it had changed hands would mean searching back through records over at least a lifetime and this "as a practical problem is extraordinarily difficult"; the extent and duration of the difficulty would depend greatly upon the attitude of the public, which if obstructive, could make the work of the Revenue very tedious indeed.

(b) Initial assessments would be awkward. Rignano recognizes the difficulties inherent in starting the scheme and proposes an arbitrary division for all estates "one third from the labour or thrift or both combined, of the present proprietor, and two thirds by inheritance from a single transfer." This is unsatisfactory. As the attitude of the taxpayers had been stressed to the Colwyn Commission as an important step in the successful implementation of the scheme[13] it would probably be more tactful if originally all estates were considered as saved and the scheme started on a "tabula rasa."

(c) Gifts inter vivos would continue to be a problem and, for the scheme to be sound, these gifts would have to be taxed at rates similar to inheritances. The general difficulties of gift taxation apply here as elsewhere, but there are some peculiar to the Rignano proposals.

Not only would the tax liability be deferred but the rate of gift taxation would be higher than that of saved wealth, therefore there is a greater possibility that the eventual estate out of which the deferred tax was to be paid might turn out smaller than the tax assessment.

---

[11] *Colwyn Commission: Appendices,* Appendix XXVI.

[12] The Colwyn Report, Minutes of Evidence, Vol. II, Question 1950.

[13] The Colwyn Report, Minutes of Evidence, Vol. II, p. 316, Questions 9154-58.

Also, although the gift is held without paying tax it is "earning" money (which is taxed at a lower rate) and there is an incentive to encourage gifts to very young people.

The Various Amendments

The chief merits of Dalton's additions to the Rignano scheme are those of:

(a) insuring successive state claims on the estate will not be defaulted on, either through waste or changes in value;

(b) helping to check the transfers of gifts inter vivos (once the entire estate is in the hands of the state it is impossible to give away any part of that estate);

(c) retaining the better qualities of the Rignano proposals in that it guarantees the man who saves during his lifetime that his savings will provide a fairly lightly taxed income to his beneficiaries, while still discriminating against older, and therefore less deserving, inherited wealth.

If, as suggested by Dalton, exemptions are allowed, including personal possessions and speculative risky shares, then this could result in some peculiar property transfers; people would prefer to risk their capital rather than see their estate pass to the state. Presumably, the reason for these exemptions on doubtful shares is to avoid the state becoming partner in ventures odd, and possibly shady, and to promote risk-taking. But if the state is setting itself up as public trustee and is willing to accept a wide variety of objects, land, shares, patents, etc., it would be invidious for it to turn selective and reject some and accept others. As in most exceptions the difficulty lies in fixing the borderline. It would be more acceptable to the people, easier to administer, and would avoid loopholes if the Dalton proposal accepted all forms of property above an initial money exemption limit (say, the amount necessary to buy a house, car, and furniture for an upper middle class family).

The suggestion that the state should appropriate all estates and pay annuities in lieu can be criticized on the grounds that such a scheme would only be politically possible if it were part of a full-scale drive to have state control throughout the economy.[14] This is, of course, precisely what Rignano intended in his original suggestion — the Dalton projection is only making the original move more efficient. British Labour Party proposals to "buy" their way into public companies

---

[14] Wedgewood, pp. 265-266.

would seem to fit into a scheme where the state could accept equities or actual businesses as part of death duty payments.

More practical objections can be raised about the actual administration of such a public trustee, about the resulting values in the property markets, and whether these would be socially acceptable, but the original Rignano proposal was basically socialistic and to criticize Dalton for implementing that scheme efficiently is unfair.

The chief objection to the second Dalton alternative — a supplemental levy and in return terminable securities — is that although insuring the collection of tax and avoiding the difficulties of changing values, it blurs the distinction between saved and inherited wealth. If the levy were varied according to the amount of *inherited* wealth (i.e., ordinary death duty rates on saved wealth, and supplementary rates on inherited), then the distinction between saved and inherited wealth is, if anything, heightened by the immediate issue of a terminable asset. It is true that this is not what Dalton proposed but it is a small amendment to meet the principal criticism.

The proposal could be criticized on other grounds. It is not true that it avoids the major pitfall of changing values completely, for if the purchasing power of the currency changes then obviously index correction will have to be made to interest paid by the state. On the other hand, if there is a free market in these terminable securities (as suggested)[15] then the capital value of the securities may alter and the inheritor finds himself worse off through holding a government security instead of say, industrial stock (a not unknown situation).

Implicit in the other amendment proposed by Wedgewood is the assumption that this deferred tax payment would encourage saving, or encourage prudent operation with the retained capital to offset both the compound interest and eventual tax payment. Administratively, a system of options spreading tax payments over a large number of years presents the Revenue with the problems of receiving continuous payments, making constant checks, and keeping complicated records. It is obviously easier to levy all tax at a specific point in time — this is one of the great natural advantages of death duties — and is the inconvenience to the state worth the incentive to the taxpayer and the possible gain to the community? Is the incentive to work and save increased by holding capital which is itself building an increasing tax burden? Only if you think you can beat the state's appreciation, and this could just as easily lead to risky ventures and capital loss as to cleverly

---

[15] *Ibid.*, p. 268.

engineered capital gains. If capital loss resulted through any cause then the shadow of the increasing tax might positively discourage work and saving. On balance, it is probably doubtful whether schemes for spreading tax burdens at the option of the taxpayer are ever administratively worthwhile unless they are correcting a glaring inequity (e.g., averaging professional incomes). One of the principal virtues of death duties is the distinct point of taxation. It is retained by both Rignano and Dalton and it is difficult to see a strong enough reason to change it.

Finally, the Rignano scheme and its derivatives do not necessarily lead to a reduction of inequality. The total amount of wealth available for inheritances would be reduced but there is no "redistributive element" in the scheme, unless we count redistribution to the state. Even if the maximum scheme is accepted the limited right of inheritance still available gives a greater advantage in saving and working to some, and thereby enables them to leave more personally saved capital to be taxed at a lower rate than the person who inherits little. In this way the relative inequalities can be continued, although absolutely the total wealth held in private hands is diminished. While, as we noted above, equity through time is not guaranteed, it is still possible to reduce Rignano tax liability by old persons deliberately leaving estates to the very young and "skipping" generations. In addition, such taxation still requires the full backing of a gifts tax which further complicates administration.

Rignano duties confuse an already complex tax structure and while they might reduce one aspect of inequity through time, they can create others and do little to check simple avoidance.

11

Wealth Transfer Taxation:
Equity Through Time, Bequeathing Power,
and Double Equity

BEQUEATHING POWER

The most sophisticated form of taxation devised to cope with the inequities resulting from estates liable to inheritance taxes at different time intervals is that of "bequeathing power."[1]

The kernel of the suggestion is to assign a "power" to every estate which can be passed to others; this includes not only inheritances but all gifts above a specified minimum. To insure that we cover both inheritances and gifts we will refer to these estates as "transferred wealth." The power so assigned is naturally larger the bigger the estate. But the estate, as well as varying "vertically" with total size and bequeathing power, varies "horizontally" through time (in this it is similar to the Rignano proposal which also varied the power to bequeath estates through time). So, like Rignano, the restriction on the inheritable estate is a function of time, but in this case the period is not the convenient (and arbitrary) one of generation. Instead the actual age difference between the donor and the donee is used. The system attempts to overcome the Rignano difficulty of identifying an estate

---

[1] First propounded by W. Vickrey, "The Rationalization of Succession Taxation," *Econometrica*, July-October, 1944, and in its final form in *Agenda for Progressive Taxation*, pp. 214-248.

115

(or part of an estate) through time by the bequeathing units representing different *net* amounts to differently aged individuals. The importance of the bequeathing units is that they remain the same, despite changes in the size of the net estate through time due to taxation. The units are the unchanging link between the taxed estate through time which enables you to tax the advantages of inherited wealth (represented by the bequeathing units) although the original estate has been continually diminished by taxation. A simple example will illustrate this:

TABLE 11:1
Bequeathing Power Units

	A	B	C	D
Age of Holder of the Estate This Year	80	40	20	10
Bequeathing Power Units	*Net Inherited Estate $'000*			
10	5	3	2	1
20	10	6	4	2
40	20	12	8	4

In this simple table the individuals A, B, C, and D of different ages can each have estates varying from $1,000-$20,000, and these estates are represented by bequeathing power units from 0-40; the choice of unit size is initially unimportant, the only criterion being that they should be sufficiently small to represent all sizes of estates within the "tranches" chosen. The distinguishing feature is that an estate of, say, forty bequeathing power units, can never represent more than $4,000 to D. If A leaves the estate of $20,000 (Case 1) to C, the tax paid is $12,000. If C then leaves this remaining estate of $8,000 to D, the tax paid is $4,000. Total tax paid by the two "generations" is $16,000. If A had given the estate directly to D (Case 2), the tax paid would still have been $16,000. The bequeathing power is transmitted horizontally unchanged and therefore it is immaterial how many times this estate changes hands before reaching D; it will always represent to D, aged ten, a bequeathing power of forty units and consequently a net estate of $4,000. As D grows older, then the amount of estate assigned to his bequeathing units will grow larger, the table above being true for a particular year. This solves the difficulty of most inheritance taxes which penalize the quick transfer and encourage the jumping of generations because by so doing a "round" of taxation is missed. Under Vickrey's system it is immaterial how many, or how few, transfers are made between donor and donee, the final recipient can only receive the same amount of net estate.

Still using the above table, if the estate of A is not transmitted totally to D in a lump sum, or by lump sum transfers, but is split between numerous intermediaries before reaching D, it is still immaterial how many "internal transfers" there are. If A leaves $20,000 to D directly (Case 3), this represents twenty bequeathing power units, and the tax paid is $8,000; A is then left with twenty further units which he decides to leave to B. This represents a net inherited estate to B of $6,000 and the tax paid on this transfer is $4,000. If B then leaves it to D, this twenty-unit transfer can only represent $2,000 net to D, and the tax paid is $4,000; D now has an inherited fortune of $2,000 plus another $2,000, $4,000 in all. The total tax paid is $8,000 plus $4,000, plus $4,000, totaling $16,000 in all, exactly the same amount as that which would have been paid had A transferred the total estate directly to D.

Even if B, instead of passing his twenty-unit estate ($6,000) to D, had split it again between C and D (Case 4), the final result is the same. Although the point is simple, it is basic to the bequeathing power theory and might be shown better diagrammatically. The figures in parentheses represent tax paid dollars at each transfer on an initial estate of $20,000 passing from A to D.

TABLE 11:2
Diagrammatic Explanation of a Transfer Tax and Bequeathing Power Units

					Total Tax
Case 1					
A (40 units)			C($12,000)	D($4,000)	$16,000
Case 2					
A (40 units)				D($16,000)	$16,000
Case 3					
A (20 units)				D($8,000)	
A (20 units)	B($4,000)			D($4,000)	$16,000
Case 4					
A (20 units)				D($8,000)	
A (20 units)	B($4,000)	(10 units)		D($2,000)	
		(10 units)	C($1,000)	D($1,000)	$16,000

For the limited explanation given above it was assumed:

(i) That there were no additions to, or subtractions from, the estates through owner savings or consumption.

(ii) That the interest earned by the estate through time was not compounded into the inheritance (i.e., that transfers were instantaneous).

(iii) That no reverse transfers were made from young to old.

We must now examine each of these assumptions.

Expanding or Contracting Estates

It is easiest to imagine the tax being paid by the legatee. If this is done then it is immaterial from what source he gets his inheritance of bequeathing units, because it is by reference to the *legatee's* holding of units, and the current amount that is transferred that the tax liability is assessed. A gift of X bequeathing units by A to B, aged y, will always be worth Xy if B holds no other bequeathing units. If he does already hold other units, whether from previous gifts from A or from other transferred wealth, then the new gift of X units at age y will have to be modified according to the stock "s" already held, Xy.

It is only the expansion or contraction of the recipient's stock of units that concerns the authorities; whether these units are *coming from* a large, small, growing, or shrinking stock is immaterial.

At the death of the donor, the entire estate will have to be assessed and the final transfers will be taxed according to the recipient's stocks of already transferred wealth. If at death it is found that a person had a negative quantity of units, i.e., less than the authorities credited him as having, knowing his previous inheritances and gifts, this only means that he has financed current consumption out of capital.

It should be noted that this penalizes the spendthrift. Under other proposals for taxation according to the circumstances of the legatee the assessment of his wealth would be at the time when he inherited anew. If he had recklessly spent his previous inherited wealth he would be in poor circumstances and consequently be taxed at low rates on this new inheritance. Under Vickrey's system the store of units already inherited is taken into account when fixing the tax rate on the new, or extra, inheritance.

A difficulty occurs when the system is first started. Some assessment will then have to be made of all the legatee's wealth before the stock of bequeathing units can be allotted.

Interest Earned

As an estate is held it earns interest; as it grows larger the tax burden grows too and therefore there is an area of discretion, apart from that of age, as to when the estate should be transferred. This is a minor point but even this can be removed if a compound rate of interest is built into the system, the rate corresponding to a given bequeathing power. Of course, this in itself could result in inequity; any rate taken[2] would penalize those whose estates did not achieve that rate, and lighten the burden on those whose growth outstripped the adopted figure.

In addition, the current rate of income tax will affect the rate of growth of estates (the richer the owner the higher his marginal rate of taxation, under a progressive system, and hence the slower the rate of growth of the estate). Although Vickrey[3] suggests a modification for the relation between the units and the size of estates to allow for the above factor, such an addition increases the complexity of the scheme without entirely closing all the loopholes (there would still be a bias in favor of the person whose income was all unearned) ; and in any case this penalty on the larger, richer estates could be counted as part of the "vertical" progressive taxation levied according to the wealth already held.

Reverse Transfers

If taxes are deducted on a transfer from A to C, and then C transfers the estate back to B, then to retain the neutrality of the system B should receive the same net sum as he would have done had the estate been given directly from A to B. If the tax on a transfer from B to C, is higher than that from A to B, then there must be a refund on the reverse transfer from C to B.

In practice refunds could not be given automatically. Vickrey mentions only two cases where it would be undesirable[4] — where wealth held at the inauguration of the scheme or wealth accumulated out of personal savings was transferred to persons below the exemption limit — but in addition extensive government payments would have to be made on simple transfers from young to old where no tax had been collected on any previous transfer. Where a young man pays a "pension" to his parents from his current income, his parents could claim in addition to the lump sum transferred a refund on the reverse transfer.

In practice, it would probably prove much simpler to disallow any refund on a reverse transfer, but levy no tax on the receiver of such gifts.

The bequeathing unit system actually embodies two taxes, one levied according to the age differential and other according to the size of the

---

[2] Vickrey suggests 4 per cent, *Agenda for Progressive Taxation,* p. 230.
[3] *Ibid.,* pp. 254-255.
[4] *Ibid.,* p. 245.

estate transferred. The two tables below are abstracts from Vickrey's own table, but they show the two taxes involved. The first shows the tax paid per twenty-year period on a $1,558 estate, the second the tax on estates of different sizes at a particular age differential of twenty years.

TABLE 11:3
Bequeathing Power Units: Tax Paid per Year Age Difference on a $1,558 Gross Estate

Years Difference	20	40	60	80
Net Estate Out of $1,558 Gross	$1,045	$635	$ 352	$ 182
Tax Paid	$ 513	$923	$1,206	$1,376
Tax Paid per Year Difference	$ 25.6	$ 23.1	$ 20.1	$ 17.2

The total tax penalty paid for each twenty-year slice increases with the growing age difference, but if this is expressed per year (assuming the tax not to be continuous, but stepped), then the amount per year is a decreasing function of increasing age difference. This is surprising, as Vickrey originally said "to establish a progressive tax which accomplishes this aim [equity through time], collects an appropriate installment of the tax at each successive stage, and yet takes into account all the various factors involved, will require a fairly radical departure from our present methods of assessing such taxes.[5] The progressive element of the whole system is supplied, not by the age tax, but by the tax on the size of the estate as shown in the following Table 11:4. But the small degree of progression indicated is misleading because this is the *transfer tax* (as shown in Table 11:4) with the size of the estate; the

TABLE 11:4
Bequeathing Power Units: Tax Paid per $ of an Estate Transferred from a Person Born in 1860 to One Born in 1880, i.e., Twenty Years Younger

Bequeathing Units	2,000	4,000	6,000	8,000
Gross Estate	$1,558	$2,452	$3,160	$3,762
Tax Paid on Transfer of Gross Estate	$ 513	$ 895	$1,206	$1,468
Tax Paid per $ Gross Estate	$ 0.33	$ 0.36	$ 0.38	$ 0.39

true progressiveness is given by a third form of the tax which is levied depending on the size of the transferred (inherited and gifted) estate already possessed from previous transfers. This form is, of course, linked to Table 11:4, but whereas Table 11:4 shows only the tax paid on a given gross estate for a transfer age difference of twenty years,

---

[5] *Ibid.*, p. 224.

Table 11:5 below shows the cumulative nature of the tax, depending on the transferred wealth already possessed by the recipient at two age differences, twenty and eighty years.

TABLE 11:5
Age Differences of Twenty and Eighty Years and Tax Paid per Additional Dollar on an Estate of $1,558

Age Difference Twenty Years			*Age Difference Eighty Years*		
Wealth Already Held $	Tax Paid on Addition of $1,558 $	Tax Paid per $ of Added $1,558	Wealth Already Held $	Tax Paid on Addition of $1,558 $	Tax Paid per $ of Added $1,558
1,558	662	0.43	182	1,497	0.96
2,452	850	0.55	243	1,524	0.99
3,160	956	0.61	277	1,527	0.99
3,762	1,012	0.67	308	1,532	0.99

The introduction of bequeathing units is a complicating factor and their significance might be difficult to convey to the public. More significantly, they suffer from a defect which any unit related to currency must bear. As changes occur in the purchasing power of the currency so must the bequeathing power unit relationship be reassessed to avoid inequity through time. It is true that as rates of tax are related to the purchasing power of the currency so should they be altered, but the bequeathing power units are a superimposition on the structure of tax rates and currency.

A system which retains the aims of Vickrey's structure but which dispenses with the complicating factor of bequeathing units and yet achieves equity through time and equity at a particular time would be the ideal. Essentially there are three parts to the tax. One tax varying with the age difference, another with the size of the transfer, and a third with transferred wealth already held. In Chart 11:1 we consider a tax structure which includes these elements.

In sector I the birth years of the donors and donees are measured on the horizontal axis. The vertical axis measures the wealth transferred. A man born in 1900 might wish to transfer an estate O'A to a young person born in 1960. Net of tax the young man can receive OB if the amount the older person gifts is O'A. This tax in sector I combines two parts of the total final tax; the tax rate on the amount transferred is proportional (i.e., O'L is half O'A, and OD is half OB), but the tax according to the age differential is progressive (i.e., a gift of O'A from

CHART 11:1
Double Equity Through Time

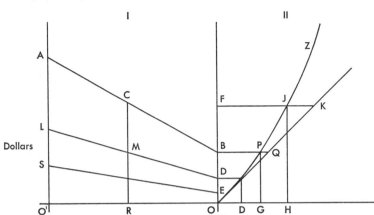

a person born in 1900 to someone born in 1960 is taxed at rate $1 - \dfrac{OB}{O'A}$, but the same amount given to someone born in 1930 would incur tax at the rate $1 - \dfrac{CR}{O'A}$; as $CR > OB$ the tax rate is progressive the larger is the age difference).

Suppose the estate passed from the person born in 1900 to the individual born in 1960 was not transferred directly, but was split in two so that O'L was gifted directly and net of tax left OD, while O'L was given to the person born in 1930 and net of tax left RM = OB, even when this net transfer OB is passed again from the 1930-born person to the 1960 person the net amount received is RM. The two transfers added together total the same net transfer as would have been passed had the whole estate O'A been transferred directly, OD + OD = OB. So there is no tax advantage to splitting an estate between generations.

If this tax in sector I is to be integrated with a tax on total gifted wealth held by the receiver we move to sector II. In sector II the vertical axis measures the amount transferred net of tax in sector I, added to this the previously transferred wealth the receiver already holds. A tax rate is applied to the total which provides the progressive feature according to size of the total wealth held, including the increment transferred.

If OD was the amount received net of the age transfer tax and this was the only transferred wealth the individual held, then by the tax schedule OZ in sector II no further tax on OD would be levied. The final net wealth held, measured on the horizontal axis, would be OD. If the receiver already held OD of transferred wealth and received a further amount OD, this total amount OB would be taxed and the net amount of wealth left would be OG. Similarly a transfer of OB added to OB already held would make the total OF liable to tax JK, leaving a net wealth JF (OH). The tax rate on the increment OB in this case is JK/OB compared to PQ/OB when the transferred wealth held was smaller.

The two sectors combined include progression by age and by wealth held and transferred. Unfortunately, the introduction of sector II destroys the neutrality through time of sector I. When the person born in 1930 receives net estate RM = OB he will be taxed on this according to his wealth holding. Even if he held no other wealth, in this example he would have to pay a further PQ tax, leaving a net amount OG. Therefore the estate OG which he then passed on to the person born in 1960 would be that much smaller than OD and the transfer cannot be the same as it would have been had the total amount been transferred directly from the person born in 1900 to the person with the 1960 birth date. The wealthier the intermediate person the greater is the penalty. This might be acceptable in terms of equity, but clearly it creates the opportunity to avoid some tax by skipping a generation. However, it is worth noting that there would be no tax penalty on the transfer through the intermediate generation if the gift were small enough to avoid tax in sector II entirely, and/or if the intermediate receiver were sufficiently poor to miss pushing the increment into the tax bracket in sector II.

This inequity through time can only be avoided completely if some system of weighting the transferred wealth at different ages is available. This is what the introduction of bequeathing power units does, but it also introduces a concept which is quite alien to the taxpayer — a measure of wealth which is not money. It is doubtful whether revenue authorities are prepared to shoulder the difficulties (and possible odium) of educating the public to this new measurement, when other ways which approximate to double equity might be devised, as in the two-sector example above.

What we must ask ourselves is whether the complication in the tax structure is compensated for by the increase in neutrality. Is it easier to view the taxation of gifts and inheritances as a means of discouraging a mild human vice, that is, clinging to wealth in old age? If so the same encouragement of distribution to very young people can be accepted as a desirable feature of a tax.

12

Wealth Transfer Taxation: U.K. and U.S. Gifts Taxes and the General Accruals Tax

Up to the moment, consideration of vertical and horizontal equity has pushed the discussion toward suggestions for a general gifts tax with rates varied according to the age of the donee (or the age difference between donor and donee) and the gifts — including inheritances — already accumulated. To examine the working of actual gifts taxes we need to regress slightly to the discussion of estate duties. All existing gifts taxes have been introduced wholly, or partially, to bolster the structure of death duties. We will find that a discussion of these gifts taxes will push us to another conclusion concerning the rates and structure of wealth transfer taxes.

First we will examine the limited gifts tax of Britain, then that of the United States.

THE BRITISH GIFTS TAX

As mentioned earlier, the simplest way to avoid estate duties is to skip the generation likely to be taxed next. So long as gifts between living persons are not taxed, then it is clearly a straightforward way to avoid payment; it is also clear that no revenue could result from such a system working without any restraints, except through accident, perverseness, or fear of a repeat of the ingratitude of Goneril and Regan. The great majority of people with anything to leave would make a formal, witnessed gift, just prior to death and thereby die penniless, leaving a happy family and a frustrated Revenue. The immediate reaction of the legislature to contain this avoidance is to "discourage" gifts inter vivos in anticipation of death by "deeming" them to pass at death, thereby making them liable to the full range of duty which they would have attracted had they remained part of the estate at death.

However, the British authorities blink at the complexity of including all gifts and are willing to settle for a specified period prior to death in which any gifts made will have to be aggregated with the estate. The only question is what should be the relevant time period? The shorter the period the greater the temptation to avoid taxation by anticipating the death, the longer the time allowed the more difficult it is for the authorities to insure that all gifts are, in fact, included. If the time period in which gifts inter vivos are included is combined with high rates of tax, then persons will continue to avoid the duty by anticipating death. Further lengthening of the period increases the difficulties of the Revenue.

The choice of the U.K. Inland Revenue for a particular number of years now stands at five.[1] In order to soften the transition from no liability at five years plus one hour to full liability at five years and under, the rates are "staggered" so that gifts made five years previously are taxed at only 20 per cent of the full rate which the aggregated estate bears, four years previously at 40 per cent, and so on. This is a mouse of a mitigation. Anyone who intends to avoid duty is not going to be swayed by the differential rate into making his gifts three years prior to death instead of five, or four; quite understandably he will, if he tries at all, attempt to anticipate the whole five years. The only reason that can reasonably be advanced for having such reduced rates is, presumably, kindheartedness on the part of the authorities, who wish to soften the sharp transition from payment to nonpayment.

What in effect the authorities are doing by having a multiplicity of rates is pandering to those who attempt to evade the main estate duties; for it is only those who so attempt to reduce their estates by gifts inter vivos that could become liable to the reduced rates. It is extraordinary that such legislation is enacted; it is even more odd that it continues to exist. It probably only does so because for those who can afford the advice and who take the trouble, property can be arranged in such a

---

[1] It was originally, in 1881, three months, extended in 1889 to a year, in 1909 to three years, and in 1946 to five years.

manner as to avoid all gift and estate taxes even at dates very close to death.

The present exemption from U.K. estate duty of gifts inter vivos made five years prior to the donor's death is especially confusing for a particular reason which is worthwhile highlighting. The confusion arises because of the divorce of duty payment from gift transfer; the lapse of time between transfer and payment is an economic gremlin which creates many confusions.

These difficulties are limited to those emphasized earlier in connection with all death duties, the desirability of insuring equity between persons at a particular time, and between persons through time. "The basic principle of estate duty is to aggregate at the date of death all property passing, or deemed to pass on that death, and to tax it on its valuation at that date."[2] If it is "deemed" that property given away five years previously is passing at death[3] the questions: "What is the property?" and "What is the value?" become much more difficult than they would be if both identity and value were current. In this respect it is odd that the authorities allow lower rates the further away from the date of death the gift is made; the difficulties, administrative time and trouble, mount with distance in time and it would seem more practical for a penalty to be attached to gifts made a long way from death to discourage these, and leniency (if any) to be given to those causing less trouble by more recent gifts. It might be claimed that the earlier a person receives a gift the higher is its marginal utility to him, so that if taxation is to equalize the sacrifice on the equi-marginal sacrifice principle then taxes should be lighter in these earlier gifts. However, it is unlikely that the Revenue authorities reason in this way, and in any case, it assumes some very large questions — for instance, the weighing of the marginal utility of the increment to wealth at an earlier date versus the increased absolute utility through holding the gift over a longer period of time than any subsequent gift.

In "deeming" gifts inter vivos to pass at death, the authorities create a "problem well-nigh insoluble"[4] as to the length of time they choose, and the rates of tax they levy. The British have extended their time

[2] G. S. A. Wheatcroft, *The Taxation of Gifts and Settlements* (3rd ed.; London: Pitman, 1958), pp. 48-49.

[3] Up to five years is the usual length, but under the provisions which do not allow a donor to keep an interest in the property, if he does so, then property given away many years previously can be liable, e.g., Re Cochrane Settlement Trusts (1945), Chap. 285, where fifty-seven years was the time period in question.

[4] See *Payne* (1939), Ch. 865, p. 876.

period and consequently enlarged their difficulties; in attempting to mitigate these difficulties by moderating the rates of duty for more distant gifts, they have operated in an inequitable manner and in a way which does not seem to compensate them for administrative inconvenience.

One of the greatest difficulties in combining the estate and gift taxes in this way is well exemplified by the authorities' distinction between "money" and "other property." The distinction arose because the law assumed that whereas the value of property in terms of money could change through time and hence the valuation of a gift for probate, money itself was the measure of value and had to be treated differently. Thus today, the law treats unsettled money gifts differently than unsettled other property. Money gifts are taxed at their transfer values and other gifts as valued at the death of the donor. The greater the time period lapse between gift and death the greater the chance for these values to be different. The actual reference to money is "a sum of money in sterling or any other currency,"[5] and this does not necessarily correlate to economic thought on the subject, nor does the law's ruling on money as a measure of value (and therefore to be treated differently), agree completely with economic ideas. It is worthwhile pursuing this line of reasoning further.

Very clearly money is not simply the coins and notes in circulation; bank credit is usually accepted as money and in present British death duty legislation, it is certainly not clear whether a check is regarded as money or "other property." Before 1957, the judiciary decided that checks were "money" and it is probable that under the new legislation this would still hold.[6] But more generally, anything which is accepted in settlement of a debt can be viewed as money and this leads to the bizarre examples of those Solomon Islanders who use cowrie shells, or the Pacific Islanders of Nap using large stones; so long as these commodities have the confidence of the community they are viewed as money. In this manner the transfer of a bank debt from one person to another is accepted in settlement of another debt. So we can coin the aphorism that the essence of money seems to be debt. By deliberately stipulating what money is in law (i.e., sterling and other currency) the Finance Acts lay themselves open to avoidance.

On the simplest grounds, if checks are *not* money then a gift made by check could be spent on goods which are to perish in the near future, food, rent, travel, etc., and which cannot, therefore, be in existence on

---

[5] *Finance Act* 1957 (5 & 6 Eliz. II) c. 49, Part V, Sect. 38.

[6] Wheatcroft, p. 54, nn. 1, 2, 3.

the death of the donor; thus as the check was not money and the duty must be levied on the goods transferred, these goods no longer exist, therefore no duty can be paid. However, it is likely that checks would be counted as money so we can move to the next possibility.

If the cash gift is used by the donee to purchase an asset from the donor — at its "proper" market value — then the cash gift is back in the original person's hands, where it will be taxed at death, but the asset is held by the donee and the donor's estate at death is reduced by the value of that asset.

As the original gift was in cash, it is not covered by the 1957 legislation and falls under the 1894 Act and in particular Sect. 7 (10) of this act, which exempts the same piece of property from paying duty twice.

If this procedure is extended, the same cash being given again and again, and repeatedly used to purchase assets from the donor, eventually stripping him of his dutiable property entirely (a nice example of the velocity of circulation), it becomes the "Repeating Trick."[7] However, this becomes so obvious an evasion that the courts would certainly try and bring the estate within the ambit of the duty.[8]

Slightly more interesting and likely is an example where if you think that cash will depreciate faster than assets over the next few years or even that particular assets will increase in constant money terms, it is then best to dispose of your gift in cash, thus making it liable for duty in cash terms, and advise the donee into what he should put his cash — old masters or shares.

It may be inadvisable to instruct the donee too closely as to what should be done with the cash. One can picture a case where the donor hands over money with instructions to buy a particular investment with it, and the receiver is obliged to follow those instructions. In such a case it might be said that the real subject of the gift is that investment[9] and this would be liable for tax at the date of death. However, the line is a very fine one. In the case quoted in footnote 9, although the deed was dated 19 December, 1946, and the sum of £5,000 was gifted on December 24 by a check "drawn in favour of the law agents to the trust, *who had already,* on 21 December"[10] applied for an allotment

---

[7] For an amusing exposition of this and other devices for avoidance of estate duty see G. S. A. Wheatcroft, "Feather-Bedding Death, or Second Thoughts on Section 38," *British Tax Review*, 1958, p. 375.

[8] Wheatcroft, "Feather-Bedding Death Further Deliberated," *British Tax Review*, 1959, p. 252.

[9] See *Sneddan v. Lord Advocate* (1954), A-C, 257, p. 280.

[10] *Ibid.,* p. 281.

of shares which two years later were worth £9,250; yet the judgment was in favor of the gift being the £5,000 and not the shares.

The idea that "money . . . itself was the measure of value," although correct, does not entitle the law to assume that it is unchangeable, or a thing apart; it remains true that money is no exception to the general laws of supply and demand; that it is valuable only for what it can be exchanged for, and this should be the valid basis of taxation. To set "money" aside as a different animal invites transference from assets to cash, and back to assets.

There are two ways out of this dilemma. Either all assets, including "money" are taxed at death but valued at date of transfer, which breaks the death duty ruling that the estate is valued at the death of the donor. Insofar as the purchasing power of the currency is expected to decline, it will increasingly pay the donor to switch his estate before death. As an alternative, all the assets (as applied to unsettled other property now) can be taxed at their value on death of the testator. The reason for the authorities' original reluctance to admit that cash was like other property — changeable in value — now becomes apparent; if a cash gift was made some years earlier, how do we value that cash at the date of death years later? Some acceptable price index would have to be used. So long as the periods did not become too fantastic (e.g., fifty-seven years) then the fairness of marking down the values of cash gifts would not be markedly on the side of the angels or the devil. There is little doubt that if the period were extended from five to ten years, substantial differences might result. The more the period is extended the weightier become the reasons for favoring a tax on *current* transfers as an alternative or supplement to death duties.

If the property is to be traced through the various mutations in order to assess its value as part of the estate at death,[11] the possibility for different valuations seems greatly increased. Possibly the most famous case in this respect[12] provided some interesting discussion of the problems resulting from variations in the value of the gift through time. If we accept that the principle underlying the 1894 and 1881 legislation[13] clearly is to prevent a person avoiding death duties by a gift inter vivos, then the opinion of Lord Sands[14] that the deceased should be assumed to have kept the property until his death, and that it should be valued

---

[11] As legislated under the "New Rules" *Finance Act* 1957, Sects. 38(1) and (8).

[12] *Lord Strathcona v. Inland Revenue* (1929), S, C. 800.

[13] *Finance Act* 1894 (57 & 58 Vict.) c. 30, Sect. 2, and *Inland Rev. Act* 1881, Sect. 38 (2).

[14] *Lord Strathcona v. Inland Revenue,* S, c. 800.

at that date of death, is the one to be followed. But this straightforward principle does produce oddities. A gift of little value enormously appreciates by the date of death by reason of the skill and exertion of the donee. Is he to pay duty on a value largely created by himself? A gift of great value becomes worthless by the date of death, through no fault of the donee. Is he to pay duty on a value which would not in any case have existed at the death of the donor? "The dull subject of duties has been agreeably illustrated by examples taken from the racecourse, such as the colt optimistically regarded as a Derby winner by donor and donee which proved to be the merest 'plater'. This and other examples from animal life enliven judgements."[15] They do indeed. They also provide very puzzling difficulties for the authorities. The extreme example of the racehorse could be argued as due to imperfect knowledge and certainly to lack of it with horses. But again the problem of "market" price can be reduced if there is no lapse of time between gift and duty payment. This, of course, does not remove the difficulties of holdings which are so large a part of the whole as to depress the market price by abrupt realization or those whose value can be altered by the parties to the transaction; these will remain with any transfer taxation. But the present distinction between money and other property and between the time when a transfer is made and its liability to tax are necessary complications in an already complex subject. They strengthen the case for some amendment to the tax structure which annihilates the time lapse between the object dutiable and the point of taxation.

THE AMERICAN GIFTS TAX

An alternative to the difficult choice of an arbitrary time period is the American concept of a gift "in contemplation of death."[16] Instead of assuming that any gift, other than tokens of affection and goodwill, made, say five years before death, is attempting to evade death duties, the legislatures in the United States tried to make the actual motive of the donor the ground on which a gift becomes taxable, at the full estate duty rates as opposed to the lower gift tax rates. It is questionable whether this is an improvement on the British system, as several new difficulties are introduced.

As the intention of tax avoidance is the justification for the taxation,

---

[15] *Ibid.*

[16] Introduced by Maryland in 1844. In 1864 Congress provided that gifts made "without valuable and adequate consideration" would be treated as a legacy (13 U.S. Statutes at Large, 288), and in 1924 used the "contemplation of death clause."

it follows that some gifts made before death will not be liable for tax at all, and this opens up a new avenue for nonpayment of estate taxes. Successive decisions in the U.S. courts have provided some clarification; sometimes the result of the gift is to relieve the donee of anxiety, to help him to achieve particular aims, house purchase, etc., and this gift, it can be maintained, is not a deliberate transfer of estate from one person or generation to another, but rather part of an economic transaction, part, if you like, of a discharge of a debt between one generation and another. Another criterion is the health of the donor; this raises subsidiary questions as to the nature of the disease, whether the donor knew from what he suffered, or whether he took it seriously; it brings in the family doctor, relatives' opinions, and a host of dubious evidence; it provides numerous possibilities of escape. Age has also been used as a gauge of motive. The older a person is the more likely is the gift to have been made in contemplation of death, so the argument runs. Because a person is 60, or 70 or 80, is he anticipating death when he makes a gift?

Generally, the American definition, although dispensing with the choice of time period, and theoretically encompassing all gifts made in a lifetime, creates so many possible loopholes that it is a dubious alternative. "It is probably correct to conclude that in many cases the more evidence is submitted to disprove contemplation of death, the greater the probability that the gift was actually made in contemplation of death."[17] And "Any tax provision becomes unduly pathetic when it gears the liability to such nonsense as the decedent's happy disposition, his practice of golfing once a week, or his entrenched habit of pottering about his garden."[18] The difficulties of this legislation were such that in 1950 Congress amended the ruling by substituting a blend of American and British practices. A time period prior to death was selected (three years); any gift made prior to that period would not be liable to the full estate duty but only to the ordinary gifts tax, levied at 75 per cent of the estate duty rates.

The American gifts tax is designed, supposedly, to back up the estate duty, an intention which is the source of most of its weaknesses. "The design is to impose a tax which measurably approaches the estate tax which would have been leviable on the donor's death had the gifts

---

[17] C. Lowell Harriss, *Gift Taxation in the U.S.* (Washington: American Council on Public Affairs, 1940), p. 19.

[18] S. Eisenstein, "Are We Ready for Estate and Gift Tax Revision?" *Taxes*, Vol. XXIII, 1945.

not been made and the property given had constituted his estate at his death."[19] It fails in this objective in five ways.

First, the gift tax involves nonintegration among three tax bases, gift, estate, and income. Each of these bases has different exemptions and different rates, not necessarily with any relationship to each other.

The nonintegration of rates will be dealt with later. For the time being the discussion will center around the differing structures. In horizontal equity through time, compared to the estate tax the U.S. gift tax is favored; it has larger initial lifetime exemptions and liberal annual allowances. Thus the donors making gifts early in their life will have a substantial advantage over those who start later, whether these later gifts are the result of choice or whether they have no option because of trust settlements, or even if they only save the money at a late date in life themselves. In this way those who inherit wealth at a younger age (and who are thereby able to start giving it away themselves) are given an advantage over those who have to earn and save and who, of course, cannot start to gift property (and take advantage of the larger exemptions and lower rates) until they have it. This horizontal equity advantage results not only from the exemption but also because the making of a gift reduces the estate which will finally be liable to estate duty, but no such saving can accompany the payment of the estate duty.

Similar difficulties occur between the income, gift, and estate taxes. It has been maintained that one of the objects of the gifts tax was "to recoup some of the income tax revenue lost by reason of transfers of income producing property by donors in high income tax brackets to donees in lower brackets."[20] When this has been presented as one of the reasons for the gift tax then the problem becomes one of confused reasoning. As already discussed above, the justification for death duties is not revenue, but equity in the total tax structure. It is a peculiar definition of equity that the state must have its pound of flesh whether the property is held by the rich or the poor. Indeed it could be held that this type of redistribution (from high income brackets to low) is precisely the sort which inheritance taxation wishes to encourage (the same argument as that used in championing inheritance taxation generally, see above). The only way in which it could be possible to recoup the income tax foregone, in this situation, would be to levy a gift

---

[19] H.R. Report No. 708, 72nd Cong., 1st Sess. (1932).

[20] Rudick, "What Alternative to the Estate and Gift Taxes?" p. 152. Apparently the first U.S. gift tax of 1924 was essentially a move to recoup income tax foregone.

(transfer) tax at rates higher than that of the death duties. In this way the transfer tax would cover the amount lost in death duties (providing all other exemptions, etc., were the same) and also have some excess to set against the income tax lost; but in some cases this could be inequitable — where the property was transferred in the opposite direction (from lower to higher marginal income tax brackets) and to correct this the transfer tax would have to be related, in some fashion, to the circumstances of the donee. In other words, it would be easier to turn the tax into a single inheritance tax rather than to deal with the inequities of two conflicting taxes, the income tax and the estate duty.

The second main difficulty is where overlap occurs. It was clearly envisaged in the original act that overlap would occur "where any property subject to the gift tax is required to be included in the donor's gross estate on his death."[21] This is one of the numerous difficulties in defining gifts. The extent of the transfer of interest can be so dubious that in some circumstances a property can be liable to two taxes. If a man buys some property which he puts in the joint names of himself and his son, he has made a gift of 50 per cent of the value of the property to his son (and is taxed on it). When the father dies his entire estate, including all the property purchased above, would be liable to estate duty. Again under insurance schemes where a person buys a life policy and assigns it to another person, a gift tax should be imposed on the policy premium paid to the date of transfer, and should continue to be levied on successive transfers. Yet the total life policy when death occurs will be liable to estate taxation. These duplications of tax are met, theoretically, by credit provisions where tax already paid can be offset against tax liability at a later date. The number of these credit decisions in the United States, and the avenues they open up for discretion as to the advantageous time to actually transfer property, indicate that a new system which eliminates overlap would be most attractive.

Third, the definition of the taxable unit has created considerable difficulty. This has been worse in the United States than it might have been in other countries if they had tried a full scale gifts tax, because the issue was bedeviled by the relationship of federal and state responsibilities and their respective tax structures. Some states had a property law derived from Spain[22] as opposed to the English common law base,

---

[21] H.R. Report No. 708, 72nd Cong., 1st Sess. (1932), 45.

[22] H. M. Groves, *Federal Tax Treatment for the Family* (Washington, D.C.: Brookings Institution, 1963), p. 60.

resulting in a "community property law" which recognized the contribution of the married woman to the income of the partnership. As the federal law levied taxes on income from property the title of which was determined by state law, the community property states had an advantage over the others in that married persons could reduce their federal income tax liability by splitting, compared to that of exactly comparable marriages in other states. Increasing friction, "a desire for tax relief and the critical community property problem accounts in large part for what seems to many an extraordinary product";[23] that is, the "marital deduction," introduced in 1948. If either married person made a gift half of it could be considered as coming from the spouse. This effectively doubles exemptions and reduces marginal rates. The community property law states still allow a spouse to enjoy a half interest in the joint property without attracting a gift tax. The result, although better than the previous position, still produces anomalies. In a community property state a husband may earn a fortune and leave his "share" of it (half) to his children. Of course, no gift tax is paid on the half property owned by the wife during the husband's life. In another state, where the community property law does not operate, if the husband makes a gift to his wife of half his savings, then one-half of it will be considered as coming from his wife herself, but that leaves a quarter (half of the half) which is liable to transfer tax. Clearly the community property state has an advantage. Other examples could be constructed to show an advantage in the opposite direction.[24] The treatment of the tax unit for gift taxation in the United States is clearly inequitable in an arbitrary manner.

In addition to the difference of the "marital deduction" outlined above there are other differences due to the limitation of 50 per cent as the maximum deduction allowed under both estate and gift taxes. Thus the 50 per cent limitation is applied to interspouse transfers.

. . . the result is to create some new and different planning tax choice problems which must frequently be resolved before all pertinent information is known. Inter-vivos inter-spouse transfers which incur gift tax may turn out to be expensive tax-wise if they result in a failure fully to use the marital deduction at death. Since property holdings and their values can fluctuate greatly over the period of a few years, the ultimate tax desirability of a transfer by gift to a spouse of a substantial portion of the donor's holdings may be very difficult to predict.[25]

---

[23] *Ibid.*, p. 65.

[24] A. W. DeWind, "The Approaching Crisis in Federal Estate and Gift Taxation," *California Law Review,* Vol. XXXVIII, 1950, pp. 87-88.

[25] *Ibid.*, p. 90.

This is similar to the British inter vivos gifts valuation problem of the divorce between valuation and full tax liability.

The final difficulty of the U.S. gift tax structure is that concerned with the creation of trusts. Trusts are a peculiarly aggravating feature of all wealth taxation because they create problems of ownership definition, of the exact timing and definition of gifts, and even of liability for tax payment. Another outline of their position in wealth taxation will be found below under the discussion of possible legal changes in wealth taxation. For the time being it is clear that in the United States instead of allowing an estate to be taxed on the death of each owner (even with allowances for marital deductions) the total tax liability will be greatly reduced if the property is settled on persons for life only and held (and invested) by trustees. There must be a great incentive to settle property in trust which in normal circumstances would never be put into trust. Trusts have enormous practical disadvantages: they are often cumbersome, involve restrictions on investment maneuver which can result in less earnings than a "free" property would earn, and they cannot be realized for purchases out of capital.

The unsatisfactory nature of the U.S. experience with its general gifts tax would be sufficient to deter anyone from copying the U.S. legislation, but as some of the defects arose from conditions unique to the U.S. federal system (the marital exemption) and others from peculiar legislative decisions (the gift tax rate set at only 75 per cent of the estate tax)[26] there are alternatives which do not embody the disadvantage of the only existing general gifts tax. These disadvantages have not been unnoticed in the United States and an authoritative draft suggesting an alternative tax structure has been presented by an Advisory Committee to the Treasury Department and by the Office of the Tax Legislative Council in cooperation with the Division of Tax Research and the Bureau of Internal Revenue.[27] The proposal[28] is simple and is the practical minimum which would achieve reasonable equity under a system of gift taxation. An integration of estate and gift taxation, treating the estate transferred at death as a final gift transfer, would insure at least that the same tax rate was used on estates and gifts. If the tax rates used were progressive, the transfers (including those at death) would have to be cumulative, much as the present

---

[26] In some way the legislature hoped that the lower rate would equal the death duty rate while allowing for the interest rate mark-up.

[27] Advisory Committee to the Treasury Department, *Federal Estate and Gift Taxes* (Washington, D.C.: U.S. Government Printing Office), 1947.

[28] *Ibid.*, especially p. 14.

basis of U.S. gift taxation is cumulative. Any exemptions would apply to all the transfers, and there should be no duplications. Thus a common set of rates and exemptions would remove many of the current criticisms of the U.S. gift and estate tax structure, and could provide a basis for other countries' gift tax, or transfer tax, structures.

One criticism is that this form of transfer tax would not produce much revenue. Under the federal and state transfer tax yields, with a tax structure largely as suggested by the Treasury 1947 discussions, an effective rate on the total tax base of 5 per cent would yield $1.113 billion; at British death duty rates applied to accumulated transfers the yield would be $5.919 billion, that is, a 29 per cent effective rate.[29]

This leaves us with the problem of exemptions. The only completely equitable way to treat exemptions is to allow a single exemption limit which can be drawn on annually, or exhausted in a single gift. Oddly the U.S. recommendations biased the tax in favor of retaining the estate until death. They recommended[30] a maximum exemption which could be claimed on inter vivos gifts, but doubled the exemption if the transfer occurred at death. There was thus a bias in favor of retaining sufficient estate to death to claim the double exemption. The committee justified this recommendation by saying that "The purpose of the exemption at death is to avoid undue hardship to dependents of the transferor once they are deprived of their primary source of maintenance and support."[31] This justification is similar to the arguments discussed above under the reasons for favoring families by consanguinity rates. Similar points can be made against them; the exemption justified on the narrow grounds of the needy widow and children, in fact, includes everyone, the child of forty who inherits, and the widow of twenty who remarries. As previously, this exemption is part of an argument for taxation according to the circumstances of the receiver and not that of the donor.

Unfortunately, the 1947 American committee's recommendations elsewhere did not insure complete equity. They left the curious anomaly whereby the transfer tax paid on transfers inter vivos did not form part of the estate at death. This created an inequity between the estate which is substantially passed during life and that which is held to death, the latter bearing a tax on the equivalent of the transfer tax which it would have paid had it been transferred during life as the other estate was. The way in which this could be neatly contained in

[29] J. C. Bowen, "Some Yield Estimates for Transfer Taxes," *National Tax Journal,* March, 1959, p. 58.

[30] Advisory Committee to the Treasury Department, pp. 15-16.

[31] *Ibid.,* p. 16.

the general transfer tax base would be to include the transfer tax paid as part of the cumulative tax base, thus insuring that the final estate at death would be the same whether it had been gifted during life or retained to death. Another simple way round this would be to swing the whole responsibility for tax payment from the donor to the receiver.

The consideration of all the difficulties of transfer taxation and these two difficulties remaining in the suggested reformation of the U.S. gift tax structure encouraged commentators to urge the adoption of a tax based on the transfer *received,* that is on the donee, not the donor.[32] This is, of course, our old friend the inheritance tax and the U.S. proposals have already been mentioned in the discussion above. This proposal is open to the major criticisms levied there, that it does not insure, or even safeguard, equity through time. That is, it is still possible under the "accretions" tax to make the transfers from very old to very young persons, thus reducing the "turnover" of the estate, and at the same time reducing tax liability.

Neither the existing gift tax of the United States nor the proposed alternatives give us a satisfactory solution to the taxation of wealth transfers. Some more continuous and broader tax structure is needed. This leads us to the proposals for an integration, not only of the estate and gift taxes (the American proposal), nor for the integrated base to be taxed according to the total transferred wealth of the individual (the accretions tax), but an integration of gifts, inheritances, and capital gains taxation, in a base which will be taxed on the receiver.[33] This is the accruals tax.

THE GENERAL ACCRUALS TAX

Once the principle of taxing the receiver of gifts and legacies is accepted it is easy to see how this tax base can be extended to include realized capital gains and windfall gains (football pool prizes, lotteries, etc.). This would neatly absorb those additions to purchasing power which escape the income tax. They are each in the nature of a capital receipt (the problems of trust income is left to later) and could be accumulated to provide liability under a progressive tax. This is the final solution proposed by C. T. Sandford.[34]

---

[32] Rudick, "A Proposal for an Accessions Tax," and "What Alternative to the Estate and Gifts Taxes?" p. 150.

[33] C. T. Sandford, "Taxing Inheritance and Capital Gains," Hobart Paper 32, Institute of Economic Affairs, London, 1965; and A. J. Merrett, "Capital Gains Taxation: The Accrual Alternative," *Oxford Economic Paper,* Vol. XVI, No. 2, July, 1964.

[34] Sandford, pp. 58-63.

Realized capital losses could be offset only against realized capital receipts. Under this structure the plea that "bunching" of realized capital gains results in inequity has been circumvented. If the capital gains so realized were to be subject to the income tax (plus surtax) rates, then the common stand is taken that gains which have accumulated over a number of years should not be taxed at the marginal rate applicable to a single year. But where, as in this proposal, the tax structure is based not on an annual basis, but on a *lifetime* then the tax structure ceases to be discriminating against these realized gains which have accrued over a long period. The essential difference between these systems is that the one treats capital receipts as a form of income and argues that they should be liable to income tax, whereas the other looks upon them as a separate taxable entity, apart from income, and liable to different rates. Thus the income tax base is on a yearly period and capital is taxed on a lifetime.

The structure, although attractive in its simplicity, has difficulties. First, with a different series of exemptions and rates from that of the income tax structure it will provide an incentive to taxpayers wishing to minimize total tax liability to switch income from one system to the other. If in any given year an increment which is represented as a capital gain would be taxed at a lower marginal rate if it were "income," then the taxpayer will try to arrange his affairs so that the capital gain is represented as "income"; perhaps by foregoing his stock option and accepting an increase in annual income in lieu, or simply by switching from capital gain stocks to income stocks. Second, and more fundamentally, this tax structure still does not insure equity through time. Capital tax liability can still be reduced by insuring that transfers are made between persons of large age differential, from grandparents to grandchildren.

To circumvent the first criticism the alternatives would be either to transform the capital accruals to an annual basis and tax them at the current income tax rates, or to regard income as accruing over a lifetime and tax all income on a lifetime accrual basis, like capital accrual. This latter proposition can be regarded as academically reasonable in that income does fluctuate from year to year, and indeed from age bracket to age bracket, and this structure might provide some interesting solutions to the problems of averaging irregular incomes through time. It could also allow remarkable flexibility especially regarding age variations in commitments, i.e., taxes could be varied according to monetary commitments of children, dependents, etc., but also by the age of the earner, with low rates for the young family, high rates for the middle aged, and low rates for the elderly; all these to be meshed in with the cumulative amounts of income and capital gain through time. Although perhaps academically acceptable, the required change in tax structure and individual and administrative outlook would be so vast to make it most unlikely in practice. Therefore, it is to the alternative that we must turn, the idea of treating capital gains on an annual basis at income tax rates.

The reasons why this was not considered in the first place are well known. There are difficulties of applying progressive tax rates to a capital gain which just takes the taxpayer into the next "bracket," so that with a basic income which would be taxed at 25 per cent, the capital gain liability is 30 per cent; yet in the next year, with the same income tax liability of 25 per cent, a capital loss of equal magnitude would only recoup a tax credit of 25 per cent. Of course, it is easy to eliminate this simple criticism. Any capital loss should be calculated as though it were a capital gain and the resulting tax liability will give a tax credit which will exactly offset the tax liability on an equivalent gain.

Again it has been held that there is a waste of effort in taxing gains one year which are offset the next year by losses.[35] By this definition, all equitable taxation must involve the likelihood of waste. To assess ordinary income tax liability, total income must be computed before allowances are deducted for dependents, etc. All tax structures must allow for repayment if circumstances during the year change and even a tax on realized gains must also allow for realized losses. The criticism is valid, but it is valid for all tax structures.

Under an annual tax on accruals, taxpayers might be forced to realize assets to meet their tax liabilities. This could impose costs on the taxpayer, as the realization of a large block of infrequently traded assets could involve a lower market price than that which might be realized by a more extended program of small outlays. This is probably a marginal problem occurring in a relatively few instances. Where a case could be made to the Revenue authorities that such a cost would be involved, then some extended time period could be allowed for tax payment. More complex systems can be devised[36] where the taxpayer would be obliged to pay only part of his tax liability based directly on the capital gains realized and the residual could be carried forward until death if not realized. This seems a large concession to all capital gains taxpayers to cover a limited case.

---

[35] See Merrett, "Capital Gains Taxation: The Accrual Alternative."
[36] Ibid.

The most serious difficulty of taxing capital gains on an annual basis is the annual valuation of all assets. This has always seemed to be a large stumbling block and proposals for current taxation of capital gains have halted at this obstacle. The block might be swallowed, though uncomfortably, if the costs of administrating an initial valuation were faced; thereafter infrequent valuations could be supplemented by a general mark-up of classified property by types. This is a hopeful but sieve-like scheme. What happens to the large, skilled valuation administration set up to cope with the original valuation after the initial phase is past? Civil service children once created are difficult to throttle. The application of mark-ups to broad classifications of property would be likely to result in mountains of litigation — disagreement would exist over geographically differential capital gains, over the classification of particular assets, and over the rate of increase. It is difficult to accept this as a realistic proposition.

The alternative, as the United States adopts in its capital gains taxation, is to require all taxpayers to submit a voluntary annual tax declaration of capital values. This, combined with large penalties for misleading returns, might produce a reasonable tax base. Unfortunately, the evidence indicates that "as much as a third or more of individual taxpayer capital gains appear to be unreported, at least in the securities field. Tighter enforcement could mean more than an additional billion dollars of revenue."[37]

Apart from securities and physical assets there must be problems in determining the cash holdings of individuals, and any attempted interference by the government in the relation of banker to customer has widespread implications.

CONCLUSIONS

The operation of neither the existing British nor American gift tax structures satisfied equity at a point in time between persons with different asset holdings, nor did they satisfy equity through time. The proposals for a general accruals tax appear more reasonable in terms of equity but have problems of valuation and do not indicate the necessary rate relationship between capital receipts and other receipts. It is consideration of this *rate relationship* that crystalizes the *structure* of tax needed.

---

[37] H. H. Hinrichs, "Underreporting of Capital Gains on Tax Returns," *National Tax Journal*, June, 1964, p. 163.

13

Wealth Transfer Taxation:
The Rates of Taxation, P.A.Y.A.

GIFTS AND RATES

Gift taxation evolved as an adjunct to the taxation of wealth at death, so its rate structure must be considered in relation to that of the death duties.

It is quite clear that to levy a gift tax at rates that are lower than those prevailing for death duties is to invite persons with property to dispose of it prior to death, e.g., the present British capital gains tax at 30 per cent. Although this could be presented as a proper aim of the taxation, that is, putting purchasing power into younger hands so that the time incidence of purchasing power coincides with a person's period of greatest family costs (children, education), no one has suggested that this form of differential taxation should be used for this purpose. It would be a rather haphazard form of incentive.

The opposite could be argued with more merit, that penal rates of gift taxation compared to those of death duties would encourage people to leave estates to be taxed by death duties rather than pay the higher gift tax rate, thus simplifying the assessment of the tax by cutting down gifts inter vivos.

The justification of the rate differential in the United States was held to be a rough approximation of the compound rate of interest which the property would have earned had it not been given away as a gift, but even this casual guess has been supplemented by exemptions and tax base evasions which leave little relevance to the idea of the compound rate of interest.

In fact, no country has interpreted the relationship of gift taxation, death duties, and income taxes correctly in its tax structure.

The countries which actually use gift taxes have introduced them as a back-up device to their death duty structure, yet in each case they have, by liberal exemptions and low rates, encouraged distribution inter vivos as opposed to their system of death duties.[1]

The reduction of gift tax liability compared to the tax liability under death duties can result from six causes. The most obvious reason is the application of lower rates. In the United States the rates applied are three-quarters of those used for estate duty. In Canada the rates, although starting at the same level, rise much more slowly than the estate duty and eventually level off at 28 per cent on gifts over one million dollars, whereas at one million dollars estate duties are 44 per cent and continue to rise to 54 per cent on estates over two million dollars. In Australia, even taking the most advantageous estate duty rates (they vary with consanguinity, and those applying to the widow or lineal issue are the lowest, e.g., 3 per cent, compared to 8 per cent on strangers), the gift tax is a lower rate of duty, and naturally if the intention was to leave the estate to a person of more remote relationship the incentive would be to gift the estate rather than have it transferred as a legacy.

The second method by which gift tax liability can be reduced is by varying the cumulative nature of the tax. Obviously, a tax which cumulates over a lifetime (United States) will create a much larger tax base than one which takes eighteen months as its time period (Australia) or one that adopts a year (Canada).

Again, the gift tax burden can be varied by the extent of initial total exemption, $30,000.00 in the United States, $4,000.00 in Canada, and $4,480.00 in Australia. This alters the impact of tax in the lower brackets.

Similar, but separate, annual exemptions can reduce the impact of a gifts tax even if it were levied at estate duty rates on a cumulative basis; thus the U.S. annual exemption of $3,000.00 means that a gift a year of $3,000.00 spread over ten years will transfer $30,000.00 with no tax liability.

---

[1] Except Sweden, where a person receiving gifts during a ten-year period which total more than the minimum exemption limit pays estate duty which assumes the gift came from the highest tranche of the estate.

In addition to the above, special reductions for gifts to spouses (50 per cent reduction in the United States), and reductions for gifts made by the married couple where they can both claim the $30,000.00 lifetime exemption when the gift is made to the third party, result in reductions of gift tax liability compared to the impact of death duties.

Finally, provisions for offsetting the gift tax payment against the liability for estate duty and deducting this payment from the gross estate taxable at death reduces the total tax base. It is rather as though you were not only allowed to credit all income tax payments made in a lifetime against liability to death duties, but you could deduct all the income as well from the base.

The result of these six influences must be to reduce the tax liability under gift taxation compared to that under death duties.[2]

The following table gives a simple indication of the change in amounts net of taxation and the average rates of tax.

TABLE 13:1

Examples of the Differential Impact of Death Duties and Gift Taxes in the United Kingdom and the United States

| Estate | United Kingdom | | | | United States | | | |
	£'000	Tax (Percentage)	£'000	Tax (Percentage)	$'000	Tax (Percentage)	$'000	Tax (Percentage)
1. Total	500	–	1,000	–	1,400	–	2,800	–
2. Net of Full Death Duties	350	30	550	45	914	35	1,643	41
3. Net of Gift Tax on Gifts Made 4 Years Previously	480	4	900	10	1,049[a]	24	1,949[a]	31
4. Net of Gifts Tax on Gifts Made 6 Years Previously	500[c]	0	1,000[c]	0	1,060[b]	24	1,963[b]	30

[a] Assumes $30,000 lifetime deductions and $3,000 annual exemption.

[b] Assumes $30,000 lifetime deductions from each spouse ($60,000 in all) and $3,000 annual exemption.

[c] It is assumed that there is no capital gain during the period and therefore no liability to capital gains tax.

[2] For a factual comparison of U.K., U.S., Canadian, and Australian estate and gift taxation, see G. S. A. Wheatcroft, "Estate and Gift Taxes — A Comparison," *British Tax Review*, September-October, 1964.

The result of these numerous influences makes it unlikely that the incidence of the gift tax would be similar to that of the death duty if that had been the initial intention of the legislature, but it is difficult to believe that any serious attempt has been made by these countries to equate the two taxes. "There has been little apparent attempt to integrate the gift tax provisions of the Income Tax Act with the estate tax."[3]

If we consider the theoretical rate appropriate to gift taxation, ignoring the actual rates which have been adopted, then the problems resolve. If gift taxes exist to supplement death duties, then it is clear that if the property is disposed of prior to death it should pay the same total tax as it would have done had it passed at death. This assumes that the legislature is not trying to achieve other aims (redistribution) by a discriminating form of taxation. If the death duty tax structure is progressive then the gift tax structure will have to be progressive (it would clearly be much simpler if a proportional rate were used). As gifts can be made piecemeal and extended over a long time period, this means that the gift tax will have to be of a cumulative nature over a long period, ideally a lifetime.

As the number of gifts made in the donor's lifetime increases, the tax rate on them increases. To make a specific net gift the donor would have to allow for his increasing tax liability.

The interrelationship between taxes on income and on capital is difficult to determine. Gifts can be considered a form of income to the recipient and taxed as part of an accrual tax. If they are so considered, a three-way relationship is established. Gifts are income and should be taxed as income at income tax rates. Gifts are also made from capital and diminish the estate taxed at death duty rates. To insure that there is not encouragement to avoid death duties by prior disbursement, the rates of gifts and death duties should be the same. Therefore, as the rates of tax on estates at death and gifts should be the same, and as tax rates on gifts and income should be the same, then the tax rates on income and property passing at death should be the same.

The statement above is striking because it fails to make explicit that in it, gifts are viewed from two different angles. When a gift is received, looked at as an addition to the purchasing power of the recipient, it is a form of income and, as such, should be liable to income tax. In other words, a gift looked upon from the receiver's point of

[3] R. W. V. Dickerson, "Estate and Gift Taxation in Canada," *British Tax Review,* July-August, 1964, p. 255.

view is income, as are capital gains and winnings. Whereas from the donor's viewpoint the gift comes from capital and reduces his estate. The remarkable conclusion that death duty rates and income tax rates should be linked comes from regarding the same transfer (gift) as capital and income. Yet some reconciliation is necessary. If there is no agreement, then when the receiver's income tax rates are lower than the donor's estate tax (average) it pays the capital owner to transfer his estate by gifts inter vivos.

Again, this form of differential tax could be justified if the intention of the legislature was to transfer capital from those who had it to those who had low incomes. In fact, this becomes a form of inheritance taxation so that the tax levied on the gift is a function of the earned and unearned income of the recipient, which in its turn is a function of his circumstances — married, children, dependent relatives, and so on. However, this base for taxation would not necessarily result in the desired redistribution of capital. So long as the younger capital owner retained his capital in non–income-yielding assets, or more precisely, non–income-taxable assets — houses, old masters, children, education — then his actual income tax rates could be quite low and consequently the gifts he received would be taxed at low rates. This could continue until the estates of all his relatives had been transferred, and had in turn been put into non–income-yielding assets, after which the young man could reorganize his capital to be income yielding.

The only way to combat this difficulty is to levy the gift tax on a cumulative basis. But this in turn leads to the difficulty of taxing a flow like income on a cumulative basis. It is as though the correct base for income taxation is not the year but the lifetime. It is theoretically correct that a completely equitable base for income taxation would be the lifetime, but administratively the year, or in some cases an average over some limited period (about seven years), has been the tried method of taxing variable incomes.

The dilemma poses itself in that incomes as a flow must be taxed over relatively short periods, while capital as a stock must be taxed in some cumulative manner. Yet if the cumulative gifts tax works out at rates lower than the income tax, taxpayers will arrange their affairs to receive their income as gifts (stock options, golden handshakes); alternatively, if the income tax rates are lower, then people will prefer to treat their gifts as income.

So the problem is to work out a relationship which will satisfy both income flows and capital stocks as tax bases, without discriminating in favor of one or the other.

It should be established first that the tax payment, whether income or accrual, should be paid by the recipient; much of the potential confusion arises from different taxpayers (donors and donees, etc.) and their differing relative tax liabilities.

What is implied in saying that there must be some relationship between transfer taxation, income taxation, and death duties is really a revision of the general tax base, and the discussion is likely to lead to varients of the "single-tax" proponents. Although in the past these pleas have often been made with a view to simplifying the tax structure, in this instance the discussion derives from desirable equitable treatment and is unlikely to simplify the tax structure. A brief discussion is merited to highlight the relationship of the rate structure for transfer taxes to the rates of other tax bases. Moreover, it could happen that the requirements of the rate structure for transfer taxation are such as to dictate much of the structure of the tax.

THE TOTAL TAX BASE

The division of the personal total tax base can be presented in five sections.

1. Wages and salaries are usually easily identifiable, and when not they will fall into one of the other categories. (ΣW).

2. The money income from capital. (ΣZ_i). Wages and salaries could be presented as money income from human capital, but this leads to confusion over the tax base since all income is thus identified with a capital source so that the tax could, theoretically, be levied on the capital invested in education, health, etc.

3. Capital accretions, gifts, inheritances, football pool winnings, etc. If all accruals were taxed on a cumulative base, then over a lifetime the total wealth of the recipient would be known — except for his savings out of salaries and wages and capital income yield. Allowance would have to be made for capital gains. Over a lifetime the accumulating accruals would embody some capital gains and this raises the problem of identifying unrealized capital gains. Without penetrating into the virtues of "roll-over" taxation, expenditure tax bases as opposed to income tax bases, etc., it does seem worthwhile mentioning a possible rough alternative, which like much rough justice has the minimum virtues of speed and simplicity, and some hope of equity. The capital gains on the known accumulated gifts could be attributed at some national average; if the assets were well managed and the owner attained a rate of return which insured his gains to be higher than the national

taxable average he would get some tax-free bonus; if not, and his rate of return was lower than the average there would be an additional tax burden. This could be some encouragement to the efficient utilization of national assets. If the accruals embody capital gains ascribed at some rate (g) for any given year, then the accrual tax base would be:

$$A_1(1 + g_1) + \{[A_2 + A_1 (1 + g_1)] (1 + g_2)\} + \ldots = \Sigma A,$$

where A_1, A_2 are the accruals in the appropriate year. Thus ΣA is the lifetime accumulation of accruals and their attributed capital gains.

4. Some "inherent capital factor." The value of holding capital is a combination of the income it yields and the command over assets (responsibility, prestige, security, etc.) which the owner enjoys. Thus, the imposition of a capital levy compared to that of an income tax is not equivalent. The capital levy removes the assets, while the income tax leaves the wealth owner still with command over his assets.

To a certain extent this is a verbal quibble (see capital levies *supra*) in that a capital levy at a rate which could be met out of the capital income would equally leave the ownership of the assets in private hands.

The Kaldor example[4] of the imposition of a capital levy compared to that of an income tax indicates that the taxpayer would rather have the income tax than the levy; thus where (r) is the average rate which equates the levy to the income tax yield at rate (i), and where $r > i$ if the taxpayer would rather pay the income tax than the levy, the "inherent factor" in capital holding is expressed by $(r - i)$ so that the summation of the inherent value of capital Z over a lifetime of (n) years is $Zn(r - i)$.

It is perfectly clear that r will vary according to the form in which the estate is held and with the expertise of those who manage the estate. The exact value of r for any two estates need not be the same. What are the attributes that contribute to r? The difference in money yields between different estates is not relevant because the ordinary income tax tZi will be based on the *actual* monetary yield of the estate (Zi), not on some national average. Thus one of the contributions to the value of (r) will be the nonmonetary income derived from nonmonetary income–yielding assets which are overlooked by the ordinary income tax.

Second, there are the security aspects of wealth holdings. These are

---

[4] N. Kaldor, "The Income Burden of Capital Taxes," *Review of Economic Studies*, Vol. IX, No. 2, Summer 1942. Reprinted in American Economics Association, *Readings in Economics of Taxation*, eds. R. A. Musgrave and C. Shoup (London: Allen and Unwin, 1959), pp. 393-415.

almost impossible to value for each person as they must vary widely between different individuals; however, it might be possible to use the amount of income that would purchase an insurance to cover the types of emergencies which are connected with security — loss of income due to accident, death leaving dependents, etc. The rate for security would be equal to the rate of interest (that is, the annual premium) required to purchase a lump sum insurance equal to Z which would be payable in these circumstances. This would vary with the age of the wealth holder, obviously becoming more important and requiring higher rates as he got older.

Third, there are those prestige advantages of wealth ownership. In actual fact it is doubtful whether any wealth owner would be prepared to forego much income to purchase prestige (his wife might), and this is so intangible, and probably negligible in most real valuations, that it is omitted here; but some coefficient could be used as a mark-up of the "prestige value." Thus the "inherent" wealth tax will consist of a non-money income factor, a security factor, and possibly a prestige factor.

As (r) is the average yield which would make the full capital tax and the income tax equivalent, then for any given year:

$$r = u + sx - i$$

where (u) is a rate of interest applied to total capital which gives a theoretical total capital income yield; (i) the actual money income yield subtracted from (u), that is (u − i) is the extent of the non-money income yield; (sx) the security rate for the wealth holder aged x years, which must be added to (u − i) to complete the value for (r). The total of r applied to capital (accruals plus savings) over a lifetime would be equal to (ΣF), that is, the total of the "inherent factor," i.e., r(ΣA) = ΣF.

5. Finally, the various constituents of the tax base outlined above have omitted savings out of current wages, salaries, and money capital income (although r, theoretically, should be applied to both accruals and savings), thus Z = ΣA + ΣS. So the total tax base, over a lifetime is:

$$\Sigma W + \Sigma Zi + \Sigma F + \Sigma A + \Sigma S$$

and theoretically, to avoid discrimination between different forms of the tax base, a single tax rate is applied to the whole expression.

Clearly this is impractical. But having established the relationship, some discussions of the approximation to the ideal are possible.

Working backward in the relationship outlined above, savings out of current income have always been a problem in any tax base. The nineteenth-century accusation was that of double taxation. The income was taxed, and then the income from the savings was taxed. Under the outline above J. S. Mill would, presumably, cry "treble taxation," because not only is the wage income and the capital income taxed, but also the saving addition to capital is taxed. The disincentive to saving and risk capital are well-known presentations against such taxation (and will be discussed below, separately) and it would appear to be common sense, given the fact that all persons (and corporate bodies) discount the future (because the dollar today is "worth" in utility more than the dollar twenty years hence, because of the potential productivity of a dollar held over those twenty years, and because of potential relative price changes of goods and services over time), to acknowledge that savings for the long-term future (as a legacy to someone after your death) are valued less than savings for the near future. This time-factor valuation is enhanced by the interpolation of death; if anything death should enormously increase the discount on the future so that present savings for near consumption are increased in value. Thus the disincentive effects of taxing receipts (legacies) as income would be much less than those of taxing savings from current income (this was, of course, the basis of the Rignano proposals). The administrative costs of discovering the full extent of current savings, a type of investigation which in many ways is repugnant to the ideals of Western political systems, and the advantages in encouraging such saving, all point toward exempting from the overall tax rate these savings out of current income. Also, on broader emotional levels the taxation of legacies is much more acceptable to a wide spectrum of reformers.

Moreover, it is clear that after one generation the savings from current income which have not been spent would be transferred and would, as accruals, become liable to taxation. Thus, after such a tax base had been in operation for some time, most of the national wealth would be included in the tax base. In these circumstances, a taxpayer would minimize his tax liability by placing his savings out of current income in non–income-yielding assets, thereby avoiding the capital-income tax as well.

Continuing the discussion of the tax base, we come to the accruals. Now it is clear that any accruals, to be taxed equitably, must be cumulated over a lifetime (further difficulties with this emerge when we consider the appropriate tax unit in Chapter 14). Each accretion would not only be liable to tax itself, but would alter the tax liability of ΣW, ΣZ_i, and ΣF. Yet taxation on a straightforward yearly basis would lead to wide fluctuations in the marginal rates of tax, and it would pay the taxpayer to lower tax liability by spreading the accrual evenly over the total period; therefore there must be a cumulative element. But the continually cumulated accruals cannot be taxed again and again each year. Some annual flow of accumulation must be ascribed. Equally it is clear that it is difficult to tax wages and salaries over a lifetime, although this would be the most appropriate time period to choose. Some means of meshing the two must be sought.

We are always mesmerized with the restraints imposed by our grandfathers. We come to accept as natural, normal, and even immutable some structure created by a past society; so it is with death duties. Even the name carries implications which we accept automatically. The plea made here is to convert death duties into lifetime duties.

If the lifetime is taken as the eventual standard tax base, then death duties instead of being the tax levied on an estate between two generations can become reconciliation of accumulated lifetime tax liabilities; the lifetime taxes become the final settlement of a deceased with his earthly auditors, the Inland Revenue; the taxpayer remains, clearly, the receiver, that is, the person who received the income and wealth through his life. The present confusion between taxpayers (donor and donee) is discontinued.

There remain numerous problems. One of these, the inequity through time, should be mentioned in this chapter. Inequity through time remains because the tax period, the lifetime, is still arbitrary and different tax burdens will fall on the same estate according to the life period of the receiver if it is his lifetime which determines the total accrual and hence total tax liability.

As the aim of the tax structure would be to insure that accruals bear the same relative tax as the other constituents of the tax base, and hence there is no gain in switching between different forms of accrual, then at death the total tax paid on accruals would be added to other taxes paid, and accruals would be added to the lifetime tax base; so that death is taken as the point of settling the overall lifetime tax base and tax payment, achieving lifetime equity between different forms of receipts.

Including an imputed "inherent factor" in the tax base was simple when it was assumed that all saving was included, and also that there was no dis-saving. With the exemption of savings out of current income the inherent tax rate is now based on an imputed nonmonetary income yield and the security aspect of wealth holdings. Thus for each year the "inherent factor," as explained above, $rZ = Z(u + sx - i)$, but as $Z = A + S$ and savings are now excluded both Z and i should be reduced by the amount of savings and their monetary yield. While $Z - S = A$ is simple to separate, to split iZ between money yield from current savings and that from accruals would be impossible.

When accruals are cumulated, imputing an income to them will have a two-fold action. It will enable at least some of the nonmonetary income which would otherwise accrue to capital to be taxed, and it circumvents the difficulty of splitting iZ. Thus each year the cumulated gross total of accruals (i.e., gifts, legacies, winnings, but not wages and salaries or capital money yield) could be increased by some coefficient representing attributed money and nonmoney yield. To this would be added a further amount representing the security yield of such capital holdings, and finally there could be added some national figure for attributed capital gains in the year. The relationship of this attributed income to the other parts of the tax base will be clearer if the method of annual or lifetime (or whatever period is selected) computation is shown.

The computation is divided into ten parts:

  (i) gross current (period selected) wages and salaries and capital money income;
 (ii) gross current accruals (gifts, legacies, etc.) ;
(iii) gross current receipts cumulated (i + ii) ;
 (iv) attributed income from ii for current period (capital gains, security, etc.) ;
  (v) cumulated gross tax base (iii + iv) ;
 (vi) exemptions in current period;
(vii) cumulated taxable base (v — vi) ;
(viii) tax liability on vii;
 (ix) previous cumulated tax payments;
  (x) net up-to-date tax liability (viii — ix).

This tax base omits saving out of current wages and salaries, and any of such saving which is invested in non–income-yielding assets. It does not discriminate between different forms of taxable property, i.e., in current terminology, between "earned" and "unearned" income.

The principal drawback is that it could involve a taxpayer in tax liabilities he could not meet. This could arise not through the sort of deficiencies of a straight moving average, but rather because the individual has dis-saved during the cumulated period, thus leaving himself with a smaller tax base than that accredited to him. This could happen even if the taxpayer did not blow all his wages, salary, and capital on consumption, but if he spent his capital faster than he accumulated capital out of current flows. There is no easy remedy to the situation in which the state has a claim on monies already disposed. The most rigorous proposition is that the state should claim its taxes as soon as the property accrues to the receiver. The problem here is that it is impossible to know what the state claims will amount to, especially if it depends on the lifetime of the taxpayer. A way around this difficulty would be to ascribe to any accrual a particular time period over which the accrual is to bear tax. The most reasonable time period to adopt would be that of a generation (thirty-one years). This means that any accrual would be assumed to be held for thirty-one years. The capital gains, the attributed income yield, and the security value would be applied at the date of acquisition; this flow of future benefits would have to be discounted at some acceptable rate to give the present value of the discounted flow. This, added to the capital sum of the accrual, would be liable to a tax rate. This tax rate could not be the actual income tax rate which would result in actuality over the coming years, because it would have to vary progressively with the capital sum accrued each year (or tax period).

The reconciliation would come over the entire lifetime. Accruals would be cumulated and known, the attributed capital gains, security, and money income yields would be cumulated as well, thus the "lifetime duties" would enable a reconciliation to be made between the actual taxes levied (and as the actual taxes levied were based on a discounted flow of benefits there would be no need to apply a compound interest rate to tax payments made during each year of accrual) and the total tax liability given the actual variations in other forms of income and tax rates. This could, of course, involve the state in payments. Depending on how leniently the "thirty-one year" rates had been levied in the first year of the accrual, the state might end up demanding still more taxes, in which case the estate of the deceased would be reduced. To save embarrassment, both to the state overcharging, and to the estate unable to pay any deficit still owing, a sensible system would be to anticipate the full reconciliation payment at a point prior to death, say at retirement, when incomes would be less erratic and when any repayments by the state would be valued more highly (although the government would still have to retain the right to a final reconciliation).

However, it is in the horizontal equity case that the thirty-one-year period is uniquely useful. Under a straightforward system of lifetime cumulated taxes, a gift or legacy left from A to B to C would be taxed more heavily than one left from A to C where all other circumstances of A, B, and C remained the same. There would be no way around this difficulty unless some means of identifying the accrual and the relative tax element were available. When, under the "thirty-one year" rule, tax is assessed and paid, then when a gift is made the Inland Revenue can assume that the gift is made out of the longest held accrual, and the age differential which dominated the debates of Vickrey ceases to be the determining factor in horizontal equity.

The generation is now built-in. It is an integral part of the tax system, and as it is fixed at thirty-one years, random deviations of actual lifetimes and age differences should cease to matter.

When the gift is made, and is assumed to be made from the oldest accrual, credit is given for those years for which tax has been paid but which have not elapsed. Thus the credit for unelapsed years out of the generation when a gift is made enables the donor to "mark-up" the gift by that amount. As implied, the "credit" is given against the donor's future tax liabilities; it is not a cash payment.

Unfortunately, such treatment for gifts re-establishes the distinction between different sorts of receipts. In this case, gifts would be favored compared to wages. Rebates, or credits, would be available on receipt of a gift which would not be available on other parts of the integrated income tax base. So this form of amendment which suggests the introduction of a specified generation time period to remove inequity through time creates its own inequity.

Although the idea of an artificial definition of "generation" is attractive, even it cannot be neutral through time. This leaves a tax base which includes wages, salaries, interest, and accruals, with a mark-up for imputed capital gains and security, levied (ideally) on a permanent up-to-date basis. This would be Pay-As-You-Accumulate (P.A.Y.A.). If the tax period could not be administered as a lifetime, and some shorter interval had to be adopted, then "lifetime duties" could correct discrepancies between the actual taxes levied under P.A.Y.A. and those which ought to have been levied over a lifetime. As P.A.Y.A. over a shorter period than a lifetime would result in tax rates at marginally higher rates than the overall accrual tax, the primary reconciliation could come, say, at retirement when some government repayment would be welcome.

Clearly the ideal period for an accruals tax and the income tax, in fact, for all personal taxation, is the lifetime. With the greatly increased capacity of data processing machinery the problems of administering such a tax are diminishing each year.

CONCLUSIONS

The thread of this section has been traced from the simple question "if we tax wealth transfers [gifts], at what rates should we tax them?" through the labyrinth of interlocking structures. The argument is that to tax such transfers leads you to insure that equity between different parts of the tax base is assured, and leads finally to a statement about the sort of overall personal tax structure that is needed to satisfy horizontal and vertical equity. It is a long way to come from a simple question, but no tax system can be simple and equitable.

What is proposed is a sort of P.A.Y.A. (Pay As You Accumulate) tax (the sector I of the double equity tax structure considered earlier) dictated doubly by the considerations of equity through time and the practical necessity for correlation of tax rates to prevent avoidance.

There would be three parts to the tax structure:

(i)   The money income tax;
(ii) The P.A.Y.A.;
(iii) The lifetime tax.

The rate of tax under P.A.Y.A. would be fixed by previous lifetime accruals (sector II of the double equity system). The final reconciliation of tax rates between I and II to insure that there was no advantage in representing income in any particular form would be the task of the lifetime tax.

14

Changes and Difficulties
of the Tax Base, Valuation, the Tax Unit,
Exemptions, Trusts, Overseas Transfers,
and Demographic Factors

The various possible changes affecting the distribution of factor shares have been examined, particularly including different tax policies. Before looking at the possible effects of the taxes, other influences on the distribution of wealth and its taxation must be examined. These problems are dealt with under seven subheads.

THE TAX BASE

Wealth taxation as used here does not deal with the commonly called "property taxes" on *particular* kinds of property, land, houses, short-term ownership of equities, etc.

With a given, inelastic supply of an asset (classically land, ignoring problems of quality, location, etc.) its value will be reduced by the capital value of the future tax payments. Thus if there are two properties both of value x, but one becomes liable for say, local property duty, while the other is exempt, then the price which a willing buyer pays for one will fall by yn, where y is the yield of the property per year, and n the number of years over which the particular individual is willing to discount. It is important to note that the price actually paid for taxed value x will be smaller by the full amount of the future dis-

155

counted tax liability yn, and therefore the property although purchased at x — yn is immediately yielding a full y or a full value x; that is, the burden of the property duty is borne at the moment of purchase (by the seller if the supply of the untaxed commodity is totally elastic, if not then by both buyer and seller) and theoretically the tax is borne at that moment unless any changes in tax rates occur during the new owner's possession of the asset. A reduction in tax rate will be a windfall gain to the owner of the reduced tax property, an increase will be a burden to the extent of the increase reduced by the amount of tax it is possible to pass onto any new buyer.[1]

This problem is implicit in all the discussions of particular exemptions under existing or proposed duties. In this discussion we are dealing with the *general* taxation of all personal wealth.

There is a fundamental problem common to all transfer tax bases — the difficulty of determining when the transfer is complete. The problems which exist with transfer taxes where they are taxed at rates different than those on other accruals (wages and salaries in particular) cease to exist if the rates are levied on a general accrual tax base; the old distinctions of bilateral and unilateral transfers which have filled numerous legal hours cease to matter; any accrual will be taxed at the same rates whether it is payment for services received or an outright gift. However, as the tax will be paid by the receiver it is important to distinguish when that liability is incurred. In other words, it is important to define when the transfer is complete.

Although the problem is complex,[2] the issues can be boiled down to three fundamentals.

First, if the donor retains any power to revoke or alter the transfer, whether he can exercise this power alone or with other interested or uninterested third parties, then the transfer must be ruled incomplete, and the capital (if it is still taxable), and any income (monetary or nonmonetary depending on the tax base adopted), will be taxed as accruing to the donor.

Second, where the donor retains any power to invade the transferred property (capital or yield) for himself, or for the beneficiaries, or for a third party, whether for education, support, or any other purpose[3] the transfer must be ruled incomplete. This must be so because, on our

---

[1] This is true of rented property also, the fall in capital values corresponding to the fall in rents. Turvey, p. 75.

[2] For some examples of the complexities involved see A. W. DeWind, "The Approaching Crisis," pp. 95-108.

[3] On this issue today in the United States see *Jennings v. Smith,* 161, F. 2d, 74 (2nd Ev.) 1947.

previous discussion, the donor by retaining such powers still has some of the security income from the property, that is he has part of the "inherent factor" of property accruing to him.

Third, where the transfer can be changed, altered, and revoked, the transfer will still be ruled complete provided that the decisions are made by an independent third party and as long as the original donor is in no way a beneficiary under the altered transfer. Under no circumstances can a transfer revert to a donor under a completed transfer.

These three basic propositions would cover most of the laws of the Meades and the Persians for an accruals tax base for a transfer. No reversions must be possible, no benefits must accrue to the donor, no discretionary control must be exercised by the donor, and the donor must have no power to alter the transfer in any way; then the transfer, for taxable purposes, will be complete.

Insurance transfers can be subsumed under the rules outlined above. Transfer is complete where the donor gifts the insurance benefits and withholds no rights to revoke or alter the benefits. The size of the gift is measured by the value of the policy at the time of transfer, plus the premium payments made after the transfer (i.e., past transfer premiums payments are treated as accruals). If the value of the insurance which finally accrues to the beneficiary at the death of the donor is different from that which was taxed at transfer, the allowance should be included for the change in value, subtracting the value of the post-transfer premiums.

VALUATION

The problem of valuation is particularly acute when there is no market transaction. This must be a basic difficulty with all transfer taxation.

The problem is small when there is a large and continuous market in the rights or commodities transferred (e.g., stock), although even this causes disagreement. If the holding to be valued is a large one then a sudden sale could depress the market price below what it would be if the sale were "leaked" out over a longer period. Is it correct to take the marginal unit price for a big holding?

A similar difficulty occurs where prices are seasonal. Should the revenue authorities be bound in their valuation by the ruling seasonal price just because the transfer is timed at, say, a period of glut? This would reduce tax revenues, and give the taxpayer considerable latitude in the disposition of assets to minimize tax liability.

Revenue authorities prefer not to tie themselves by legislation or judicial decisions to the narrowest interpretation of the going market price; the Commissioner "shall not make any reduction in the estimate on account of the estimate being made on the assumption that the whole property is to be placed on the market at one and the same time."[4] By this the authorities are assuming that the executors must act as prudent men, "leaking" out the estate in such a manner as to avoid swamping the market. Or another case where seasonality would not be accepted as a reason for low prices (for cattle) when by waiting a known period it was reasonable to expect a "proper season" to arrive and higher prices to be received sufficient to more than compensate for the waiting period.

However, generally valuation of transfers is based on the idea of the "open market price." The concept of "open market" is elaborated by reference to the price fixed; the "principal value" is held to mean "the price which the property would have fetched on the death of the deceased in the open market if it had then been sold in such a manner and subject to such conditions as might reasonably be calculated to obtain for the vendor the *best price* for the property,"[5] and this is further defined as "the best price possible that is obtainable."[6]

This "best price" in an "open market" is, presumably, close to the economist's concept of the "fair" price, which is "historically closely bound up with the notion of cost under fully competitive conditions."[7] But such an outlook presupposes, at least, large numbers of buyers and sellers and perfect knowledge, to say nothing of homogeneity and the "efficient" working of the market.[8] The courts have tried to satisfy the demands of freedom of entry: "the property must be assumed to be offered under conditions enabling every person desirous of purchasing to come in and make an offer, proper steps being taken to advertise the property and let all likely purchasers know that the property is for sale."[9] Indeed, the freedom of entry and the number of buyers and sellers involved is beyond the academic economist's usual dreams. "The

---

[4] *Finance Act* 1910 (10 Edw. VII & 1 Geo. V) c. 8, Sect. 60(2). This is the American problem of blockage. See Harriss, p. 80.

[5] *E. Ellesmere v. I.R.C.* (1918), L.T. 568 at p. 573, per J. Sankey. Italics inc.

[6] *Ibid.* (1918), 2 K.B. 735 at p. 740.

[7] Sir D. Robertson, *Lecture on Economic Principles* (London: Staples Press, 1957), p. 96.

[8] For a full discussion of this issue see A. A. Tait, "The Economic and Legal Interpretation of 'Open Market Price,'" *British Tax Review*, June-August, 1965.

[9] D. J. Lawday and E. J. Mann, *Green's Death Duties* (5th ed.; London: Butterworth, 1963), p. 398.

whole world was hypothetically there, making hypothetical bids."[10] Yet sometimes the law is obliged to accept specific limitations. If I am prepared to offer a higher price for a piece of property than others, whether this results from the ignorance of my underwriter, my ability to avoid restrictions which others would be obliged to incur, or my own caprice and whim, seems to matter little. If any motive is ascribed to those participating in this theoretical market it is that buyers should seek to maximize their satisfaction of desires within the limits of their income and wealth, and sellers should seek to maximize their net revenue. If it is assumed that the bids reflect the assessment of the buyer in maximizing his satisfaction then it is to the actual bids that we should look, and if the seller is maximizing his net revenue then it is the highest bid which should prevail.

If freedom of entry creates difficulties in the valuation of transfers, the assumption of perfect knowledge can create more. In bidding for a property the buyer will, if it is, say, an auction, know other prices; but he cannot make a realistic assessment of the ability of the property in question to satisfy his desires vis-à-vis other properties unless he has perfect information about the background of each property. When valuing, say, unquoted stocks and shares in a private company, all information relevant is assumed known. This is clearly impractical and judgments have had to defer to the real limitations upon perfect knowledge.

It is true that where an actual imperfection existed a valuation under the assumptions of free entry and perfect knowledge might produce a more favorable result for the executor than for the Revenue. As the real world is usually imperfect valuations are, therefore, commonly weighted against the authorities. For instance, it is usual to assume that a limitation on entry (usual in private companies, and in a broader sense, in most markets, even if only for geographical reasons) and imperfections in knowledge (very common, most men not aspiring to omnipotence) both act to increase the price of goods above that which they would have under "perfect competition." Therefore, both these conditions being much more likely than the assumptions outlined above should, normally, result in properties undervalued by the state. It is true that these imperfections can both act in the opposite manner, inducing price drops and not rises.

Generally, the valuation of a transfer has to be made on the basis of actual, assessed possible bids for the property, rather than by the complete application of the economic theory of the fair market price.

---

[10] *I.R.C. v. Crossman* (1937), A.C. 26 at p. 69.

THE TAX UNIT

There is an extensive, interesting, recent, and well-argued literature on the claims of the various social units as a base for taxation.[11] We do not intend to reiterate the arguments presented, as the relative positions are easy to understand and require little comment.

The broad difficulties of the taxable unit raised by accrual taxation of any form are the basis for taxing transfers between spouses, between parents and children, and between donors and dependents.

The overwhelming consensus of academic opinion is that the marriage unit is a proper basis for taxation; that two sets of spouses with the same total income should pay the same tax, regardless of the division or source of that income. This would appear to be equally true in the case of accruals. The accruals add to the security of the marriage unit, and they add to its income (however defined) in the same manner as the existing incomes do. If the marriage unit is the taxable unit under an accruals tax of any form, then transfers between the partners cannot be taxed and this would have to hold good even at the death of one partner where the entire asset holding would then be in the hands of one partner; for tax purposes no transfer would have taken place. Any credit (under the integrated income tax outlined above) would be on the jointly held assets and would continue even if one of the partners died. As the law does not permit polygamy in the United Kingdom or the United States there is no avoidance avenue by splitting the tax base between numerous wives.

Although, under a lifetime accruals tax, the dissolution of the marriage by death does not create any insuperable problems the creation of the marriage and its dissolution by means other than death do.

When two persons who until marriage have accumulated assets independently marry, how should their joint property be rated under a cumulative system? To insure equity between two marriages with the same total income but differently apportioned, the two cumulated totals would have to be added together and taxed at the full marginal rate, the allowances for marriage being made by means of marriage exemptions.

When the marriage is dissolved, other than by death, the exemptions

[11] D. Throop Smith, *Federal Tax Reform* (New York: McGraw-Hill, 1961), pp. 43-52; Groves, *Federal Tax Treatment for the Family*, pp. 56-83; R. Goode, *The Individual Income Tax* (Washington, D.C.: Brookings Institution, 1964), pp. 241-251; J. M. Buchanan, *The Public Finances* (rev. ed.; Homewood, Ill.: Irwin, 1965), Chap. 23; Vickrey, *Agenda for Progressive Taxation*, Chap. 10; U.K. *Royal Commission on the Taxation of Profits and Income*, 2nd rep., Cmd. 9474, 1954.

cease (except for dependents) and the accumulated tax liability incurred during the marriage is apportioned with the cumulated income equally between the partners. To avoid the hardship of a sudden liability to tax on regaining single status a tax credit could be given for the difference between the accumulated tax paid as a marriage partner and that which would have been paid as a single person in receipt of the same income over the same period.

Trusts would be considered as created mutually by both partners, and no powers of invasion, revocation, or alteration could be admitted by *either* partner. A settlement to a spouse would not be taxable but when it passed outside the family (defined as including children — see below) it would become liable to tax.[12]

The next problem, the place of children in the tax unit, is more difficult. In the first place, it is difficult to define the point when children cease to be children. Each definition has its disadvantages. The age of legal responsibility could well be an age far beyond that at which a child has assets and income of its own, and the child could easily be married. Similar difficulties emerge if, say, the age of completing education is adopted. The most sensible course might be to tax the child as a separate taxable entity from birth with full individual initial allowances, thus insuring that in most cases of small earnings or petty gifts accruing, no tax liability would be incurred. Under a system using exemptions, the amounts set to be tax free would have to be very low to avoid evasion by parents deliberately channeling part of their income/accruals through their children. In any case, there is the major criticism that a progressive tax structure treating the child as a separate individual does lead to avoidance by income splitting, so that up to some age the child has to be included in the family unit if only to discourage this form of avoidance. The argument that the child can be included in the tax base, perhaps by using some coefficient (as in France, where adults are counted as one unit and children as a fraction which can be varied according to age), could be used but this requires a definition of "child." Perhaps a reference to full-time education might be the best way around this problem. It should be noted that under a structure where the child is included in the marriage tax base, his accruals are likely to be taxed at high marginal rates, determined by his parents' liability. At the abrupt point in time when he ceases, for tax purposes, to be a child, this will not necessarily involve him in unfairness, because his accruals will have been accumulated and his current tax liability (probably on a low accrual basis as he will just be starting to earn) will

---

[12] See below for further comment on trusts.

be related to the tax already paid; so that it is likely, if his accruals by gift or legacy have been large while he was a child, that his earnings will for the first few years as an independent person be lightly taxed. There would be a large initial difference in impact between say, a child still fully dependent but with only a month to go before he becomes fully independent, and another who has just become fully independent; the accrual of say, a large legacy to these two youths would involve the first one in a large tax liability under his parents' marginal tax rate, while the other, just starting to accrue, would have a low tax rate. However, in the succeeding years, the youth who had incurred the very high tax would have this included in his cumulated tax paid and this would automatically reduce his tax burden, whereas the other youth would proceed on the normal cumulating accrual base.

Dependents who are not children have to be defined carefully. In common sense a dependent is a person who is wholly dependent on the family (whether this consists of one or a number of persons) in much the same way as a child is. The difficulties cluster round persons who are only partially dependent in this way, such as old people whose other sources of revenue are not sufficient (or are not deemed sufficient by the family) to support them and who are supplemented by transfers from the family. The most extreme case of this might be where the "family" was legally obliged, even if unwilling, to make the transfer, e.g., alimony, or maintenance grants to illegitimate children. This difficulty can be covered by a combination of minimum exemptions and accumulations. Where, for instance, alimony must be paid, this will be treated as completed transfer to be taxed at the rate appropriate to the accumulated previous accrual of the recipient.

It should be pointed out that in all the instances discussed above, if accumulation was not included or if the accumulation were incomplete either by not including all forms of receipts (including wages and salaries) or by expending over limited time periods, substantial problems of avoidance and inequity must result.

EXEMPTIONS

Exemptions are justified because of the saving in administrative costs on the collection of small tax revenues from low income and wealth groups. This also enables progression to be introduced according to the size of the family, a point discussed above. As far as an accruals tax, or an integrated income tax, is concerned, the problems of exemptions are those of the sizes and allocations of the individual exemptions.

The larger the initial, say, annual exemption then the easier it is to administer much of the tax; however, if this exemption is extended to children then the larger it is the greater is the avoidance avenue by income splitting. Some convenient amount must be chosen which will balance the convenience and practicality (for small spontaneous gifts at Christmas, etc.) against the danger of substantial avoidance. One writer has held[13] that the annual exemption with a gift tax should be set against the gift from each individual donor, but this hardly seems a reasonable situation with either a gift, accrual, or integrated income tax; one person could receive x gifts up to the limit of the exemption in each case. It would make the annual exemption totally open-ended, an undesirable feature.

There remains the question as to whether there should be any lifetime exemption?

The point of having such exemptions is relevant only in tax structures where there are separate tax bases, as the lifetime exemption plays the same role for a capital tax as the annual exemption does for the income tax — it cuts out the small estate and small transfers similar to the elimination of the small incomes. Under a completely integrated income tax structure the annual exemptions would cumulatively give a lifetime exemption in themselves, as a function of the length of life, and the need for a double set of exemptions vanishes.

TRUSTS

Under an ideal wealth transfer tax, decisions to leave property in trust as opposed to leaving it outright would not be affected by the tax code. Yet this basically simple proposition is difficult to implement if we accept that a life interest (or shorter period) in a trust property is not equivalent to the outright transfer of the property itself. In particular, the beneficiary of income from property in trust does not have control over the assets and cannot thereby affect his own income (say between capital gains and yield), nor does he have the power to realize the capital, to consume out of the capital, or to enjoy income in kind (houses, pictures, objets d'art) from the capital stock. There is, in this sense, a very real reduction in the satisfaction to be gained by a benificiary under trust compared to the beneficiary of an outright transfer. Nor can any precise money measurement be applied to this difference. Perhaps the security aspect could be measured as suggested in Chapter

---

[13] DeWind, "The Appproaching Crisis," p. 179.

12, but it is difficult to measure the loss of satisfaction by removal of control over asset structure and realization.

However, it is worthwhile questioning the entire legal base of settlements. If we ignore the patina applied to trusts by the accumulation of estate tax avoidance procedures, and return to the original, essential element of the trust, we must consider that it was originally created as a legal means of insuring that an estate would either remain intact, and/or would be well managed (i.e., the implication is that the beneficiaries would be minors, wives, or other unreliables who would not be able to conduct the arrangement of the capital in a responsible or dispassionate manner). That is, the donor reckons that by putting a property in trust he is doing better by his beneficiaries than he would if he transferred the property outright; their welfare is greater than if he had transferred the property outright. This must be true otherwise (tax considerations apart) the donor would not put the property in trust in the first place. If, in fact, the beneficiaries are better off, is there any reason for arguing that settlements are less advantageous than outright transfers? There is sufficient doubt here to let us maintain, legitimately, that for tax purposes the settled gift and the outright gift are equivalent. Certainly, when we replace the patina of trust avoidance procedures that give settlements an appearance more attractive than that of outright gifts because, eventually, they attract less tax, then the argument for treating the two transfers as the same is irresistible. Why should a creation of the law become a tax avoidance avenue when there is a valid presentation of the case (above) for treating them equally; the fact that it is used for avoidance makes it all the more reasonable that it should cease to be treated favorably.

Under existing tax law in both the United States and the United Kingdom, estate duty liability can be reduced by the creation of a settlement in which the creator is not beneficially involved but which will benefit his descendants over a long period.[14] Under any legislation designed to encompass property left in trust the legislature will have to rely, to some extent, on the cooperation of the courts in interpreting the acts with the *intention* of preventing avoidance rather than aiding avoidance.

It does appear that the methods of tackling trust creation, trust capital, and trust income for liability to taxation have been undertaken in a very unimaginative manner on the part of the legislator and in a too imaginative manner by the tax lawyers. In the United Kingdom the life estate is fully taxed by death duties as part of the deceased's estate

---

[14] Wheatcroft, "Estate and Gift Taxes — A Comparison," pp. 357-359.

but the discretionary settlements are not taxed so long as there are at least two discretionary beneficiaries alive. The beneficiaries of settlement in the United States similarly can avoid tax, because the federal estate tax applies to property transfers over which the owner has powers of disposition when he died (there are exceptions to this, e.g., gifts inter vivos made "in contemplation of death").[15] With this method of avoidance there have emerged cancerous growths which multiply yearly; for instance the problems of appointment of trustees and their independence of action from the donor, and the powers of discretion and the difficulties of trusts where the income accumulates until payment is made as a lump sum. Under a transfer tax such as an inheritance or integrated income tax, legislation could reduce many of these difficulties. The basic affirmation would be that the tax would be liable, on the capital sum settled, according to the marginal tax rate that the beneficiaries' circumstances justified.

When the beneficiary became entitled to receive the income from the trust then that portion of the trust (half, third, etc.), to which he was entitled would be taxed at his marginal accrual rate, as though he had received the lump sum as an outright accretion. With accumulating trusts there would be no tax liability until the beneficiary actually received the income or capital sum.

EXTRATERRITORIAL TRANSFERS

Finally, there is the problem of transfers made to persons outside the political boundaries of the country. If an accruals tax is related to the donee's circumstances, an easy method of avoidance for a rich potential recipient of a substantial gift would be to leave the country for a few years.

Depending on the current political attitude to capital transfers a tax could be levied on any such transfer at a penal rate (say the maximum accrual tax rate) sufficient to discourage such transactions.

Any tax differential between countries can encourage the movement of capital and labor. The contemporary "Western" outlook increasingly appears to condone government regulation of capital flows; usually, a similar effort to limit the free movement of individuals is considered an intolerable constraint on personal liberty. Essentially, a tax structure must reflect some social consensus in the country and those

---

[15] The use of trusts for avoidance is well illustrated by a speech by F. D. Roosevelt in 1935 in which he alleged that one family divided its holdings into 197 separate family trusts to avoid income taxes and surtaxes. For further reference see Ratner, p. 471.

who disagree with the prevailing opinion should be free to "vote with their feet" if they wish, but perhaps a government can legitimately lay claim to retaining some of the individual's capital while still allowing expatriation of the earnings of that capital.

There is no complete answer to the difficulties of the free movement of capital until international economic differences greatly diminish. As this takes us into the realm of science fiction it is, perhaps, more reasonable to accept government limitation on capital flows.

DEMOGRAPHIC FACTORS

Demographic factors affecting future flows are those which tend to favor the long-lived rich who have few children, and whose children tend to marry those of other rich persons.[16]

The rich do tend to live longer (in most countries it is, literally, possible to buy health) and hence the incidence of estate duty is lighter upon them than would be an annual wealth tax. If they also have low fertility rates, this is likely to condense property into fewer hands. The likelihood is that children brought up in the same milieu as other rich children will tend to marry rich children.

SUMMARY

The tax base is the general taxation of personal wealth. The main difficulty is to determine when the transfer is complete. A new wealth transfer tax would not allow a donor any possibility of reversion, any benefits, any discretionary control, or any power to alter the transfer.

Valuation must be at the assessed market price bids, even if these are made without perfect information and by privileged buyers.

The taxable unit is the marriage unit. Problems of death, divorce, children, and dependents can be met by exemptions and allowances.

Trusts would be taxed on the lump sum represented by the beneficiaries' income.

To control extraterritorial transfers of capital made to avoid tax, some government control of overseas capital would have to be accepted.

Demographic factors work to increase the inequality of wealth holding. Government spending on education and health and the rise of a "meritocracy" would help to work against this demographic force.

---

[16] On this approach see Meade, *Efficiency, Equality and the Ownership of Property,* pp. 46-52.

15

The Effects of Personal Wealth Taxes

The effects of the various tax structures we have been discussing are not strictly our concern. We have argued that the desirability of one effect (redistribution) cannot be proved by economics, and the other effects, on work effort, consumption, saving, risk-taking, prices, etc., are secondary as far as we are concerned, because the essential point is that a wealth tax is necessary to complete an equitable tax structure. If the tax structure is to be fair some form of wealth tax is desirable. Given that, the effects of the tax come next. However, we will look at these effects for two reasons. First, because the attractiveness or unattractiveness of some of these effects compared to those of different types of wealth tax might influence the choice between particular forms of wealth taxation. Second, because the most usual and pungent criticism of any wealth tax is that apart from the administrative difficulties, it has undesirable effects on work effort, saving, and risk-taking.

The chapter divides into three main subsections, the "traditional" view of wealth tax incidence, a partial equilibrium analysis, and a general equilibrium discussion.

TRADITIONAL INCIDENCE

Basically we follow the Musgrave analysis of incidence believing that "the traditional distinction between direct incidence and indirect effects involves an arbitrary separation between various elements of the total change that are neither separately identifiable nor of separate significance as matters of policy."[1]

The idea of "ultimate burden"[2] in taxation is misleading; when new taxes increase the resources in the hands of the public sector it also means that if the government increases its transfers, other individuals (possibly the same individuals) gain, or if government expenditure on goods and services is increased then the community as a whole, or part, may benefit. Thus the "ultimate burden" is not something which can be located, and consequently, the concept is misleading.

When resources are increasingly moved to the public sector by a given tax this can be termed budget incidence; when the resources in the public sector are unchanged, but the method of financing them is altered, this is tax incidence. It is in tax incidence that we are interested.[3] However, we must examine some of the aspects of traditional incidence theory because the taxation of wealth can be on transfers and this involves two persons, the predecessor (testator) and the successor (the inheritor), and the traditional discussion about the division of the tax "burden" between the two is interesting.

In the writings on this subject, there appears to be a circle of opinion from the "death duty no burden" idea to the tax on "things"; we deal with them under five headings:

   (i) No Burden at All,
  (ii) Successor's Burden,
 (iii) Both Predecessor and Successor's Burden,
 (iv) Predecessor's Burden,
  (v) A Burden on No Person.

No Burden at All

Under a tax on successions a man is led in the first place to look upon the whole in a general view as his own; he is then called upon to give up a part. His share amounts to so much: this share he is to *have;* only out of it, he is to *pay* so much *per cent.* His imagination thus begins with embracing the *whole:* his expectation fastens upon the whole: then comes the law putting in for its *part*, and forcing him to quit his hold. This he cannot do without pain: if he could, no tax at all, not even a tax on property, would be a burden.[4]

This led to a suggestion (put forward in 1794 to Charles Long, Pitt's

---

[1] Musgrave, p. 228.

[2] E. R. A. Seligman, *The Shifting and Incidence of Taxation* (5th ed.; New York: Columbia University Press, 1926), Chap. 1.

[3] For a detailed discussion of traditional incidence and a presentation of an alternative see Musgrave, Chap. 10, pp. 385-401.

[4] W. Stark, *Jeremy Bentham's Economic Writings* (London: Allen and Unwin, 1952), I, 292.

co-secretary to the Treasury) that where the deceased left no direct lineal descendants then one-half of his estate should go to the public treasury and the other half remain subject to the power of bequest.[5]

The crux of this theory is that "in matters of property in general, and succession in particular . . . *hardship* depends upon *disappointment; disappointment* upon *expectation; expectation* upon the dispensations, meaning the *known* dispensations of the law."

This assumes that the successor "feels" the burden and that it is in his disappointed expectation that the burden lies.[6] From this we might say that where expectation is not confounded (as when the legatee *knows* the estate is to be taxed at a particular rate) there can be no burden. Patently, this implies that if by custom and convention a tax becomes accepted, known, and expected, it ceases to be burdensome; this is difficult to accept as a theory of incidence.

Burden on the Successor

The basis of this view is that of "dead men tell no tales," nor do they, apparently, pay any taxes. "The predecessor must be dead before the tax can be levied and dead men, like other inanimate objects, can pay no taxes."[7] This has respectable antecedents in that Adam Smith wrote about transfer taxes at death that they "fall finally as well as immediately upon the person to whom the property is transferred";[8] and Ricardo concurred.[9] Numerous other writers[10] follow similar reasoning,

---

[5] An indication of the difficulties involved in eighteenth-century taxation is provided by Bentham's admitting that to carry the proposal through "the Upper House, would . . . incline me to exempt the Peerage from its operation," *ibid.*, p. 284.

[6] This must be the source of Gladstone's argument for consanguinity rates.

[7] H. Dalton, *Principles of Public Finance* (3rd ed.; London: Routledge and Sons, 1936), p. 53; but to be fair to Dalton he amended his view for in the 4th edition, 1957, we read "The actual payment when the tax falls due, an inheritance tax will probably be paid out of capital to a greater extent than an income tax will be paid, year by year, out of money which would otherwise have been saved" and further "effects" are allowed in that the inheritor will in expectation "be less inclined to work and save . . . and indulge in dis-saving."

[8] A. Smith, Book V, Chap. 2, Appendix to Articles 1st and 2nd.

[9] D. Ricardo, *Principles of Political Economy and Taxation* (McCullach ed.; London: Murray, 1876).

[10] Sir F. Schuster, Colwyn Report, Minutes of Evidence, I, 13, argues that saving for tax payment prior to death only increases the tax liability; therefore the tax is likely to fall on the successor. T. S. Adams, "Effect of Income and Inheritance Taxes on the Distribution of Wealth," *American Economics Association Proceedings*, Vol. V, 1915; J. Harrington, "The Inheritance Tax," *Annals of American Academy of Political and Social Science,* March, 1915; S. Huebner, "The Inheritance Tax in the American Commonwealths," *Quarterly Journal of Economics,* Vol. XVIII, August, 1904, p. 548.

ignoring or belittling the argument that taxes can be anticipated, felt, parried and avoided before payment falls due. Indeed the reactions of individuals to proposed changes in tax (say, as between income and capital taxes), as we shall argue later, form a realistic assessment of the effects of alternative forms of tax. If knowledge that accumulated wealth will be taxed encourages present consumption, this is an effect (burden) of the tax. To argue that "If the term incidence is interpreted and applied with reference to the attachment of the immediate burden of the tax, it seems that the extent to which personal motives to accumulate are affected by the duties should be regarded as an economic effect of incidence"[11] introduces a needless distinction between the money burden (incidence) and its effects; the money burden is of little interest, it is its effects which are of use in policy decisions.

Burden on Both Predecessor and Successor

This concept is similar to that encountered in descriptions of other taxes; the effect of commodity tax is often illustrated in elementary texts by a graph showing the "incidence" of a tax distributed between buyer and seller in the ratio of the elasticity of supply to the elasticity of demand;[12] again the estate duty can be likened to the income tax where both the taxpayer (the father) and the son may be hit by taxation (poorer education, health, etc.) ; so does the estate duty hit both father (predecessor) and son (successor).[13]

Similarly, we find a set of schizophrenic presentations of the estate duty where the actual duty is part postponed income tax and as such is paid by the predecessor, and part capital tax paid by the successor.[14] This cannot be accepted because who is to delineate that part which is "debt accumulated by the deceased"?[15] Why should the state not claim that all estate duties are of this nature? This supposition is suggested and used as a basis for representing the "burden of death duties."[16] From our viewpoint, interested as we are in the effects and not in the elusive "ultimate burden," this approach where both are affected can be reasonable. It must be clear that a man may make moves to antic-

---

[11] J. K. Hall, "The Incidence of Death Duties," *American Economic Review*, Vol. XXX, March, 1940, p. 58.

[12] W. J. L. Ryan, *Price Theory* (New York: Macmillan, 1958), pp. 118-119.

[13] See The Colwyn Report, p. 170.

[14] De Viti De Marco, *First Principles of Public Finance* (London: Cape, 1952), pp. 361-362.

[15] *Ibid.*, p. 362.

[16] N. Kaldor, "The Income Burden of Capital Taxes."

ipate the inheritance tax, and it is likely that his heirs may alter their behavior in the anticipation of their inheritance. It does appear reasonable to keep in mind that both may be affected.

On Predecessors

If the transfer tax is viewed not from the angle of expectation but instead simply as the addition or subtraction of purchasing power then a strong case can be made for the tax falling on the testator. The inheritor undoubtedly gains purchasing power, a "fortuitous income,"[17] and his potential consumption is increased above that which he would have provided for himself; on the other hand, the testator has foregone his enjoyment of consumption during life, part of which has gone toward tax payment. This payment can be considered as a property tax, levied each generation, against which eventuality, if he wishes, the testator may take out insurance policies.[18]

A Burden on No Person

"Duties upon the succession to property at death are not taxes upon the dying, because they are not levied until they have ceased to own the property, and not taxes upon the inheritors, because they only inherit by the will and permission of the state itself."[19] The tax in this case is paid by "property." But property as a concept separate from those who own it is hardly a useful tool for examining the effects of wealth taxation.

From this brief excursion into past controversies on the "incidence" of death duties it appears reasonable for the examination to proceed by examining the effects of taxation on the individual; further, the effects on both the testator and the legatee will have to be considered, but the analysis will proceed by considering the position of the individual faced with a tax either current on income, or future on his estate, or payable on the transfer of a gift, or even annually on his net wealth, and the probable reactions to these will be the meat of the discussion. At some points it will be convenient to introduce the behavior of the legatee, the gift or wealth receiver, especially where this might appear to offset the effects of the tax on the predecessor.

---

[17] Hall, p. 58.

[18] A. C. Pigou, *A Study in Public Finance* (New York: Macmillan, 1929), p. 161; G. F. Shirras, *Science of Public Finance* (3rd ed.; New York: Macmillan, 1936), I, 386, II, 542.

[19] U.K. *Memoranda on the "Classification and Incidence of Imperial and Local Taxes,"* Cmd. 9258, 1899.

There is left the transition from the individual to the group, and this can only be discussed where specific assumptions are made, or facts known, about the composition of the group.

DIFFERENTIAL TAX INCIDENCE

It is useful to further delineate what we are dealing with at the moment. The earlier discussion has described and commented on the various tax *structures* which can be used to tax wealth. These structures, as has been noted, are usually progressive; in a narrow sense this means only that they have rates which increase more than proportionately with increases in wealth holdings; some have double progression (e.g., capital levies with progressive rates with size of wealth held, and length of time held), but this progressiveness refers only to the *rate* structure of the individual taxes. More generally, progression is taken to refer to redistribution between individuals, or between groups. Clearly the tax structure and the result of that structure must be separated.[20] A tax might have a progressive rate structure but its effects could be regressive. What is under consideration are the alternative effects of the taxes examined previously, the structure of which has been determined by (it has been held) the taxes already in operation (particularly income tax) and by the rates of taxes already levied. Following Musgrave these overall alternative effects are referred to as tax incidence.

When we look at the introduction of a wealth tax it must be quite clear what initial position we are positing. Is it a *change* in an already existing wealth tax? The effects of this we would refer to as "specific tax incidence."[21] The alternative is to assume a given level of real expenditure and consider different ways of financing this, e.g., with a wealth tax or an income tax, thus "differential tax incidence" becomes the difference in "the distributional results of two tax policies that provide for equal yield in real terms."[22] The usual case, as existing wealth taxes are rare in practice, would be the introduction of a wealth tax into an existing system. This allows a reduction in other taxation, which could be either a reduction in other direct taxes (e.g., income tax) or a reduction in indirect taxes resulting in an overall greater reliance on direct taxes.

---

[20] For a similar, extended discussion, see D. Dosser, "Tax Incidence and Growth," *Economic Journal*, September, 1961.

[21] R. A. Musgrave, "On Incidence," *Journal of Political Economy*, August, 1953, p. 306.

[22] Musgrave, *The Pure Theory of Public Finance*, p. 212.

EFFECTS OF PERSONAL WEALTH TAXATION ON WORK EFFORT

As mentioned elsewhere, we are discussing only "tax incidence," not "budget incidence." The tax is assumed to be met by the wealth owner and not a wealth receiver (if a transfer is involved), although this possibility must be kept in mind. More particularly we are covering the case of "differential tax incidence,"[23] that is, holding real budget expenditure constant and examining the effects of tax substitution.

Substituting Taxes on Wealth for a Personal Income Tax

The usual way to consider an estate tax is as a delayed income tax, paid at death.[24] The annual tax is the insurance premium required to purchase a lump sum sufficient to meet the tax at death. In this way estate taxation can be said to have the same effects as an annual income tax.

The effect of a proportional income tax on work effort depends on the assumptions about the marginal role of substitution between income and leisure. The most reasonable assumptions are those of the marginal utility of income decreasing and the marginal utility of leisure either constant or decreasing also.[25]

If, with an income tax imposed, the percentage rise in the marginal utility of income is greater than the percentage decline in the net wage rate, then work effort must be raised (i.e., leisure reduced) so that the marginal utility of income may be reduced. With successive increases of tax the percentage rise in the marginal utility of income is less than the percentage decline in the net wage rate, so that work effort is reduced and leisure increased. The effect of tax depends on the part of the labor supply at which the initial equilibrium position rests. A similar, indeterminate result is produced if the marginal utility of both income and leisure is assumed to be decreasing. A progressive tax involves a stronger substitution effect and is likely, therefore, to reduce work effort further than a proportional tax. On this basis, the substitution of an estate tax for an income tax would produce no changes in the overall effects.

But the effects of an estate tax replacing an income tax (budgetary real expenditure constant) are not exactly comparable to the annual

---

[23] For a discussion of the advantages and disadvantages of "differential," "budget," and "absolute" tax effects see R. A. Musgrave and T. Krzyzaniak, *The Shifting of the Corporate Income Tax* (Baltimore: Johns Hopkins University Press, 1963), Chap. 1.

[24] N. Kaldor, "The Income Burden of Capital Taxes," pp. 141-151.

[25] Musgrave, *The Pure Theory of Public Finance,* pp. 232-238.

premium which would purchase the lump sum for tax payment at death. To take the extreme case, if all income taxation were replaced by an inheritance tax[26] then there is a triple choice between work effort (untaxed), leisure, and accumulating capital to leave to heirs (untaxed until death); this last has the added, but incidental, advantage of yielding income during the owner's lifetime.

An interesting and elegant presentation of the problem can be constructed in a three-dimensional diagram[27] but the results are indeterminate, except that the change from an income tax to a capital tax will never lead to more saving and more leisure; this could happen only, of course, at the expense of consumption. This tax change will be reflected in reductions of leisure or saving.

Another difference between the income and wealth taxes would be the extension of the tax base to non–income-yielding assets. An individual who found that assets, previously untaxed, were not liable to taxation could be discouraged from saving for such assets (houses, pictures, objets d'art, etc.) which previously he had considered as an untaxed source of income-in-kind.

An important distinction in the effects of the two taxes could result from the latitude each tax leaves the taxpayer in arranging his tax payment. The essence of a modern income tax structure should be the short lapse between liability and payment, exemplified by P.A.Y.E., but even an annual tax liability does not give the individual much opportunity to avoid the tax. However, if the income tax is replaced by a death duty then the liability to tax is postponed to the end of a person's life, and indeed the payment of tax at all becomes an option which can be exercised or not, during life. This was part of the problem of Rignano (see Chapter 10) where an individual may avoid payment by consuming his capital and dying without an estate to tax. Obviously, if total (or partial) income tax liability is to be deferred until death, the temptation to avoid payment by consuming the estate becomes very strong indeed.

For the individual the result of substituting an estate tax for income tax would depend not only on his work/leisure preferences as discussed above, but also on his age. As a young man the substitution would probably encourage work and saving. As an older man it is likely to

---

[26] Not as N. Kaldor, "The Income Burden of Capital Taxes," p. 398, suggested, owners of estates "confronted with the choice of compounding all future death duty liabilities by paying a permanent annual tax (additional to other annual taxes to which they are liable)."

[27] A. Williams, *Public Finance and Budgetary Policy* (London: Allen and Unwin, 1963), pp. 103-104.

encourage leisure and consumption; the combined attractiveness of more leisure, consumption, and tax avoidance would be hard to resist.

For the group, the overall effect would depend obviously on the age distribution.

An *inheritance* tax introduces another consideration. The individual making the gift can reduce his tax liability by splitting his estate into numerous parcels, and/or by giving it to the poorer members of society. Thus the effect on work effort would depend on the circumstances and number of the persons to whom he wished to leave a legacy. All else equal, the more numerous and poorer the legatees the greater the incentive to work if an inheritance tax is substituted for an estate duty. As the likelihood is that the legatees will be poorer (because there are far more poor persons in society and because it is by inheritance that many persons in rich families become rich) then the inheritance tax might encourage work effort.

The effects of a *gift* tax are similar to those of an inheritance tax. In a like manner the tax on the gift could be paid by an annuity paid by annual premiums. There is one significant difference between the two taxes. An inheritance tax leaves the individual with no option as to when he pays the tax; he must wait until death before actual payment. But a gift tax leaves the individual with the option of timing the transfer and by his decision to give he also includes a decision to pay tax. As long as the tax rates are so arranged that no advantage can be gained by delay or by any subtleties in timing, then the effects of the gifts tax on work effort appear similar to those of the inheritance tax.

Important differences should be noted as soon as we turn to lags in response and "dynamic" aspects. As noted, under an inheritance tax structure any change in rates or structure will only affect those whose estates fall in that year; under a gifts tax, the maximum time for the change in structure to affect all wealth would be the same as that under the inheritance tax, but it is likely that the "turnover" of wealth through gifts would be more rapid than that normally associated with the generation, therefore the total time lag in response to a change in tax structure would probably be smaller under the gift tax than under the inheritance tax.

Again, under a gift tax there is discretion as to the timing of the tax liability. The individual making the gifts can decide when to make the gift and thereby when he will incur the tax. In this way an astute person might deliberately time his gifts to coincide with the troughs of depressions, so that his assets are valued at a lower level than usual. See Chart 15:1.

CHART 15:1
Timing and Gifts Taxation

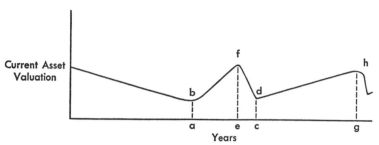

By making his gifts at times a and c instead of e and f, his total gift would be only ab + cd instead of ef + gh. If these decisions were random and some made gifts at the peaks and others at the troughs then the effects might cancel out; but this would be unlikely in practice, since some years would be recommended by financial advisors as "good years to make gifts" and there would be a bias towards most people attempting to "hit" the troughs. It is, therefore, likely that even if inheritance and gift taxation had the same degree of wealth turnover, the valuation under gifts taxation, other things remaining equal, would be lower than that of inheritance taxation; to maintain equal yield the rates of tax would have to be higher.

Insofar as the taxpayer can minimize the tax "burden" by his timing of gifts, and to the degree that this encourages him to work harder and leave more, this would reinforce the incentive to work provided by the removal or reduction of the income tax. It seems probable, therefore, that a gifts tax replacing (partially) a direct income tax would be encouraging to work effort if paid by the donor.

If paid by the donee and accumulated with either his total gifts or total income the effect would depend on the flexibility he had in the timing of the receipt. If the lifetime was the base then the substitution of the tax on gifts for part of the tax on other income would not affect his work effort, except that there might be some small advantage in the timing of the tax-free gift to meet particular expenditures which could compare unfavorably to the cumulated tax liability on all income and gifts. If we compare two situations, one where the donee has an income for x years taxed at a higher rate of tax to compensate for the lack of a gifts tax, to another with the same income for x years taxed at a lower rate because a gifts tax is in force, then probably the final total absolute tax liability will lead to greater work effort, especially as the *expectation* of receiving a gift is open to many forms of uncertainty.

The unforeseen *capital levy* is no problem in terms of its effects on work effort, for it can have no effect before its imposition, and the only subsequent effects (provided there is a convincing guarantee against repetition) will be those promoted by the removal of the income tax. But clearly, it is a little unreal to discuss a capital levy in the context of differential tax incidence, for by its very nature it cannot replace another tax on any permanent basis.

An annual *net worth* tax reduces the source of "unearned" income and thereby reduces the attractiveness of saving to accumulate the capital necessary to produce that income. Therefore such a tax reduces the potential future yield of current work effort and can be expected to operate against work effort. This assumes that the net worth tax will be levied on capital already accumulated and will continue to be levied on new capital accumulation; obviously, if there were discrimination against old capital, and not against new, then work effort would be increased.

The effect of replacing a direct income tax by the net worth tax providing an equivalent revenue is similar to that outlined above, where the estate duty replaced the income tax. However, it should be noted that the analysis had to be limited to a single time period (a lifetime), and that there should be an alternative presentation where account is taken of the different impacts of an estate duty which impacts only once in a lifetime (an unfortunate phrase but it would be odd to speak of "once in a deathtime") and a recurring capital tax which will act more often than once in every, say, thirty years. This can be done in a three-dimensional diagram assuming three time periods but the limitation of this particular diagrammatic approach is that it must also be assumed that the level of wage income is fixed. Ideally, what is needed is a representation where income, consumption, saving, and leisure, are allowed to change through time, but the results would be very indeterminate.

The effect of replacing a direct income tax by the wealth tax providing an equivalent revenue, if the income tax is levied on both wage and capital income, should depend in part on the relative sizes of the tax base. If the wage tax base is small, and the capital income (and capital) base are large, then the capital tax rates (replacing the income tax) can be low, and the "impact" effect on current effort probably favorable (the combined weight of the total relief from income tax and the low rate of the capital tax).

With a large wage tax base and a small capital ownership, the net worth tax rates would be high, and the "impact" effect could discourage the accumulation of capital out of current work effort.

Note that the relative impact rates of income and capital are not based only on income-producing capital, but between a tax on all income (from work and from capital) and a tax on all capital including non–income-yielding capital. So that although the capital income base might appear small this does not necessarily imply that the total wealth tax base would be small.

For the group, the effect of the tax must be a function of both the numbers and the "responsibility intensity" of those composing the group. Obviously large wealth owners will form a small percentage of the total whereas the wage receivers will be large; the greater the inequality of distribution of wealth the more numerous will be those favorably affected by the relief from income tax and thereby the more favorably affected towards work effort. It can be held that the more responsible persons, the people necessary to make decisions for economic growth, the persons who have freedom of choice whether to work or not, or to work less intensively, are those wealth owners who will be most adversely affected towards work effort by the net worth tax. Once again the greater the inequality the fewer are those persons affected in this way and the more likelihood that total group work effort would be increased.

Substituting Taxes on Wealth for Consumption Taxes

Saving out of current income to provide an inheritance is not in anticipation of future consumption. If the work effort is undertaken to earn the current income with full forethought that this saving will not be for future consumption but is deliberately intended to be a legacy, then the imposition or removal of consumption taxes does not affect that judgment, except so far as present consumption is made more, or less, attractive.

The imposition of the inheritance tax (and the reduction of consumption taxation) reduces the attractiveness of leaving legacies, so that work effort, although unaffected by the increased attractiveness of future consumption, is affected by two forces, the increased attractiveness of present consumption and the unfavorable prospects of reduced legacies in the future.

To the extent that the favorable aspect of future legacies was always discounted, compared to current enjoyment, the reduced attractiveness of working to provide an inheritance may not be as powerful as the increased attractiveness of present consumption. Therefore, work effort might increase slightly or leave the change indeterminate.

When changing circumstances are introduced allowance must be made for the growth of capital. If the overall expected growth of capital saved over the period is sufficient to pay the inheritance tax (as is quite possible even at present) the situation is changed. The comparison now is between an inheritance tax introduced, which will now not only tax the savings for legacies but also the capital growth of those savings over the period, and, on the other hand, the consumption tax which the inheritance tax has replaced, which was never a tax on capital gains. The introduction of this tax is thereby a dual disincentive to work effort. It taxes the savings and the capital gains, and this must be offset against the increased attractiveness of present consumption. In this way the possibility of growth reinforces the incentive to consume today and to the extent that this is financed from that which otherwise would have been saved, the effect is to leave work effort unchanged.

If the effect of the *inheritance* tax replacing a consumption tax is felt by the inheritor, then the comparison is between lower consumption taxes encouraging present consumption and either encouraging or discouraging work effort depending on the substitution of consumption and leisure, and a smaller inheritance. Once more the uncertainty of the timing and amount of a gift in the future probably weight the decreased consumption tax more heavily than the smaller inheritance.

In the same way that income earned and saved to provide inheritance is unaffected by the taxation of future consumption, so savings to provide gifts are not for consumption, and therefore a tax on future consumption will not affect the decision to work and save for such gifts. Thus the removal of the consumption tax does not affect the decision to provide gifts except insofar as present consumption is made more attractive.

The introduction of a *gifts* tax alters the future value of the net gift, making it less attractive. With present consumption made more attractive by the removal of the consumption tax, consumption out of that which previously had been saved may take place; whether present consumption will be made so attractive vis-à-vis saving for legacies that work effort will increase is difficult to judge.

When the possibility of fluctuations is introduced, then the gift tax, compared to the inheritance tax, as discussed above, may allow the taxpayer to reduce his tax liability by timing his transfer, in which case the disincentive to work effort would not be as great as in the static case.

Again, capital appreciation could offset part of the tax payment, but as this appreciation would have existed without tax, this only makes the gift tax a tax on capital gains as well.

However, the discretionary element in gifts results in another difference; as it gives discretion to the timing of the gift, it also gives a
choice as to what shall be transferred. In this way, if assets appreciate
at different rates, which is most probable, then the person making the
gift cannot only choose a time when generally assets are lower than the
"trend" but can also select those particular assets which are out of
favor at present, but which have a reasonable chance of appreciation in
the near future.

Thus the gift tax would probably not reduce work effort by as much
as the inheritance tax, but the result of their substitution for consumption taxes would still have to be indeterminate.

The reactions to the alternative of a *net worth* tax replacing a general tax on consumption depend on the assumptions affecting consumption out of capital.

If the consumer is presented with reduced taxes on consumption and
lower prices in the market, his real income has increased, but to counter
this there is tax on his net worth which lowers his future consumption
and real income. The effect on work effort depends on the extent by
which the marginal utility of present income has increased vis-à-vis the
marginal utility of leisure, compared to the decrease in marginal utility
of future income vis-à-vis future leisure. If we accept that the future
is discounted by some amount then we see that the higher present real
income will be worth more to the individual than his future reduced
real income.

The above has assumed that saving is for future consumption,
whereas one form of taxation under discussion is that on wealth which
is destined for future generations who may or may not consume it, but
certainly the idea of consumption is undoubtedly relegated to a distant
date, usually beyond the lifetime of the present owner. The argument
above is not fundamentally changed. Instead of the net worth tax
lowering future consumption out of capital, it can be thought of as
lowering future capital, and hence the income yielded by that capital;
thus future consumption out of capital income is reduced. It seems
likely, therefore, that work effort, because of the higher present real
income, may be increased.

Summary of Effects and Work Effort

Most of the results on work effort of substituting a wealth tax for an
income or consumption tax are indeterminate. Generally, gift taxes do
not reduce work effort as much as inheritance taxes do. Overall, of all

the taxes on wealth net worth taxes look as though they might encourage work effort the most.

EFFECTS OF PERSONAL WEALTH TAXATION ON CONSUMPTION AND SAVING

Saving is undertaken either for future consumption, or just for the sake of accumulation which in itself provides security, power, etc. Admittedly, some of the estates taxed under death duties may have been intended for consumption, but that intention was never fulfilled, because death, unexpectedly and inconsiderately, intervened.

Generally, from an observation of human nature as evidenced by the large number of estates accumulated in the past and not consumed, it is reasonable to assume that some people save not for consumption, but for publicity of dying rich, security, insuring continuity for a well-provided family line, etc.

Substituting Taxes on Wealth for an Income Tax

The estate and inheritance taxes replacing the income tax must discriminate strongly against accumulation for bequests, while the relative attractiveness of consumption versus savings for consumption within a lifetime is restored to pre–income tax positions.

As argued when discussing work effort, if an *inheritance* tax is paid by the legatee then this could result in lower income tax rates, and uncertainty about the future receipt of legacies might push the individual, in the short run prior to actual receipt of the legacy, towards greater saving. On actual receipt of the inheritance total saving and consumption over the period are unlikely to be altered; thus the only outcome would be an alteration in the timing of the saving.

With a *gift* tax replacing the income tax it is probable that by timing the gifts carefully and choosing particular assets, the total tax liability could be reduced compared to the liability under estate or inheritance taxation. Thus the introduction of gifts taxation although operating in favor of consumption and saving for future consumption, might not operate as powerfully against inheritance as does estate duty.

The effect of a capital levy on saving was debated, particularly, by the Colwyn Commission. A prominent argument was that of the discouragement and penalization of "thrift." "The levy would penalize the thrifty, while in no way reaching the spendthrift,"[28] the old worry (see the Rignano proposals) that some forms of taxation may favor the

---

[28] The Colwyn Report, p. 286.

reckless and prodigal, beloved by novelists but not by the Inland Revenue. As evidence, the worthies of the Chamber of Commerce gave a moving example of the married man with liabilities (dependents) taxed hard on his provident pile while the spending bachelor escaped the tax.[29] Although a moving cautionary tale (a modern fable that he who saves is lost) the appeal to thrift is often made to blind us to more pressing social needs.

As the minority report put it, "We are disposed to think that disproportionate weight is often attributed to the virtue of savings as compared with the importance of securing a wider diffusion of something to save."

This aspect of thrift is geared to that of accumulation and time. The point at issue here is that of the "generation burden." The older generation who have had their working lives in which to save, and who are anticipating the pleasure of utilizing their former frugalities in the comforts of retirement, are most hard hit by a sudden levy on wealth at this particular point in their life. To the young with little capital and hopes of a rewarding vocation the levy can be lightly set aside in the knowledge of their capacities for work and saving; also in the comforting belief that the levy has been and gone like a Biblical rain of frogs, which is unpleasant, but unlikely to return in our lifetime. With current income taxes increasing it is more difficult to save now compared to previously, and thereby the levy, in retrospect, might not appear so unfair.

The most serious consequences for saving would follow from the fear of another levy, although generally the effects of the levy might (especially if income taxes were reduced) be encouraging for saving. The question of guarantee against repetition emerges as a permanent one in any levy discussion. No political party can bind its successor to guarantees of this sort, but neither can overall domestic agreement prevent external emergencies producing another levy. If the levy were instituted not for debt redemption, but for extraordinary wealth taxation, then providing it was sufficiently effective it is unlikely that it would be repeated. But specific guarantees cannot be binding or enforced on or by political parties; the main sanction lies in the next general election.

If a *net worth* tax is used the results depend on the definition of savings and the lapse between tax payments. If the individual in fact saves, but consumes his savings before the net worth tax is levied, then he avoids tax. But it is reasonable to assume that medium-term savings

---

[29] The Colwyn Report, Minutes of Evidence, Vol. II, p. 578, 1927.

would be affected by the tax although there would exist a strong encouragement to consume savings in anticipation of the wealth tax. A three-dimensional discussion can be conducted showing that the individual will prefer the income tax to the recurring capital tax of equal yield.[30]

Between the estate duty and the periodic net worth tax with equal yields the results are again inconclusive,[31] but a priori it does appear that the estate duty operates against "hump" saving less harshly than the recurring capital tax simply because there is a longer time period during which decisions to save and consume can be made and executed.

Again, the *gifts* tax is probably preferred to the recurring capital tax because it allows more discretion as to the timing and form of asset transfer, and hence liability to tax.

One motive for saving often held to be powerful is the desire for power and prestige, as these are associated with wealth holding. The taxation of the wealth, it is held, will reduce the desire to work and save for power and prestige. However, increasingly power and prestige are associated with the management of large corporate bodies where actual wealth ownership is immaterial. No longer is it necessary to have wealth in order to run a company; the professional manager has much of the power and prestige that once was synonymous with wealth. To the extent that this is true, and increasingly true, the taxation of wealth on this issue is unlikely to affect motives to work and save.

Summary

The net worth tax encourages present consumption and, compared to the other taxes, operates against both hump saving and inheritance saving.

A capital levy could penalize saving, but with a convincing guarantee against repetition it might encourage saving.

The individual would probably prefer the income tax to the recurring capital tax, and possibly, to the estate duty, and will prefer the estate duty to the recurring capital tax, and the gifts tax to either.

THE EFFECT OF PERSONAL WEALTH TAXATION ON RISK-TAKING

The problem before the individual investor can be represented as one of choosing some mix of net income streams, where net income is defined as yield plus changes in capital value, net of investment costs.

---

[30] A. Williams, p. 99.

[31] *Ibid.*, pp. 105-108.

CHART 15:2
Risk-Taking with Complete Loss Offset

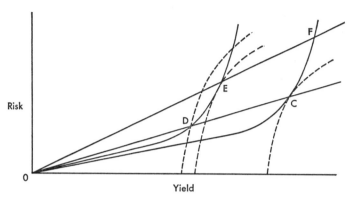

The choice of the mix depends on the individual's weighting of the chance of gain or loss for each investment.[32]

The most widely accepted analysis of this problem concludes that if full loss offset is allowed an income tax will increase total risk-taking.[33] There are important caveats to this conclusion. Private risk-taking may increase or decrease; total risk may be difficult to define, and full loss offset is unlikely to exist.

In Chart 15:2 the initial equilibrium position is at C and the post-tax position with an unchanged portfolio and full loss offset on the post-tax optimum asset curve is at D; but a more favorable alternative, and an equilibrium point on a higher indifference curve, is possible at E. The total risk and yield of the post-tax combination (D) remained unchanged and, therefore, when there is a readjustment to a higher risk combination of assets at E, this must mean that *total* risk at point F rises. Consequently, total risk post-tax will exceed total risk before tax, but private risk is not necessarily increased — although E could be above C. With full tax loss offset against the capital tax, similar conclusions to the income tax follow (i.e., that total risk-taking under a capital tax would be increased).

This conclusion is limited by the provisions for total loss offset and the fact that it applies to *total* risk, not necessarily to *private* risk. We claim, however, that comparing an income tax to a capital tax, the individual investor will prefer, in welfare terms as far as risk-taking is

---

[32] On this approach see R. A. Musgrave and E. D. Domar, "Proportional Income Taxation and Risk Taking," in Musgrave and Shoup, eds., *Readings in the Economics of Taxation*, p. 493.

[33] Musgrave, *The Pure Theory of Public Finance*, pp. 320-322.

concerned, the capital tax. To show this, some further discussion of risk is required.

What constitutes risk and the effect of taxation on that risk, has been a field of considerable recent controversy. We can itemize four "kinds" of risk.[34]

(i) The risk of a rise in interest rates or a change in the market assessment and hence a fall in capital value. Even where a stock is redeemable at par on a specified date, there is the risk of wishing to sell the stock before redemption (prior realization) and facing a capital loss. This risk we can term the illiquidity risk.

(ii) The risk of capital and income loss through changes in the general purchasing power of money. This is best exemplified by the contrast of fixed interest securities redeemable at par which have high yields on current market valuation, whereas equities whose interest payment can be increased often have low yields because the assessment of the market is that the likelihood of falls in the general purchasing power is large and therefore the insurance against this is more important than the guarantee of yield.

(iii) There are the two risks associated with borrowed money; the risk that the borrower may not repay, and

(iv) the risk that in borrowing the yield of the investment must be such as to cover the cost of the borrowed capital in addition to the yield looked for on invested capital.

It can be held that (iii) could be subsumed under (i), because a change in the market assessment is partially based on the likelihood of nonrepayment, collapse, etc. Similarly, the earning capacity itemized as (iv) can again be included in the market assessment. Thus for our analytic purposes, that is to discuss differential tax incidence, it is clearer to look to two principal risks faced by the individual investor, the illiquidity risk, and the purchasing power risk. To call the second the "capital risk" would be confusing since illiquidity involves the possibility of capital loss — though from different reasons; so we have our two categories:

(i) Illiquidity risk,

(ii) Purchasing power loss risk.

Isolating these particular two risks enables us to discuss the effects of wealth taxation on risk more clearly. Some discussion at this point must be made of the expectations of the investor regarding government

---

[34] Kaldor, *An Expenditure Tax,* pp. 106-108, for a discussion of a division into five types of risk.

expenditure, because it is clear that different views on this radically affect his attitude toward changes in the purchasing power of money, and possibly toward his willingness to commit his assets to illiquid forms. If the investor considers that the proposed tax is to be used to provide a budget surplus which will be anti-inflationary, then the risk of losses through changes in purchasing power are diminished; on the other hand, it could be felt at the same time that the reduction in purchasing power implied by the tax reduced the possibility of rises in the market estimation of assets. If the tax is obviously to finance current expenditure then the purchasing power risk is increased. If the tax is to finance a balanced budget expansion, then it depends on the composition of the budget whether the investor considers the tax to be inflationary or not.

The combination of these two types of risk can be represented diagrammatically by assuming an investor with an amount of liquid capital OA in Chart 15:3; this is a given amount and does not change through time, all investments (increasing illiquidity) are represented as yield on axis OX, which as mentioned above, is a combination of interest and capital gains.

The yield is best thought of as available from one asset only (e.g., bonds), so that at the prevailing price the investment of the total liquid funds OA in this illiquid form would yield OB. The question now is: Does the individual investor want to invest all his liquid funds or does he prefer some combination of assets and cash? His assessment of the risk of illiquidity involved in the investment and of the risk of purchasing power loss through remaining liquid can be represented by indifference curves. Both remaining liquid and getting a yield have positive utilities, both have diminishing marginal utilities, and the investor is assumed never to be entirely liquid or totally invested. The indifference curves would be shaped as indicated in Chart 15:3 and in a pre-tax situation the investor would be at an equilibrium point, such as C.

An income tax on both yield and capital gains is introduced, changing the budget line to AD and establishing a new equilibrium at E, where cash held is OJ and bonds held are AJ and the yield is JE. Depending on the exact shape of the indifference curves E could be at a point higher than C, giving greater liquidity (cash) and lower yield. However, in any case, the alternative imposition of a capital tax paid out of capital reduces both the available capital (OA) and thereby the potential yield to a net tax budget line FG. The capital tax and the income tax will have an equal yield where their post-tax budget lines

CHART 15:3
Individual Welfare and Risk-Taking Under a Capital Tax and an Income Tax

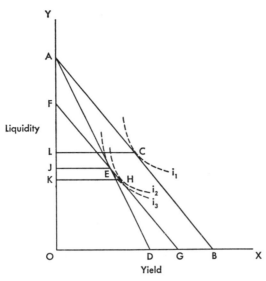

intersect at E, but the investor under the capital tax will prefer to move to an equilibrium point on FG at H. At H the investor holds less cash OK than at C or E, but through this illiquidity receives a higher yield HK than he did under the income tax, and is on a higher indifference curve. The investor prefers the capital tax to the income tax.

The exact form of the capital tax (estate, gift, or net worth) may modify the analysis of the actual amount of risk-taking undertaken in each case.

The effect on the proportion of liquid assets devoted to investment is uncertain as it depends on the relative changes of $\frac{AJ}{OA}$ and $\frac{FK}{OF}$ as the capital tax alters the base of the assets.

The *gifts* tax is unlikely to alter the investor's assessment of the future purchasing power of money, but it will tax capital gains when they are transferred, and all personal capital must at some time be transferred; therefore the gifts tax will affect the yield and the asset base as did the inheritance tax. As the investor is left some discretion as to when he will accomplish the transfer (gift), thereby choosing a moment and an asset which will attract a low capital tax, this form of tax may have slightly less disincentive to risk than the inheritance tax. As the gifts tax does reduce the assets base, the actual effect on the proportion of private assets invested vis-à-vis the income tax is, as above, indeterminate. But the individual on welfare grounds will prefer the gifts tax.

The effect of a *capital levy* on risk-taking depends, as it has for the other effects, on the unexpectedness of the levy and the guarantee against repetition. The effect on risk-taking is likely to be directly related to the use of the levy receipts. The British type of levy to reduce debt would contract the range of government fixed-interest securities, future borrowing could be on more favorable terms (i.e., lower rates of interest), and this would affect the whole market. Fear was expressed that as collateral would be reduced so would there be a restriction in credit creation and a reduction in the money supply. From the evidence collected, it appeared that the actual assets held by businesses greatly exceeded their trading collateral; a removal of a portion of their assets would simply call into action assets hitherto unused. Also, of course, the redemption of the debt would place fresh (liquid) assets in the hands of others which could be used for collateral.

Broadly, it was thought that if another levy were not anticipated, and possibly, if the resultant saving were used to reduce current income tax rates, then, if anything, enterprise might be encouraged.[35]

The periodic *net worth* tax taxes both the capital gain and the assets which give rise to that gain, so that its effect is similar to that examined for the inheritance tax and the gift tax. However, it is possible that the regularity of the net worth tax may alter the individual's assessment of purchasing power changes, as this form of taxation is bound to be more closely linked to current government revenue and annual budgets than the "generation spread" of inheritance and gifts taxation. If the effect of the net worth tax is thought to increase the likelihood of, say, inflation, then there will be a shift from liquid into high capital gain stocks (even though these are taxable they offer the chance of appreciation which cash cannot).

It does seem possible to increase risk-taking under this tax change, especially if the discussion includes the reaction of the investor to government expenditure from the changed source of revenue. It should be noted that this reaction will only matter if the individual's view changes with the tax change; if he considers the two taxes as equally inflationary then change is neutral in this respect. Generally, capital taxes are more likely to be considered inflationary than taxes on current expenditure or income, especially when the government views the revenue as current and uses it for current expenditures.

Generally, the result of this substitution on the proportion of private

---

[35] The Colwyn Report, paras. 766-768, 779-785, 828-831.

assets will be indeterminate, because, as previously, the asset base is changed. Again, the welfare of the individual will be higher under the net worth tax.

The net worth tax can be evaluated between "safe" and "risky" assets in terms of the relative current valuation of those assets. For instance, until the middle 1950's in the United Kingdom, the risk of capital loss in a business venture was rewarded by high yields. With increasing anticipation of capital loss through inflation, "safe" fixed interest securities have replaced risky equities as the high yielding shares; risky equities with likelihood of expansion and earnings matching inflationary price increases now yield very low amounts.

In the pre-1955 position, a wealth tax could be imposed if it was expected that there would be a falling price level when capital was not likely to be readily available for risky ventures; the tax, based on capital value, would have hit the safe holder of low yielding (high capital value), gilt-edged securities (the rentier), and have let the risky entrepreneur off relatively lightly.[36]

The reversal of the yields changes the position and it can be maintained[37] that a wealth tax penalizing high capital values (low yields) would hit precisely those equities with high risk contents. If the low yield was due to the "growth prospects for dividends and capital"[38] then a wealth tax would operate against risk-taking.

On the other hand, the low yield, high risk equity was a product not only of the growth prospects for dividends and capital, but also of the expectation of inflation and surtax avoidance. The surtax avoidance was and still is due to the large differential in tax rate between surtax and long-term capital gains tax; in its simplest form due to the taxation of current income from property but not of the income from capital gains; thus assets with a high capital gain possibility have an enhanced value (which literally enhances their market value) due to their double attraction of low current income and high capital increment. If this discrepancy in tax treatment were abolished, then there is a possibility that the reverse yield gap might be closed, because it would then be relying solely on the prospect of general monetary inflation.

A wealth tax introduced would itself automatically tax capital gains

---

[36] Kalecki, "The Economics of Full Employment," *Bulletin of the Oxford University Institute of Statistics* (Oxford, 1944).

[37] T. Balough, "A Note on the Wealth Tax," *Economic Journal,* March, 1964, pp. 222-223.

[38] *Ibid.,* p. 223.

and thereby reduce the attractiveness of low yield, high gain stocks, thus contributing to a position where the effectiveness of a wealth tax against the "rentier" would be increased.

Essentially, it can be argued that between safe and risky investments a wealth tax will discriminate against the safe if there is an expectation of deflation and no tax advantage in capital gains exemption; if there is inflation and capital gains advantage then the wealth tax will remove the capital gains advantage (if care is taken to relate the wealth tax rate to the income tax base). The whole discrimination revolves around the *expectation* of inflation. The greater this is, the more will wealth taxation discriminate against risk.

This discrimination against risk-taking due to a high expectation of inflation will have to be offset against the arguments that wealth taxation will increase risk-taking.

Summary

Wealth taxes will increase total risk-taking if full loss offset is allowed. Private risk-taking could be increased with the capital tax. Compared to a similar income tax risk-taking is unlikely to be changed but the individual will prefer the capital tax. The substitution for a sales tax results in indeterminate changes in risk-taking. The greater is the expectation of inflation the more will wealth taxation discriminate against risk.

GENERAL EQUILIBRIUM ADJUSTMENT

Taxes on wealth are on a stock as opposed to the more usual taxes on flows. Of course, if income earning assets are valued by capitalizing the income stream and the capital tax is only on income-yielding wealth, then the wealth tax is the same as a tax on capital income.

If factor shares remain unchanged, substituting a wealth tax on income-earning assets favors wage earners and consumers, and discriminates against savers and those who have income from capital.

A similar wealth tax replacing a general sales tax will favor consumers and discriminate against savers and capital interest recipients. The wage earner's position is improved relative to that of the interest receiver.

A tax on wealth including cash and non–income-yielding assets is not equal to a tax on interest. This tax includes assets or income in kind that was previously tax free. It broadens the tax base and reduces the necessary rate of tax on interest to yield an equal rate of return to the wealth tax on income-yielding assets. Hence the severity of the effects is reduced but not the direction. There will be a reassessment between income-yielding and non–income-yielding assets. Capital owners, finding that both are now taxed, will switch to those that yield a money income until the rate of return on money income–yielding assets and income-in-kind assets, net of tax, is the same.

Lower prices of nonmoney income–yielding assets (e.g., owner occupied houses) may result in lower returns to factors producing those assets. There may be shifts of labor and capital into other products.

If factor shares change, numerous alternatives open up. Lower rewards to capital may reduce the supply and encourage firms to change their factor mix. Or capital holders may attempt to maintain some real net rate of return so that the increased tax on interest would be reflected in higher depreciation charges and interest rates, and passed on to consumers in higher prices for goods and services.

If total private saving is reduced under a wealth tax does this necessarily indicate that the tax should be rejected? No more than the probable increase in total risk-taking indicates that the tax should be adopted. The question is a relative one: Do we need more risk-taking? Is more risk-taking necessarily a desirable object? Similarly, do we need more saving? The answers depend, broadly, on the particular economy and the time chosen. In conditions where unemployed resources exist less saving and more risk-taking might be desirable; there is no a priori way of determining that the total value of private saving after the introduction of a wealth tax will be less desirable from the point of view of economic welfare than the value of savings undertaken today. In any case, the government can extend its role as a saver to compensate for a reduction in private saving.

WEALTH TAXES AS A BUILT-IN STABILIZER

It can be held that if new taxes are imposed they should extend the "built-in-stabilizing" tendency of the tax structure.[39] Recent measures of the existing built-in flexibility of the British tax structure have shown it to be about 50 per cent if both personal and company taxation is included, and if no allowance is made for indirect taxation.[40]

A wealth tax would be subject to two conflicting tendencies. As

[39] C. A. R. Crosland, *The Conservative Enemy* (London: Cape, 1962), Chap. 1.
[40] A. R. Prest, "The Sensitivity of the Yield of Personal Income Tax in the U.K.," *Economic Journal,* September, 1962. A. R. Pearse, "Automatic Stabilization and British Taxes and Income," *Review of Economic Studies,* February, 1962.

wealth grew the tax base would expand and with a fixed rate the yield would increase; but as the taxation was increasingly effective in cutting down the large wealth holdings the yield would fall. The net result depends on three factors:

(i)   The increase in wealth broadening the tax base of existing estates;
(ii) The increase in wealth holdings of new estates;
(iii) The reduction in size of the upper estates.

If (i) and (ii) outstripped (iii), then changes in the size of national income could be slightly counterbalanced by the built-in effectiveness of the wealth tax, but this is unlikely to be as effective as the personal income tax or corporate taxation.

Finally, it is clear that the discussions outlined above are in forms of a political entity, a country with defined geographical boundary; of course, the arguments can be couched in terms of the world where the discussion could be on world growth of wealth, on the growth of capital in capital rich countries, as opposed to its growth in labor rich/capital poor countries. Wealth taxation can be considered in an international context as taxing those capital rich states to provide capital for poorer countries, effecting an international redistribution of capital.[41]

The problems are similar but larger and more intransient and in many ways more interesting, but they require not a separate chapter, but a different book.

WEALTH TAX EFFICIENCY

Finally, we can ask: Is wealth taxation the most efficient way to alter the future distribution of wealth and the flow of factor payments? What is the most efficient form of government action?

The detailed discussion is in Appendix III, but overall, government expenditure changes appear the most efficient way of altering the factor payments (while maintaining investment equal to savings). But this is probably politically inexpedient and as it works through diminishing consumption it is likely to be antiexpansionary, whereas taxing the profits does not necessarily act in the same depressing manner.

If we are to examine methods of altering the flow of factor payments, or even of achieving equity over the tax structure, by using taxes on wealth, we should mention that the public sector can tax wealth in ways

---

[41] D. Dosser, "Towards a Theory of International Public Finance," *Kyklos,* Vol. XVI, 1963, espec. pp. 74-79.

other than those of net worth taxes, capital levies, or taxes on the transfer of wealth. When the government sells extra bonds and extends the national debt this is likely to decrease the value, not only of existing government debt, but possibly the value of all other market securities, and even all other assets. In this respect the sale of debt could be likened to a tax on wealth.

Again, the government can tax the accumulation of wealth in excess of that already existing by extending its role as a saver at the expense of the private sector.

Wealth is not only taxed and redistributed by the public sector however; the sale of goods and services by monopolies could be considered a tax; so could the sale of *anything* be considered (like government debt above) to be altering the valuation and distribution of other assets. We are interested only in the decisions of the public sector, so we have ignored the actions of the private sector insofar as their buying and selling affects the distribution of wealth; additionally we are interested only in those decisions of the public sector to tax wealth which are primarily for that specific purpose, and which are not incidental to other policies, e.g., borrowing or budget surpluses, etc.

SUMMARY

Overall, there are no determinate statements that can be made about the effects of wealth taxes. Work effort may or may not be increased; the same is true of saving. Changes in risk-taking depend upon very restrictive assumptions.

If an attempt is made to give some broad coherence to the discussion of the effects of wealth taxes, then it could be said that gift taxes do not discriminate against work effort as much as inheritance taxes do, and that net worth taxes would probably discriminate against it least of all.

Although an unusual tax, the capital levy, with accepted safeguards against repetition, would not affect work effort adversely and might encourage saving and risk-taking.

A general wealth tax (replacing an income tax) which taxes non–income-yielding assets could result in a fall in demand for those assets, and either a switch of more saving into income-yielding assets, or a more general decline in total saving. Changes in aggregate saving do not necessarily damn or recommend a wealth tax; the important factors are the prevailing employment conditions and the actions of government as a saver.

As a built-in stabilizer, wealth taxes are likely to be less effective than personal or corporate taxation.

The most efficient means of altering the future flow of factor payments by government action would be to alter government expenditure on goods and services, but as this is likely to be politically inexpedient wealth taxes are a more efficient means in practice.

16

Implementation and Conclusions

Some attempt should be made to relate the examination to the problems of implementation, so below is a short consideration of the major practical difficulties, followed by a summary of the whole discussion.

IMPLEMENTATION

In terms of political expediency there are five questions appropriate to any tax change.

1. What size of change is involved? It is always easier to tinker than to rebuild. The citadels, bastions, and ramifications of the acts affecting taxation (sixty statutes on U.K. estate duty alone) are eloquent witnesses to the urge to add, modify, or marginally alter an edifice rather than tear it down and start again.

  (i) Policies which represent minor improvements (or objectively, changes) to taxes which already exist are more likely to be adopted than major changes.

 (ii) Major changes are those which require considerable alterations but which are substantially within the ambit of existing taxes.

(iii) Fundamental changes are those based on different concepts and requiring large amounts of new legislation.

2. Is there any revenue loss involved? Clearly, the Inland Revenue commissioners will be unhappy about new proposals which involve a possible reduction in tax revenue (e.g., legacy duties).

3. Is it an attractive part of a political platform? No party wants to be saddled with unpopular legislation. On the other hand parties will often look for particular rallying positions and a different proposal can be a useful identification mark when all parties are grey.

4. How far will it inconvenience the civil service? The Inland Revenue never has enough people to cope with the demands made upon it. Any proposal which adds to the administration's burdens without some compensating relief in other directions will run into the quicksands of departmental delay and procrastination.

5. Is there any obvious vested interest which will support it? Universal apathy is not a good launching pad for taxation changes and if the legislation is likely to appeal to a particular pressure group, obviously its chances of success are improved.

If a proposal attracts the support of a vested interest, does not inconvenience the civil service, is attractive as a plank in a party platform, involves no loss of revenue, then it might be possible to force through a major or fundamental change. Basically all signs must be "go" before there is a serious chance of change.

How do the conclusions of this short discussion square with the questions of implementation?

The conclusions for policy can be split into three forms. First is a fundamental change based on a different appraisal of the tax structure. This would entail the introduction of "Pay-As-You-Accumulate" personal taxation linked to income taxes and lifetime taxes. Basically these embody the two-sector principles of equity outlined in Chapter 11. It should be noted that this system would comply with the best of liberal tradition by encouraging distribution to younger persons and penalizing the concentration of property held for a long time in few hands. It also encourages saving.

But no vested interest is particularly committed to such a change; although it would be more equitable, the process of educating the majority to understand how it would be advantageous to them, and to overcome the (fundamental) opposition of wealthy vested interests would be lengthy and probably inconclusive. If such a change were to attract support it would probably have to be that of disinterested equalitarians (in the sense of tax equity). The inconvenience to the civil service would be large, requiring a reformulation of departments and methods. Depending on the tax rates chosen there need be no loss of revenue. It could form a basic part of a political party program.

The difficulties of changeover could be acute. The change envisaged is a fundamental reassessment of the personal direct tax structure, away from the annual base to a lifetime base. Although both income taxes (P.A.Y.E.) and accrual taxes (P.A.Y.A.) would be collected currently and cumulated, there would be a reconciliation on a cumulative base over a lifetime. There is probably no more difficult changeover than one which substitutes a long tax liability period for a short one. Those who are earning already could not be put in the new cumulative system, because their tax rate could not be related to their past income and accruals. Therefore, some very long transition period would have to be accepted. The usual trouble with transitions is the danger of taxpayers opting for whichever base is the most advantageous, thereby creating potential inequity. However, one advantage of this particular transition is that it is quite impossible to misrepresent your generation — at least that is fixed; so taxpayers could not switch from one tax base to the other. All new wage earners would be taxed under the cumulative base. All those already earning and already having accruals would continue to be taxed as previously.

The dual transition tax structure, although inconvenient, would have one significant advantage. As the older tax base shrank through deaths, the new tax base would expand not only by the increasing number of people joining, but through the cumulative nature of the tax base; the death of the older persons automatically increases the tax base through the transfers of wealth augmenting the accrual base of the newer generation. Although the tax rates of the two transition bases would be totally different, persons of the same age would be treated equally, and there would be no opportunity for switching between the two bases because the criterion of the tax base is no longer the definitional one found in current taxes (earned, unearned, corporate, unincorporated, capital gain, income in kind, etc.) but the natural one of the date of birth.

In a country with a highly organized tax structure and numerous groups sensitive to change, an alteration so fundamental as this would be extremely difficult. Such a proposal would require time to be adopted by a party, time to be thrashed out, and time to be assimilated by the administration and the public. Some sort of change may be desirable, but it cannot happen quickly. Is it reasonable to expect the Labour Party in Britain to swing away from its recent preoccupation with nationalization to concentrate on issues where there is obvious existing personal inequity? In countries which are only starting to create their tax structure, where the existing modes of taxation are not so immutable nor the pressure groups completely entrenched, it might be possible to begin with the cumulative tax base, rather than change at a later, inconvenient, date.

The second group of conclusions for implementation comes into the category of major but not fundamental. It would be possible to adapt P.A.Y.A. to act as a form of net worth tax at the local level. One of the repeated difficulties of local government is the inflexible nature of rates (in the United Kingdom) or the so-called "property tax" (in the United States). If it were possible to harness the desires of local authorities for greater fiscal autonomy to the proposal this would form a very strong vested interest in favor of it. If the local governments were given responsibility for levying a double-equity accumulation tax it would provide them with a much broader tax base than that which they enjoy at present. Checking and inspection could be represented as more properly the responsibility of local government, especially in densely populated areas where there are economies of scale in training and using expert valuation officers. To some extent this could be presented as an extension of the property taxes already levied by local governments.

There should be some reconciliation between the local tax on accruals and the central government tax on other income, to avoid the problems of taxpayers representing increments under either tax base depending on which happens to be the most advantageous. If the central government's income tax were on a cumulative basis then reconciliation might be possible (through the lifetime taxes) at the national level; if the central government's income tax were not on a cumulative basis then all the problems of definition reemerge. But even with a local cumulative property tax, and a central government noncumulative income tax, the inequity should be less than that which exists today.

This sort of proposal is easier to implement in a nonfederal tax structure, where the form of local taxes can be dictated by the central government. The rapprochement necessary to implement the two taxes at the two levels of government would be difficult to create in a federal system.

Finally, there is a third group of conclusions, those which are changes in the texture of existing taxes or indications for policy. The discussions in the text have yielded a crop of these:

   (i) minimize exemptions, particularly those to:
      (a) agriculture,

      (b) industrial hereditaments,

      (c) charities and objects of national interest;

(ii) eliminate multiple exemptions, and substitute a lifetime exemption limit;

(iii) all gifts (including "money") should be taxed at their value on transfer;

(iv) trust capital should be taxed;

(v) differential rates between gift taxes and death duties should be removed;

(vi) the importance of control over monopoly influences;

(vii) the importance of the "assumed" split in factor incomes when national growth plans are formulated;

(viii) the importance of government expenditure on education and health;

(ix) the need for worker retraining schools;

and most of these would meet the "go" signals discussed earlier, but none of them involve any fundamental rethinking of objectives or relationships; they are all, in some way or another, embodied in our present economic thinking.

CONCLUSIONS

The discussion concerned the personal ownership of assets as recognized by the current legal code of a country. These assets are very unequally distributed in both developed and underdeveloped countries (Chapter 1). Economic analysis cannot "prove" that any of the sociopolitical arguments are a justification for taxing wealth — although many of them give a strong indication that personal wealth is a reasonable subject for taxation (Chapter 2) — but if the tax system already includes taxes on income in some form then the taxation of personal wealth is necessary to insure the equity of the total tax structure (Chapter 2).

The unequal distribution of wealth will continue to be a problem in the future as any "automatic" solution through the "euthanasia of the rentier" is most unlikely and in any case would still leave inequities. Future factor payments are likely to continue to favor capital (Chapter 3); economies of scale, technology, and differential price changes (Chapter 4) point toward an increasing flow to capital. National "growth plans," monopoly legislation, and trade union activity can help to stem the likely increase in payments to capital (Chapter 3). Income taxation worsens the situation by reducing the reasonable aspirations of the low wealth groups, and the nonprovision of education can be likened to a highly progressive wealth tax falling on those who have innate skill but neither the opportunity nor the money to develop their talents (Chapter 4). Greater expenditure on education and more reliance on merit promotion would be forces to counteract the demographic features which favor the already rich (Chapter 14), but the taxation of wealth is still necessary (Chapters 4 and 5).

Part of the kernel of tax equity concerns the expectations of individuals (Chapter 4) and the reasonable aspirations of society (Chapter 2) which consider certain differentials as acceptable, and taxation should help to mold and satisfy these expectations and aspirations.

Personal wealth taxes were introduced originally to provide revenue for the government, especially in times of emergency; later (United Kingdom, 1894, and United States, 1916) they were justified mainly as a redistributive agent (Chapter 5).

Capital levies are an extraordinary form of taxation, if tolerated, only because they are temporary. The minimum conditions for levying such a tax are a minimizing of the time lag between valuation and payment, the maintenance of a stable purchasing power over the levy period, a degree of acceptance by the public, control of capital flight, and some guarantee against repetition. There must be better ways of taxing wealth (Chapter 6).

Net worth taxes although attractive are limited by the administrative need to rely on realization or infrequent valuations. It has been suggested that the time of accumulation might be better, a form of Pay-As-You-Accumulate tax, but which swings attention to transfers (Chapter 7).

Although attractively simple taxes to administer, estate duties have not been very effective in redistributing wealth. The forces which limit this method of redistribution are the growth of capital, the "freezing" of ownership, intermittent imposition, trusts, and capital movements. Skipping a generation and erosion of the tax base by differential rates (particularly in the United Kingdom) on agricultural land, industrial hereditaments, and objects of national interest are major ways of avoiding estate duty. Problems of avoidance and valuation are not unique to estate duties, but simple avoidance is, and this results in substantial inequity (Chapter 8).

Although consanguinity rates are used in many countries the only justification for them is under conditions which make taxation according to the circumstances of the legatee a more reasonable alternative.

Such taxation, although having many advantages, cannot insure equity through time (Chapter 9).

The Rignano proposals attempted a crude method of achieving some equity through time; however, they foundered on the administrative problems (Chapter 9).

The most formidable attempt to achieve equity through time was that which used bequeathing-power units; the major difficulty is the confusing nature of these units as intermediaries between age differences and wealth transferred. However, the concept isolates the problem of double equity, and a double sector system has been devised which achieves almost the same result without using "extraneous" units. But some inequity through time still remains, which can be annihilated only by using the type of mechanism embodied in bequeathing-power units. Is the complication in the tax structure compensated for by the increase in neutrality, or is it better to view the taxation of gifts and inheritances as a means of discouraging a mild human vice, that is, clinging to wealth in old age? (Chapter 11).

The disadvantages of a gift tax to back up legacy and estate duties is exemplified by the United Kingdom and the United States. There are problems concerning the period during which gifts will be liable to taxation, the motive of the donor, the different forms in which gifts can be made, exemptions, overlaps, the tax unit, and the position of trusts (Chapter 12).

An accruals tax does not satisfy the necessary relationship between capital receipts and all other receipts (Chapter 12).

The relationship of transfer taxes to stocks of property and income flows is such that equity throughout the system can be realized with three basic parts to the personal tax system:

(i) the income tax,
(ii) the P.A.Y.A. (Pay-As-You-Accumulate),
(iii) the lifetime tax (Chapter 13).

The proposed system would stop avoidance through gifts inter vivos, and also that through trusts. The problems of defining a completed transfer, the tax unit, exemptions, and extraterritorial transfers, do not seem insuperable (Chapter 14).

The effects of personal wealth taxes on work effort, consumption, saving, and risk-taking are not presented as either justifying or condemning the use of such taxes but we have attempted (in Chapter 15) to assess the differential incidence of a net worth tax, a gift tax, and an estate duty, compared to an income tax and a sales tax.

Overall, there are no determinate statements that can be made about the effects of wealth taxes, but none of the effects discussed appeared sufficiently important to prevent the introduction of a more comprehensive, cumulative, wealth tax.

The importance of what *The Economist* has recently called "tired egalitarian arguments" is not diminished because they have been with us a long time, nor are the arguments reduced because the complexity and richness of modern society obscure many of the inequalities. When you cover the floor with a rich carpet it does not alter the fact that there is a hole in the floor, or when Mussolini built cardboard houses to impress Hitler it did not alter the slums behind. So the multitude of avoidance and evasion schemes, the different forms in which persons can collect their rewards, the insidious changes in wealth and income through price changes or automation, do not alter the fact that great inequity exists in most modern tax structures. It is not true that what the public does not know will not harm it; of course it harms it by making it relatively less well off and it is all the more reprehensible that those who are aware of the process do not do something to alter it.

The situation is worse in underdeveloped economies. Most such countries "show a degree of inequality in the distribution of income comparable to, if not greater than, that of the 'developed' countries of Western Europe or North America. The statistical evidence is sketchy and not very reliable; yet such as there is all tends to show that the degree of concentration in the ownership of property is quite as great in the poor or semi-developed countries of the Middle East, Asia or Latin America, as in the countries of advanced capitalism."[1] Thus the problem of "reasonable expectations" which we have discussed is all the worse in those countries. The inequities are naked instead of concealed as in developed economies, but the problem of equitable wealth is just as great, if not greater, in Europe and North America.

Essentially, all of us have an interest in fair taxation. Tax structures which connive at avoidance, are arbitrary in their liability, and which prolong historical inequities, are the concern of everyone. To paraphrase Donne, Ask not for whom the tax is levied, it is levied for thee.

---

[1] N. Kaldor, *Essays on Economic Policy* (London: Duckworth, 1964), I, 256.

Appendix I

Selection of Data to Examine the Effects of Price Changes on Different Wealth-Owning Groups in the United States and United Kingdom

The asset groups chosen were in part dictated by the official split of estates and also by the desire to get some comparability between the U.S. and U.K. data. Six groups for each country were selected; bonds (which include government and private), cash and mortgages (a distinction between these could not be maintained as the earlier U.S. figures were not split), corporate stocks, insurance (U.S. insurance was taken as "gross," which meant that up to and including 1945 "an exemption with respect to insurance receivable by beneficiaries other than the estate, not to exceed in the aggregate $40,000, for any one estate — allowable for estates of individuals who died prior to October 22, 1942"[1] had to be added to each wealth-owning group's net insurance to give the gross amount comparable to the years post-1945), real estate (house and business property, and land), and other (mainly household goods and some "trade assets"). These groups, it was felt, would give an indication of how asset holdings were changed with changing prices, e.g., stocks, versus bonds, cash, and real estate.

[1] *Statistics of Income, 1944,* U.S. Treasury Department, Internal Revenue Service, Part I, p. 333, n. 16.

YEAR

Ideally, it would be preferable to include each year 1920-60. To get a division of wealth groups for the United States which would be comparable over the entire period we were obliged to start with the figures for 1927. A peculiarity of the U.S. data is that the earlier statistics provide a more comprehensive and continuing series than the later years. As we move into the fifties, the data become very patchy; altogether the returns were not available in the form necessary for this examination for 1946, 1950, 1951, 1952, 1953, 1956, 1957, 1958, 1960. This meant, for instance, that it was impossible to make corrections for differences in the timing of returns between the United States and the United Kingdom (see below). The data for the United Kingdom started in 1920-21, but there are gaps in it, too. Sometimes it refers to a different political entity (e.g., 1921-22 "England" only, as opposed to "Great Britain"), or is nonexistent (e.g., during World War II) or unusable (e.g., 1934-35), so that the following years had to be omitted: 1921-22, 1934-35, 1939-47.

Another difficulty is that estate tax returns filed during a calendar year do not necessarily refer to that year (in the United States they must be filed within fifteen months). For the United States generally "these data [if filed 1961] are presented as estimates of income and gifts during 1960 and of estates of those who died in 1960. The presence of a very few earlier returns does not appreciably affect the validity of the statistics."[2] The table and graphs are presented for what we shall call "inferred years." That is, we infer that the data is of the year shown, although the year in which it is filed may be different. For the United States, the inferred year is the year prior to the year in which the data is filed. For the United Kingdom, the inferred year and the file year are the same. This weights the U.K. data more heavily toward earlier years than the U.S., as approximately two-thirds of the data for each country is actually applicable to the inferred year, while two-ninths of the data for the United States and none for the United Kingdom refer to subsequent years, but one-ninth of the data for the United States and one-third for the United Kingdom refer to preceding years. Because of the discontinuity of the series it is impossible to make corrections for these discrepancies. Since our primary concern is with the *relative* position of wealth groups in each country, as long as the time bias is not unevenly spread between the wealth classes the discrepancy is

---

[2] *Statistics of Income, 1960. Gift and Estate Tax Returns,* U.S. Treasury Department, Internal Revenue Service, p. viii.

not too imperfect. The correction to inferred years does allow a rough comparison of the U.S. and U.K. data.

WEALTH-OWNING GROUPS

The comparison is made between three wealth-owning groups, lower, middle, and upper. To obtain a reasonable comparison through time and to insure that particular years were not dominated by unusual estates coming up for probate, considerable aggregation was necessary; after some experimentation the wealth-owning groups £5,000-£25,000, £25,000-£100,000, and over £100,000 seemed reasonable categories for the United Kingdom. There is no meaningful sense in which these can be converted into U.S. $'s for a long time period during which rates of exchange fluctuated and living standards changed greatly. Eventually the U.S. categories chosen, again partially dictated by comparability through time, were $60,000-$200,000, $200,000-$800,000, and over $800,000. To get these it was necessary to correct the pre-1939 figures in the lowest category which were given for $50,000-$100,000, to $60,000-$100,000, assuming proportionality.

PRICE INDICES

The base year adopted for both the U.S. and the U.K. series was 1958. Sources are given with Tables 3 and 4.

Appendix II

An Estimate of the Extent of Avoidance
of the Estate Tax in Great Britain

It is likely that the amount of avoidance is directly related to the rates of tax; high taxation results in large amounts of avoidance and vice-versa. When progressive rates were first introduced into British death duties in 1894, they ranged from 1-8 per cent; although unpopular it is doubtful that they were sufficiently high to incite large scale avoidance. As the period in which gifts inter vivos were deemed to be part of the estate was only three months, there was a considerable temptation to use such gifts; this is borne out by the decision to raise the period, in 1889, to one year, and again in 1909 to three years. However, compared to today, with rates from 1-80 per cent, the incentive to avoidance in the early part of the century was small.

To the extent that the yield of death duties in the early years of the century is a "true" yield (i.e., that there is little avoidance), then if standardized tax rates are applied to those figures we can obtain a ratio of revenue to wealth for the two dates, and an estimate of the potential present-day yield of death duties, and thus an estimate of the amount of avoidance.

To do this we can derive a yield for, say, 1912, using 1960 tax rates; express this as a fraction of the total wealth held in 1912; then compare the actual 1960 yield as a fraction of wealth held in 1960, and if there is a difference in the ratios (1960 smaller) this will indicate the extent of tax avoidance.

The assumptions are:

(i) That the 1912 figures for estates passing at death are reasonably complete, i.e., that there is little avoidance.

(ii) That the distribution of wealth estimates are comparable.

It is reasonable to take 1912 as a base. By that time death duty tax rates had reached a maximum of 15 per cent; at the same time the period during which gifts inter vivos were liable to tax had been extended (in 1909) to three years. Three years is a long time compared to the original three months and it seems likely that this was a considerable deterrent to avoidance, while the rates had not yet reached heights that encouraged the widespread use of other, more complicated, methods of avoidance.

The second assumption is much more uncertain. The estimates for total wealth are obtained by using the estates passing at death as random samples of the living, and these taxed estates are multiplied by a reciprocal of the appropriate (sex and age) mortality rate to provide the estimate of total wealth. There are a number of difficulties about this approach,[1] one being that there is an exemption limit to estate duty taxation and therefore the estimates of total wealth do not include small wealth holdings, unless these are interpolated. To the extent that these exemptions are left out then the estimates of total wealth will overstate the proportion of wealth held in higher wealth brackets. Again, as the total wealth estimates are derived from the estate duty figures then the wealth totals themselves are skewed by the avoidance; if there is large scale avoidance in 1960, then the estimates of total wealth will be that much smaller as they are derived from the "shrunken" estate duty returns.[2] However, although the total wealth estimates are smaller than they "should" be in 1960, so is the tax revenue, and the resulting fraction or ratio is comparable to the one for 1912. If the ratio is lower in 1960 than that for 1912, it will be some measure of avoidance.

So our statement is that if the same tax rates are applied to 1960 and 1912, and the tax revenue expressed as a percentage of total wealth,

[1] Lydall and Tipping, "The Distribution of Personal Wealth in Britain."

[2] Although not by gifts inter vivos as a number of the recipients of gifts inter vivos die each year and these gifts are included in their estates and multiplied by the appropriate mortality rate. It could be held that these receivers of gifts inter vivos were not a random sample of such receivers as it is unlikely that persons would give gifts to people who were likely to die, but this is a small error and is offset slightly by the fact that some gifts are taxed twice if the receiver also dies within five years.

then, if there has been no avoidance and the distribution of wealth has not been particularly skewed in the period, the two ratios should be the same.

TABLE II:1
1912 Estate Duty Returns at 1960 Rates

Selected Wealth Groups £'000	Number 1912	Number 1960	Rate 1960 (Per Cent)	Mid Value of Estates	Estate Duty Return at 1960 Rates £'000
0.1–0.5	6,130	–	–	–	–
0.5–1	11,160	–	–	–	–
1–5 }	15,188	–	–	–	–
3–5 }		6,210	2	4,000	496.8
5–7.5 }	3,419	2,085	3	6,250	390.9
7.5–10 }		1,334	4	8,750	466.9
10–12.5		861	6	11,250	581.2
12.5–15		525	8	13,750	577.5
15–17.5 }	1,935	323	10	16,250	524.9
17.5–20		226	12	18,750	508.5
20–25	434	434	15	22,500	1,464.8
25–30		316	18	27,500	1,564.2
30–35 }	678	217	21	32,500	1,481.0
35–40		145	24	37,500	1,305.0
40–45 }	219	123	28	42,500	1,463.7
45–50 }		96	31	47,500	1,413.6
50–60 }	261 }	151	35	55,000	2,906.8
60–70 }		155	40	67,500	4,185.0
70–75	45 }				
75–100	137	137	45	87,500	5,394.4
100–150	118	118	50	125,000	7,375.0
150–200	69	69	55	175,000	6,641.2
200–250	30	48	60	250,000	7,200.0
250–300	–	–	–	–	–
300–400	38 }	34	65	400,000	8,840.0
400–500	14 }				
500–600	4 }	8	70	625,000	3,500.0
600–750	4 }				
750–800	– }	5	75	875,000	3,281.3
800–1m	5 }				
1m–1.5m	8 }				
1.5m–2m	2 }				
2m–2.5m	– }	11	80	2m	17,600.0
2.5m–3m	– }				
3m+	1 }				
Total					79,162.5

In 1912, estate duty receipts were £78.7 million at 1960 rates. Wealth is estimated[3] for 1912 at £9,310 to £10,500 million. Therefore, the proportion of estate duty receipts at 1960 rates in 1912 is 7.5-8.5 per cent.

The actual receipts from estate duty in 1960 were £235.9 million, representing 5.6 per cent of the national wealth.[4]

The 1912 figures exceed those of 1960 by between 1.3 and 1.5 times; multiplying the estate duty yield in 1960 by these factors gives the yield which might be expected under our assumptions, for 1960:

$$£235.9 \times 1.5 = £355.7 \text{ million} \quad (50 \text{ per cent larger})$$
$$£235.9 \times 1.3 = £315.4 \text{ million} \quad (34 \text{ per cent larger})$$

These figures indicate that avoidance is on a very large scale, between 34 and 50 per cent.

A check can be made on this estimate to insure that it is not totally ridiculous. Recently the Commissioners for Inland Revenue have included in their annual reports the figures for those gifts inter vivos which become liable to taxation under the present five-year ruling. If it is assumed that the "average" age at which people attempt to avoid death duty by gifts inter vivos is, say, sixty, then from life-expectancy tables we take the percentage who will probably die between the ages of sixty and sixty-five. At age sixty years, life expectancy is 15.2 per cent and the number surviving from 10,000 is 8,999; similarly for sixty-five, expectancy is 12.1 per cent, and the number surviving, 6,859. Thus: for the age group sixty to sixty-five, the percentage expected to die is 12.95. Inter vivos gifts accounted for £25.198 million of the estates taxed in 1960. This represents money which, but for the unexpected or unfortunate death of the testator, would have escaped taxation; therefore the total amount of avoidance through gifts inter vivos is:

$$£25.198m \times \frac{100}{12.95} = £194.58m.$$

This means that the amount of capital which successfully avoids taxation is £169.38m. The average rate of duty in 1960 was 22.77 per cent, and this applied to the theoretical, successful avoidance gives a figure of £38.57m. This, expressed as the percentage increase in yield which could be expected over that obtained in 1960, gives 16 per cent.

---

[3] H. Campion, *Public and Private Property;* Langley, "The Distribution of Private Capital, 1950-1951," and "Distribution of Capital in Private Hands 1936-39 and 1946-47"; Lydall and Tipping, "The Distribution of Personal Wealth in Britain."

[4] *Ibid.*

So that if all possible means of avoidance are included the amount of revenue lost might be 34 per cent of the 1960 total; of this 34 per cent, some 16 per cent could be attributed to gifts inter vivos. As gifts inter vivos are the simplest way of avoiding this tax they could be expected to bulk large in the total avoidance; all the other means of avoidance could reasonably contribute the other 18 per cent. At least the figure of 34 per cent avoidance is not ludicrous, as it would have been had our "check" figure of 16 per cent turned out to be higher than 50 per cent.

Appendix III

The Efficiency of Wealth Taxes

Profits, income, capital, investment, and savings are represented by P, Y, K, I, and S. The marginal propensity to save of capitalists is shown as sc, and that of wage receivers as sw.

Let us use the Kaldor full employment equilibrium model expressed in real terms to start with, where:

$$\frac{P}{Y} = \frac{1}{sc - sw} \cdot \frac{I}{Y} - \frac{sw}{sc - sw} \tag{1}$$

$$\frac{P}{K} = \frac{1}{sc - sw} \cdot \frac{I}{K} - \frac{sw}{sc - sw} - \frac{Y}{K} \tag{2}$$

This assumes $S = I$, but if we introduce a government sector (G) into this, then:

$$Y = C + I + G$$
$$Y = C + S + T_z + Tw - R$$

where T_z, Tw, and R are taxes on capital, wages, and transfers, respectively. Then:

$$I = S + T_z + Tw - R - G.$$

To demonstrate the most simple position where there is only one tax on

211

capital (T_z) and the only government expenditure is on transfers which accrue to wage earners (W represents wages):

$$I = S + T_z - R$$
$$Sw = sw(W + R)$$
$$Sc = sc(P - T_z)$$

$\therefore$ $\qquad I = sw(W + R) + sc(P - T_z) + T_z - R$

as $\qquad Y = W + P$, then $W = Y - P$, so:

$$I = swY + T_z(1 - sc) + P(sc - sw) - R(1 - sw)$$

$$\frac{P}{Y} = \frac{1}{sc - sw} \cdot \frac{I}{Y} - \frac{sw}{sc - sw} - \frac{1 - sc}{sc - sw} \cdot \frac{T_z}{Y}$$

$$+ \frac{1 - sw}{sc - sw} \cdot \frac{R}{Y} \tag{3}$$

The first two terms of the right hand side are identical to those in (1) but the whole expression is now modified by the capital tax and the transfer. Perhaps it is clearer and should be pointed out that the same expression results if we assume government saving instead of the rather clumsy $Y = C + S + T_z + Tw - R$: if

$$I = Sw + Sc + Sg$$

and $\qquad Sg = T_z - R$

then the same expression, (3), results. The possible policies, assuming income and investment constant, are:

$$\Delta T_z \quad \bar{R} \qquad \Delta P = -\frac{(1 - sc)}{sc - sw} \cdot \Delta T_z \tag{2a}$$

$$\bar{T}_z \quad \Delta R \qquad \Delta P = \frac{(1 - sw)}{sc - sw} \cdot \Delta R \tag{2b}$$

$$\Delta T_z = \Delta R \qquad \Delta P = \frac{(1 - sw)\Delta R}{sc - sw} - \frac{\Delta T_z(1 - sc)}{sc - sw}$$

$$= \frac{\Delta T_z(sc - sw) - (\Delta T_z - \Delta R)}{sc - sw} \tag{2c}$$

as $\qquad \Delta T_z - \Delta R = 0$

$$\Delta P = \Delta T_z = \Delta R.$$

The effectiveness of policy (2c) is exactly what would be expected in the balanced budget case, where the increase (or decrease) in profits would be precisely equal to the change in capital taxation and transfer payment.

Between the other two policies, the larger the marginal propensity to save differential (sc — sw) the less effective will be the tax change; as sc moves towards unity and sw towards zero policy (2a) becomes less effective and policy (2b) increasingly effective. Clearly, the larger the marginal propensity to consume of those with capital $(1 - sc)$ the more effective will policy (2a) be, and the smaller the marginal propensity to consume of wage earners $(1 - sw)$ the less effective (on profits) will be policy (2b). Thus, if the object is to reduce the rate of factor flow to profits, the most effective policy would be to reduce transfer payments. As long as sc $\geqq$ sw, taxation increases will not be as effective in altering the share of profits as reductions in transfer payments. Essentially, as *reductions* in transfer payments are usually ruled out on grounds of political expediency, this points towards the view that *new* policies should rely on increased taxation rather than on the redistributive character of transfer payments.

The larger the marginal propensity to save differential (and this is, presumably, related to points in the time of economic development) the truer this policy indication will be.

If government expenditure on goods and services replaced the expression for transfers then the goods and services would accrue to both wage earners and capitalists. The relationship is complicated by a modification of expression (2) to allow for public expenditure to both groups:

$I = S + T_z - Gw - Gc$ where (G) government expenditure on goods and services is split between wage earners (Gw) in the form of payments to workers in government employ, etc., and capitalists (Gc) in the form of profits on government contracts, etc. Then $Y = P + W + Gc + Gw$.

$$Sw = sw(W + Gw)$$
$$Sc = sc(P + Gc - Tz)$$
$$Sg = Tz - Gc + Gw$$

$$I = P(sc - sw) + Tz(1 - sc) - Gc(1 + sw - sc) - Gw + swY$$

$$\frac{P}{Y} = \frac{1}{sc - sw} \cdot \frac{I}{Y} - \frac{sw}{sc - sw} - \frac{(1 - sc)}{sc - sw} \cdot \frac{Tz}{Y}$$
$$+ \frac{1 + sw - sc}{sc - sw} \cdot \frac{Gc}{Y} + \frac{1}{sc - sw} \cdot \frac{Gw}{Y} \qquad (4)$$

Once more the first two expressions on the right hand side are as in (1) and (2). The possible policies are changes in the tax rate with government expenditure constant (3a) as in (2a), and:

$$\bar{G} \qquad \Delta Tz \qquad \qquad \Delta P = \frac{(1 - sc)}{sc - sw} \cdot \Delta Tz \qquad (3a)$$

$$\bar{T}z \qquad \Delta Gc \qquad\qquad \Delta P = \frac{1 + sw - sc}{sc - sw} \cdot \Delta Gc \qquad (3b)$$

$$\bar{T}z \qquad \Delta Gw \qquad\qquad \Delta P = \frac{1}{sc - sw} \cdot \Delta Gw \qquad (3c)$$

$$\Delta Tz = \Delta Gc + \Delta Gw \qquad \Delta P = \frac{1}{sc - sw} \cdot (\Delta Tz - \Delta Gc) \qquad (3d)$$

As in expressions (2a)-(2c), the expenditure policy remains the most effective way of altering profits (providing sc > sw) and of the two possible policies for changed expenditure those accruing to the wage earners are the most effective, that is, cutting government expenditure, wage payments, etc., that accrue to workers. Once again this is both politically and socially inexpedient. The balanced budget policy (3d) is interesting because the result depends on the split of the government expenditure on goods and services between capitalists and workers, the larger the amount of increased expenditure channeled to capitalists the less effective will this policy be in changing profits. Depending on the split of the expenditure between capitalists and workers the balanced budget policy can be more or less effective than (3a), (3b), or (3c), but it can never be negative; that is, a balanced budget increase — as long as sc > sw — can never *reduce* profits. A balanced budget reduction could be more effective than a reduction in government expenditure accruing to capitalists.

Again, the policy indication is for new changes to be concentrated on capital taxes.

If the possible taxes are spread to include taxes on wages, retaining only expenditure on goods and services, split between workers and capitalists, then:

$$Y = W + P + Gc + Gw$$
$$I = S + Tz + Tw - G$$
$$Sw = sw(W + Gw - Tw)$$
$$Sc = sc(P + Gc - Tz)$$
$$I = P(sc - sw) + Tz(1 - sc) + Tw(1 - sw)$$
$$\quad - Gc(1 + sw - sc) - Gw + swY$$

$$
\begin{aligned}
\frac{P}{Y} = {} & \frac{1}{sc - sw} \cdot \frac{I}{Y} - \frac{sw}{sc - sw} - \frac{1 - sc}{sc - sw} \cdot \frac{Tz}{Y} \\
& - \frac{1 - sw}{sc - sw} \cdot \frac{Tw}{Y} + \frac{1 + sw - sc}{sc - sw} \cdot \frac{Gc}{Y} \\
& - \frac{1}{sc - sw} \cdot \frac{Gw}{Y}
\end{aligned}
\qquad (5)
$$

The possible policies are:

$$\bar{G} \qquad \Delta Tz \qquad \Delta P = \frac{(1 - sc)}{sc - sw} - \Delta Tz \qquad (4a)$$

$$\bar{G} \qquad \Delta Tw \qquad \Delta P = \frac{(1 - sw)}{sc - sw} - \Delta Tw \qquad (4b)$$

$$\Delta Gc \qquad \bar{T} \qquad \Delta P = \frac{1 + sw - sc}{sc - sw} \cdot \Delta Gc \qquad (4c)$$

$$\Delta Gw \qquad \bar{T} \qquad \Delta P = \frac{1}{sc - sw} \cdot \Delta Gw \qquad (4d)$$

As long as $sc > sw$ then policy (4b) will reduce profits more than (4a). The tax on wages will reduce consumption by more than the tax on capitalists' income. Similarly, as before, changing the government expenditure to wage earners will reduce profits by a greater amount than an equal change in the government expenditure on capitalists. Regrettably, under this limited presentation, the most efficient policy involves taxation of the wage earners and a reduction of government expenditures on wage earners to reduce the profits of capitalists.

The Pasinetti criticisms that the capital owned by wage earners, through wage earners' savings, must be included and should be discussed here. If reformulations of the expressions are attempted to take account of this, including a government sector, they yield complicated and not very informative relationships. However, it could be more simply argued that the policies already outlined approximate to the Pasinetti position because the marginal propensity to save of workers as *capitalists* (i.e., receiving capital yield) is the same as that of any capitalist. That is, the sw and sc used above are the marginal propensities to save of capitalists (all persons owning capital) and wage earners — all persons receiving a wage. In a previous discussion it was argued that much of the saving in the lower income and wealth brackets was contractual and that the marginal propensity to save was a function of the *source* of income, and any receiver of capital yield, if his total income (whether mixed from wages and capital or purely from capital) was low, would have a high marginal propensity to save (sc) because of the contractual nature of low income saving.

Bibliography

BOOKS AND ARTICLES USED

Ackley, G. "The Wealth-Saving Relationship," *Journal of Political Economy*, April, 1951.

Adams, T. S. "Effect of Income and Inheritance Taxes on the Distribution of Wealth," *American Economics Association Proceedings*, Vol. V, 1915.

Alessi, L. de. "Re-Distribution of U.K. Wealth by Inflation," *Southern Economic Journal*, October, 1963.

Altman, G. T. "Combining the Gift and Estate Taxes," *Tax Magazine*, May, 1938.

Anderson, W. H. *Taxation and the American Economy*. Englewood Cliffs, N.J.: Prentice-Hall, 1951.

Aron, R. "Social Structure of the Ruling Class," *The British Journal of Sociology*, June, 1950.

Arrow, K. J. *Social Choice and Individual Values*. 2nd ed. New York: Wiley, 1963.

St. Augustine. *Homily VI*, 25, Migne, *Patrologiae Latinae*. Vol. XXXV. Translated in *A Library of the Fathers*. Oxford: J. H. & J. Parker, 1848.

Bach, G. L. "The Re-Distributional Effects of Inflation," *Journal of Political Economy*, February, 1957.

Balough, T. "Taxation, Risk Bearing and Investment," *Bulletin of the Oxford University Institute of Statistics*, Vol. VII, September, 1945.

———. "The Unimportance of a Capital Levy," *Bulletin of the Oxford University Institute of Statistics*, Vol. VI, No. 3, February, 1944.

———. "A Note on the Wealth Tax," *Economic Journal*, March, 1964.

Barna, T. "The Burden of Death Duties in Terms of an Annual Tax," *Review of Economic Studies*, May, 1958.

Bates, J. A. "The Finance of Small Businesses," *Bulletin of the Oxford University Institute of Statistics*, May, 1958.

Beckwith, B. *The Economic Theory of a Socialist Economy*. Stanford: Stanford University Press, 1949.

Bell, C. *Civilization*. London: Chatto and Windus, 1928.

Benham, F. C. *The Taxation of War Wealth*. Economica, N.S., Vol. VIII, 1941.

Bentham, J. *The Works of Jeremy Bentham*. Bowerings ed. Edinburgh: William Tait, 1839.

Berle, A. A. *Power Without Property*. New York: Harcourt Brace, 1959.

Berle, A. A., and G. C. Means. *The Modern Corporation and Private Property*. New York: Macmillan, 1932.

Bernstein, E. M. "Inflation in Relation to Economic Development," *I.M.F. Staff Papers*, Vol. II, No. 3, November, 1952.

Bittker, B. I. "Recommendation for Revision of Federal Estate and Gift Taxes," *Federal Tax Policies for Economic Growth and Stability*. Washington, D.C.: U.S. Government Printing Office, 1955.

Blackburn, J. O. "Intangible Taxes: A Neglected Revenue Source for States," *National Tax Journal*, June, 1965.

Blackstone, Sir William. *Commentaries on the Laws of England*. 3rd ed. Oxford: Clarendon Press, 1768.

Bloomberg, W. *The Age of Automation*. New York: League for Industrial Democracy, 1955.

Bollinger, L. L., J. K. Butters, and L. E. Thompson. *Effects of Taxation: Investments by Individuals*. Cambridge, Mass.: Harvard University Graduate School of Business Administration, 1953.

Boulding, K. "The Fruits of Progress and the Dynamics of Distribution," *American Economic Review, Papers and Proceedings*, May, 1953.

Bowen, J. C. "Some Yield Estimates for Transfer Taxes," *National Tax Journal*, March, 1959.

Bowley, A. L. *Wages and Income in the U.K. Since 1860*. Cambridge: Cambridge University Press, 1937.

Brazer, J. E. "A Program for Federal Tax Revision," *Michigan Pamphlets, No. 28. Institute of Public Administration*. Ann Arbor: University of Michigan, 1960.

Brems, H. "The Distributive Shares, Wage, Price, and Tax Policy," *Journal of the American Statistical Association*, September, 1962.

Bronfenbrenner, M., and F. D. Holzman. "A Survey of Inflation Theory," *American Economic Review*, September, 1963.

Brown, E. Carey. *Effects of Taxation Depreciation Adjustments for Price Changes*. Cambridge, Mass.: Harvard University Graduate School of Business Administration, 1952.

———. "Mr. Kaldor on Taxation and Risk-Taking," *Review of Economic Studies*, October, 1957.

Brown, E. H. Phelps. "The Share of Wages in National Income," *Economic Journal*, June, 1952.

———. "Accumulation, Productivity and Distribution," *Economic Journal*, June, 1953.

Buchanan, J. M. *The Public Finances*. Rev. ed. Homewood, Ill.: Irwin, 1965.

Butters, J. K., and J. Lintner. "Taxes and Mergers," *Harvard Business Review*, March, 1951.

Butters, J. K., J. Lintner, and W. L. Carey. *Effects of Taxation: Corporate Mergers*. Cambridge, Mass.: Harvard University Graduate School of Business Administration, 1951.

Bye, R. T. "Capital Formation and Inequality," *American Economic Review*, December, 1936.

Campion, D. J. M. "Estate Duty Saving," *British Tax Review*, November-December, 1959.

Campion, H. *Public and Private Property in Great Britain.* Oxford: Oxford University Press, 1939.

Campion, J., and O. Daniels. *The Distribution of National Capital.* Manchester: Manchester University Press, 1936.

Cannan, E. *Wealth.* 2nd ed. London: P. S. King and Son, 1924.

Carl-Saunders, A. M., and C. Jones. *A Survey of the Social Structure U.K.* Oxford: Clarendon Press, 1958.

Cartter, A. M. "A New Method of Relating British Capital Ownership and Estate Duty Liability to Income Groups," *Economica,* August, 1953.

Cerenville, P. *Les Impôts en Suisse.* Lausanne: Corbaz and Lie, 1898.

Chambers, S. P. "Taxation and the Supply of Capital for Industry," *Lloyds Bank Review,* January, 1949.

———. "The Capital Levy," *Lloyds Bank Review,* January, 1951.

Clark, C. "Public Finance and Changes in the Value of Money," *Economic Journal,* December, 1945.

———. *Welfare and Taxation.* Oxford: Catholic Social Guild, 1954.

Clark, J. B. *The Distribution of Wealth.* New York: Macmillan, 1899.

Clay, Sir H. *Property and Inheritance.* The New Way Series, No. 5. London: The Daily News Ltd., 1926.

Cohen-Stuart, A. J. "On Progressive Taxation," in *Classics in the Theory of Public Finance,* R. A. Musgrave and A. T. Peacock, eds. New York: Macmillan, 1958.

Cole, G. D. H. *The Simple Case for Socialism.* London: Gollancz, 1935.

———. *Socialist Economics.* London: Gollancz, 1950.

———. *A History of Socialist Thought.* New York: Macmillan, 1953.

Comstock, A. *Taxation in the Modern State.* New York: Longmans, Green & Company, 1929.

Conrad, A. N. "On the Calculation of Tax Burdens," *Economica,* November, 1955.

Copeland, M. A. "Determinants of the Distribution of Incomes," *American Economic Review,* March, 1947.

Copper-Willis, E. "Towards Equality. A Study of the Ownership of Wealth," *Fabian Publications.* London: Gollancz, 1930.

Crosland, C. A. R. *The Future of Socialism.* London: Cape, 1956.

———. *The Conservative Enemy.* London: Cape, 1962.

Crum, W. L. *The Distribution of Wealth.* Cambridge, Mass.: Harvard University Graduate School of Business Administration, 1935.

Dalton, H. *The Capital Levy Explained.* London: The Labour Publishing Company, Ltd., 1923.

———. *Some Aspects of the Inequality of Incomes in Modern Communities.* London: Routledge and Sons, 1925.

———. *Principles of Public Finance.* 3rd and 4th eds. London: Routledge and Sons, 1936, 1957.

De Jouvenal, B. *The Ethics of Redistribution.* Cambridge: Cambridge University Press, 1951.

Denison, E. F. "A Note on Private Saving," *Review of Economic Statistics,* August, 1958.

De Viti De Marco. *First Principles of Public Finance.* London: Cape, 1952.

DeWind, A. W. "The Approaching Crisis in Federal Estate and Gift Taxation," *California Law Review,* Vol. XXXVII, March, 1950.

Dickerson, R. W. V. "Estate and Gift Taxation in Canada," *British Tax Review*, July-August, 1964.

Dickerson, Z. C. "Fred M. Taylor's Views on Socialism," *Economica*, February, 1960.

Diebold, J. *Automation, Its Impact on Business and Labor*. Washington, D.C.: National Planning Association, May, 1959.

———. *Beyond Automation*. New York: McGraw-Hill, 1964.

Dobb, M. H. *On Economic Theory and Socialism*. London: Routledge and Paul, 1955.

———. *Capitalism, Yesterday and Today*. London: Lawrence and Wishart, 1958.

Dobrin, S. "Lenin on Equality, and the Webbs on Lenin," *Soviet Studies*, April, 1957.

Domar, E. D. "Capital Expansion, Rate of Growth and Employment," *Econometrica*, April, 1946.

Donnahoe, A. S. "Measuring State Tax Burdens," *Journal of Political Economy*, June, 1947.

Dosser, D. "Tax Incidence and Growth," *Economic Journal*, September, 1961.

———. "Towards a Theory of International Public Finance," *Kyklos*, Vol. XVI, 1963.

Due, J. "Net Worth Taxation," *Impôts sur la fortune y inclus droits de succession*. Institut International de Finances Publiques, Congrès de Zurich, September, 1960.

Dunlop, J. T. *Wage Determination Under Trade Unions*. New York: A. M. Kelley, 1950.

Dunn, Leroy. "A History of British Death Duties." Unpublished Ph.D. dissertation, London School of Economics, 1955-56.

Durbin, E. F. M. *Problems of Economic Planning*. London: Routledge and Paul, 1949.

Ecklund, G. N. "Our Federal Estate and Gift Taxes: Loopholes and Remedies," *University of Illinois, Current Economic Comment*, August, 1953.

Economist, The, 4 April, 1964.

Eigner, R. M. "Indian Income, Wealth and Expenditure Taxes," *National Tax Journal*, Vol. XII, June, 1959.

Eisenstein, S. "Are We Ready for Estate and Gift Tax Revision?" *Taxes*, Vol. XXIII, 1945.

Ellul, J. *The Technological Society*. New York: Knopf, 1964.

Fabricant, S. *Revaluations of Fixed Assets, 1925-34*. New York: National Bureau of Economic Research Bulletin, 1962.

Fagan, E. D. "Recent and Contemporary Theories of Progressive Taxation," *Journal of Political Economy*, August, 1938.

Federation of British Industries. *The Effects of Inflation on Industrial Capital Resources*. London, 1951.

———. *Estate Duty and the Family Business*. London, 1953.

Fijalkowski-Bereday. "The Equalizing Effects of Death Duties," *Oxford Economic Papers* (N.S.), June, 1950.

Finer, S. E. "The Political Power of Private Capital," *The Sociological Review*, July, 1956.

Fisher, J. A. "Taxation of Personal Incomes and Net Worth in Norway," *National Tax Journal*, March, 1958.

Gaitskell, H. "The Economic Aims of the Labor Party," *The Political Quarterly*, January-March, 1953.

Goldsmith, D. "Capitalism and Equality of Income," *American Economic Review*, Vol. XL, No. 2, May, 1950.

Goldsmith, R. W. *A Study of Saving in the United States*. Vol. III. Princeton: Princeton University Press, 1956.

Goodchild, W. P. "Some Points Arising in the Valuation for Estate Duty and Stamp Duty," *Journal of Institute of Actuaries*, Vol. LXXXIV, Part 3, 1958.

Goode, R. *The Individual Income Tax*. Washington, D.C.: Brookings Institution, 1964.

Graham, F. D. *Social Goals and Economic Institutions*. Princeton: Princeton University Press, 1948.

Groves, H. M. *Postwar Taxation and Economic Progress*. New York: McGraw-Hill, 1946.

————, ed. *Viewpoints on Public Finance*. New York: H. Holt, 1947.

————. "Retention of Estate and Gift Taxes by the Federal Government," *California Law Review*, Vol. XXXVIII, March, 1950.

————. *Federal Tax Treatment for the Family*. Washington, D.C.: Brookings Institution, 1963.

Groves, H. M., and L. Prober. "Equity Grounds for Property. Taxation Reexamined," *Land Economics*, May, 1951.

Gurley, J. C. "Fiscal Policy in a Growing Economy," *Journal of Political Economy*, December, 1953.

Hall, C. A. *Effects of Taxation: Executive Compensation and Retirement Plans*. Cambridge, Mass.: Harvard Business School, 1951.

Hall, Sir D. *Reconstruction and the Land*. London: Macmillan, 1941.

Hall, J. K. "The Incidence of Death Duties," *American Economic Review*, Vol. XXX, March, 1940.

Hamburger, W. "The Relation of Consumption to Wealth and the Wage Rate," *Econometrica*, January, 1955.

Hansen, B. "Aspects of Property Taxation," *Travaux de l'Institut International de Finances Publiques*, 1962.

Harberger, A. C. "Taxation, Resource Allocation and Welfare," in *The Role of Direct and Indirect Taxes in the Federal Revenue System*, J. F. Due, ed. Washington, D.C.: Brookings Institution, 1964.

Harding, C. D. *Green's Death Duties*. 4th ed. London: Butterworth, 1958.

Harrington, J. "The Inheritance Tax," *Annals of American Academy of Political and Social Science*, March, 1915.

Harrington, M. *The Accidental Century*. New York: Macmillan, 1965.

Harriss, C. Lowell. *Gift Taxation in the U.S.* Washington: American Council on Public Affairs, 1940.

————. "Estate Taxes and the Family Owned Business," *California Law Review*, Vol. XXXVII, March, 1950.

————. "The British Revaluation of Real Estate for Local Taxation," *National Tax Journal*, 1952.

————. "Sources of Injustice in Death Taxation," *National Tax Journal*, Vol. VII, December, 1954.

————. "Valuation of Property for Taxation," *Public Finance,* Vol. IX, No. 1, 1954.

von Hayek, F. A. "The Maintenance of Capital," *Economica,* August, 1935.

Hecht, J. S. *Unsolved Problems: National and International.* London: Jarrolds, 1930.

Henderson, H. D. "Inheritance and Inequality." *Daily News* pamphlet. London: 1926.

Hicks, J. R. "Distribution and Economic Progress," *Review of Economic Studies,* October, 1936.

————. *Theory of Wages.* New York: St. Martins Press, 1963.

Hicks, J. R., U. K. Hicks, and L. Rostas. *The Taxation of War Wealth.* 2nd ed. Oxford: Clarendon Press, 1942.

Hicks, U. K. *Public Finance.* Welwyn, Eng.: Nisbet, 1948.

————. "Direct Taxation and Economic Growth," *Oxford Economic Papers,* October, 1956.

————. "Mr. Kaldor's Plan for the Reform of Indian Taxes," *Economic Journal,* 1958.

Higgins, B. "A Note on Taxation and Inflation," *Canadian Journal of Economics and Political Science,* August, 1953.

Hill, T. P. "Income, Savings and Net Worth — the Savings Surveys of 1952-54," *Bulletin of the Oxford University Institute of Statistics,* May, 1955.

Hinrichs, H. H. "Underreporting of Capital Gains on Tax Returns," *National Tax Journal,* June, 1964.

Hobson, J. A. *Poverty in Plenty: The Ethics of Income.* New York: Macmillan, 1932.

Holt, C. C. "Averaging of Income for Tax Purposes," *National Tax Journal,* December, 1949.

Hoover, G. "The Economic Effects of Inheritance Taxes," *American Economic Review,* Vol. XVII, March, 1927.

Huebner, S. "The Inheritance Tax in the American Commonwealths," *Quarterly Journal of Economics,* Vol. XVIII, August, 1904.

Hunter, M. M. "The Inheritance Tax," *Annals of American Academy of Political and Social Science,* May, 1921.

Ilersic, A. R. "Estate Duty and Private Companies," *Accounting Research,* Vol. V, 1954.

————. *The Taxation of Capital Gains.* London: Staples Press, 1962.

International Tax Program, Harvard Law School, The World Tax Series. *Taxation in Australia,* 1958; *Taxation in Sweden,* 1959.

Jay, D. *The Socialist Case.* London: Faber and Faber, 1946.

————. "Labour and Tax Reform," *British Tax Review,* March, 1957.

————. *Socialism in the New Society.* New York: Longmans, Green & Co., 1962.

Jenkins, H. P. "Fiscal Equity in the Unequal Treatment of Unequals," *Journal of Political Economy,* August, 1951.

Jenkins, R. H. *Equality in New Fabian Essays* (pp. 76-81). London: Turnstile Press, 1952.

Jensen, J. P. *Property Taxation in the U.S.* Chicago: University of Chicago, 1931.

John of Paris. *De Potestate Regia et Papali* (ca. 1303), Chap. 7.

Johns, R. K. *Dymonds Death Duties.* 14th ed. London: Solicitors Law Stationery Society, 1965.

Jones, R. "An Essay on the Distribution of Wealth and on the Forces of Taxation (1790-1855)," *Reprints of Economic Classics.* New York: Kelly and Millman, 1956.

Kahn, H. *Personal Deductions in the Federal Income Tax.* New York: National Bureau of Economic Research, 1960.

Kaldor, N. "The Income Burden of Capital Taxes," *Review of Economic Studies,* Vol. IX, No. 2, Summer 1942.

———. "Alternative Theories of Distribution," *Review of Economic Studies,* Vol. XXIII, 1955-56.

———. "A Model of Economic Growth," *Economic Journal,* December, 1957.

———. *An Expenditure Tax.* London: Allen and Unwin, 1958.

———. "Economic Growth and the Problem of Inflation," *Economica,* N.S., Vol. XXVI, August-November, 1959.

———. *Essays on Economic Policy.* Vol. I. London: Duckworth, 1964.

Kaldor, N., and J. A. Mirrless. "A New Model of Economic Growth," *Review of Economic Studies,* June, 1962.

Kalecki, M. "A Theory of Commodity, Income and Capital Taxation," *Economic Journal,* September, 1937.

———. "The Determinants of the Distribution of the National Income," *Econometrica,* April, 1938.

———. *Essays in the Theory of Economic Fluctuations.* London: Allen and Unwin, 1939.

———. "The Economics of Full Employment," *Bulletin of the Oxford University Institute of Statistics* (Oxford, 1944).

———. *The Theory of Dynamic Economics.* New York: Rinehart, 1954.

Katona, G., and J. B. Lansing. "The Wealth of the Wealthy," *Review of Economics and Statistics,* February, 1964.

Keith, E. G. "How Should Wealth Transfers Be Taxed?" *American Economic Review,* Vol. XL, May, 1950.

Kessel, R. A. "Inflation Caused Wealth Re-distribution," *American Economic Review,* March, 1956.

Keynes, J. M. *Economic Consequences of the Peace.* London: Macmillan, 1920.

———. *The General Theory of Employment, Interest, and Money.* London: Macmillan, 1936.

Khan, E. M. "The Distribution of Wealth in Islam," *Pakistan Economic Journal,* June, 1951.

Kimmel, L. J. *Taxes and Economic Incentives.* Washington, D.C.: Brookings Institution, 1950.

Kirkaldy, A. W. *Wealth, Its Production and Distribution.* London: Methuen, 1920.

Klein, L. R., K. H. Straw, and P. Vandome. "Savings and Finances of the Upper Income Classes," *Bulletin of the Oxford University Institute of Statistics,* November, 1956.

Knight, F. H. "The Ethics of Liberalism," *Economica,* February, 1939.

———. "Idealism and Marxism," *Economica,* August, 1939.

Korah, V. L. "Estate Duty Testamentary Trusts of Foreign Lands," *British Tax Review*, March-April, 1960.

Kravis, I. B. "Relative Income Shares in Fact and Theory," *American Economic Review*, December, 1959.

Kuznets, S. *Shares of Upper Income Groups in Income and Housing*. New York: National Bureau of Economic Research, 1950.

———. "Economic Growth and Income Inequality," *American Economic Review*, March, 1955.

Labour Party. *Labour and the War Debt, a Statement of Policy for the Redemption of War Debt by a Levy on Accumulated Wealth*. London: The Labour Party, 1922.

Lampman, R. J. "Changes in the Share of Wealth Held by Top Wealth Owners, 1922-1956," *Review of Economics and Statistics*, November, 1959.

———. *The Share of Top Wealth Holders in National Wealth 1922-1956*. Princeton: National Bureau of Economic Research, 1962.

Langley, K. M. *Capital Gains Taxation*. London: Fabian Research Series, No. 150, 1952.

———. "Distribution of Capital in Private Hands 1936-39 and 1946-47," *Bulletin of the Oxford University Institute of Statistics*, December, 1950, February, 1951.

———. "An Analysis of the Asset Structure of Estates 1900-1949," *Bulletin of the Oxford University Institute of Statistics*, October, 1951.

———. "The Distribution of Private Capital, 1950-1951," *Bulletin of the Oxford University Institute of Statistics*, January, 1954.

Lansing, J. B., and H. Lydall. "A Comparison of the Distribution of Personal Income and Wealth in the U.S. and Great Britain," *American Economic Review*, March, 1959.

Lauderdale, J. N. *An Inquiry into the Nature of Public Wealth*. London: Constable and Company, 1804.

Lawday, D. J., and E. J. Mann. *Green's Death Duties*. 5th ed. London: Butterworth, 1963.

Lee, G. "Death Duties and the Private Company," *The Banker*, February, 1954.

Lent, G. E. *The Ownership of Tax Exempt Securities, 1913-1953*. New York: National Bureau of Economic Research, 1955.

Lepper, S. J. *Effects of Alternative Tax Structures on Individuals' Holdings of Financial Assets*. Yale Economic Essays, Vol. IV, No. 1, 1964.

Lewis, W. A. *The Principles of Economic Planning*. London: D. Dobson, 1959.

Lindahl, E. "Some Controversial Questions in the Theory of Taxation," in *Classics in the Theory of Public Finance*, R. A. Musgrave and A. T. Peacock, eds. New York: Macmillan, 1958.

Lindgreen, G. "Net Taxable Wealth, Income and Wage of Executive Directors of Large Swedish Companies," *Accounting Research*, January, 1954.

Lingard, J. R. "Estate Duty on Disclaimers of a Life Interest," *British Tax Review*, June, 1958.

Little, I. M. D. "Review of Kaldor's 'Expenditure Tax,'" *Economic Journal*, 1956.

Little, L. T. "Direct Taxation and the Inflationary and Deflationary Effects of Fiscal Policy," *Accounting Research*, July, 1950.

London and Cambridge Economic Service. *The British Economy: Key Statistics, 1900-1964.* London: Times Publishing Co., 1965.

Looker, C. "The Impact of Estate and Gift Taxes on Property Disposition," *California Law Review,* March, 1950.

Lydall, H. F. "Personal Savings and Consumption Expenditure," *Bulletin of the Oxford University Institute of Statistics,* October-November, 1953.

Lydall, H. F., and D. G. Tipping. "The Distribution of Personal Wealth in Britain," *Bulletin of the Oxford University Institute of Statistics,* Vol. XXIII, No. 1, February, 1961.

Lyndall, H. "The Life Cycle in Income, Saving and Asset Ownership," *Econometrica,* April, 1955.

MacGregor, D. H. *Public Aspects of Finance.* Oxford: Clarendon Press, 1939.

————. *Economic Thought and Policy.* Oxford: Oxford University Press, 1949.

Machlup, E. "The Effects of Income Re-distribution," *Review of Economic Studies,* February, 1943.

Magee, J. D. *Taxation and Capital Investment.* Washington, D.C.: Brookings Institution, 1939.

Magnus, P. *Gladstone, a Biography.* London: Murray, 1954.

Marshall, A. *Principles of Economics.* 8th ed. New York: Macmillan, 1950.

Meade, J. E. *A Neo-Classical Theory of Economic Growth.* London: Allen and Unwin, 1961.

————. "The Rate of Profit in a Growing Economy," *Economic Journal,* December, 1963.

————. *Efficiency, Equality and the Ownership of Property.* London: Allen and Unwin, 1965.

Meade, J. E., and F. H. Hahn. "The Rate of Profit in a Growing Economy," *Economic Journal,* June, 1965.

Meredith, H. O. "Rates and Taxes," *Economic Journal,* September, 1939.

Merrett, A. J. "Capital Gains Taxation: The Accrual Alternative," *Oxford Economic Paper,* Vol. XVI, No. 2, July, 1964.

Metzler, L. A. "Wealth, Saving and the Rate of Interest," *Journal of Political Economy,* April, 1951.

Mill, J. S. *Principles of Political Economy.* London: Longmans, Green, Reader, and Dyer, 1875.

Mincer, J. "Investment in Human Capital and Personal Income Distribution," *Journal of Political Economy,* August, 1958.

Mitchell, B. E. *Abstract of British Historical Statistics.* Cambridge: Cambridge University Press, 1962.

Monroe, J. G. "The Finance Act, 1957 — Estate Duty," *British Tax Review,* 1957.

Morgan, E. V. *The Structure of Property Ownership in Great Britain.* Oxford: Clarendon Press, 1960.

Morrison, H. *Socialization and Transport.* London: Constable, 1933.

Mortensen, C. M. "Estate and Trust Taxation from C.P.A.'s Point of View," *The Journal of Accountancy,* August, 1953.

Moulton, H. G. "Capital Formation and Inequality — A Reply," *American Economic Review,* December, 1936.

Musgrave, R. A. "On Incidence," *Journal of Political Economy,* August, 1953.

———. *The Pure Theory of Public Finance.* New York: McGraw-Hill, 1959.

Musgrave, R. A., and E. D. Domar. "Proportional Income Taxation and Risk Taking," in *Readings in the Economics of Taxation.* American Economic Association. London: Allen and Unwin, 1959.

Musgrave, R. A., and T. Krzyzaniak. *The Shifting of the Corporate Income Tax.* Baltimore: Johns Hopkins University Press, 1963.

Musgrave, R. A., and M. S. Painter. "The Impact of Alternative Tax Structures on Personal Consumption and Saving," *Quarterly Journal of Economics,* August, 1948.

Musgrave, R. A., and A. T. Peacock, eds. *Classics in the Theory of Public Finance.* New York: Macmillan, 1958.

Newsom, G. H. "Assessment of Estate Duty: The Basis of Valuation," *British Tax Review,* 1956.

———. "Assessment of Estate Duty: Goodwill and Court Proceedings," *British Tax Review,* 1956.

Norris, H. "Fiscal Policy and the Propensity to Consume," *Economic Journal,* 1946.

Northcliffe, E. B. "European Fiscal Systems," *British Tax Review,* 1958 and 1959.

Oakes, E. "The Federal Offset and the American Death Tax System," *Quarterly Journal of Economics,* August, 1940.

Oliver, H. M. *A Critique of Socio-economic Goals.* Bloomington: Indiana University Press, 1954.

O'Mahoney, J. C., ed. *The Challenge of Automation.* Washington, D.C.: Public Affairs Press, 1955.

Panter-Brick, J. "The Re-distribution of Wealth," *The Political Quarterly,* October-December, 1952.

Parsons, T. *The Structure of Social Action.* Glencoe, Ill.: Free Press, 1949.

Pasinetti, L. L. "Rate of Profit and Income Distribution in Relation to the Rate of Economic Growth," *Review of Economic Studies,* October, 1962.

———. "A Comment on Professor Meade's 'Rate of Profit in a Growing Economy,'" *Economic Journal,* June, 1964.

Peacock, A. T. *Income Re-distribution and Social Policy.* London: Cape, 1954.

———. "Economics of a Net Worth Tax for Britain," *British Tax Review,* November-December, 1963.

Peacock, A. T., and J. Wiseman. *The Growth of Public Expenditure in the United Kingdom.* National Bureau of Economic Research. Princeton: Princeton University Press, 1961.

Pearse, A. R. "Automatic Stabilization and British Taxes and Income," *Review of Economic Studies,* February, 1962.

Pechman, J. A. "An Analysis of Matched Estate and Gift Tax Returns," *National Tax Journal,* June, 1950.

———. *Essays in Federal Taxation.* New York: Committee for Economic Development, 1959.

Pesek, B. F. "Distribution Effects of Inflation and Taxation," *American Economic Review,* 1950.

Phillips, J. A. "Tax Factors Effecting Operation of Closely Held Corporations," *The Journal of Accounting,* February, 1953.

Phillips, W. "On Death," *British Tax Review,* March, 1958.

———. "How Income Tax Came Home to Roost," *British Tax Review,* September-October, 1959.

Pierson, N. G. *Principles of Economics.* New York: Macmillan, 1902.

Pigou, A. C. *A Study in Public Finance.* New York: Macmillan, 1929.

———. *The Economics of Welfare.* 4th ed. New York: Macmillan, 1932.

———. *Socialism v. Capitalism.* New York: Macmillan, 1937.

Poole, K. E. "The Problem of Simplicity in the Enactment of Tax Legislation, 1920-1940," *Journal of Political Economy,* December, 1951.

Potter, P. C. "Modern Methods of Minimizing Taxation: The Deed of Covenant," *British Tax Review,* June, 1956.

Preiser, E. "Property and Power in the Theory of Distribution," *International Economic Papers No. 2.* The International Economic Association. London: Macmillan, 1952.

President's 1963 Tax Message. *Hearings Before the Committee on Ways and Means.* Part 1. Rev. ed. House, 88th Cong., 1st Sess., 1963.

Prest, A. R. "On the Calculation of Tax Burden: A Rejoinder," *Economica,* August, 1956.

———. *Public Finance in Theory and Practice.* London: Weidenfeld and Nicolson, 1960.

———. *Public Finance in Underdeveloped Countries.* London: Weidenfeld and Nicolson, 1962.

———. "The Sensitivity of the Yield of Personal Income Tax in the U.K.," *Economic Journal,* September, 1962.

Preston, E. "Personal Savings Through Institutional Channels," *Bulletin of the Oxford University Institute of Statistics,* September, 1951.

Ratner, S. *American Taxation: Its History as a Social Force in Democracy.* New York: W. W. Norton, 1942.

Reuther, W. *The Challenge of Automation.* Washington, D.C.: Public Affairs Press, 1955.

———. "U.S.A. — A Free Society Faces the Age of Automation," *Times Review of Industry and Technology,* March, 1965.

Revell, J. R. S. "Settled Property and Death Duties," *British Tax Review,* May-June, 1961.

———. "Assets and Age." *Bulletin of the Oxford University Institute of Statistics,* Vol. XXIV, No. 3, August, 1962.

Rhodes, E. C. "The Distribution of Earned and Investment Incomes in the U.K.," *Economica,* February, 1949.

———. "The Distribution of Incomes and the Burden of Estate Duties in the U.K.," *Economica,* August, 1951.

———. "Earned and Investment Incomes, U.K. 1952-53," *Economica,* February, 1956.

Rhodes, James R. *Roseberry.* New York: Macmillan, 1965.

Rhys-Williams, Lady. *Taxation and Incentive.* Oxford: Oxford University Press, 1953.

Ricardo, D. *Principles of Political Economy and Taxation.* McCullach, ed. London: Murray, 1876.

Rignano, E. *The Social Significance of the Inheritance Tax*. New York: Knopf, 1924.

Rignano, E., and J. C. Stamp. *The Social Significance of Death Duties*. London: Noel Douglas, 1926.

Robbins, L. "Notes on Public Finance," *Lloyds Bank Review*, October, 1955.

Robertson, Sir D. *Lecture on Economic Principles*. London: Staples Press, 1957.

Robinson, J. *The Accumulation of Capital*. New York: Macmillan, 1956.

Robson, P. "Capital Levies in Western Europe After the Second World War," *Review of Economic Studies*, October, 1959.

Rolph, E. *The Theory of Fiscal Economics*. Berkeley: University of California Press, 1954.

Ropke, W. *Civitas Humania: A Humane Order of Society*. London: William Hodge, 1948.

Rose, J. R., and G. L. Wilson. "Valuation of Equity Capital," *American Economic Review*, December, 1939.

Rostas, L. "Capital Levies in Central Europe 1919-1924," *Review of Economic Studies*, Vol. VIII, October, 1940.

Rostow, W. W. *The British Economy of the Nineteenth Century*. Oxford: Clarendon Press, 1948.

Rudick, H. J. "A Proposal for an Accessions Tax," *Tax Law Review*, Vol. XXV, 1945.

———. "What Alternative to Estate and Gifts Taxes?" *California Law Review*, Vol. XXXVIII, March, 1950.

Ryan, W. J. L. *Price Theory*. New York: Macmillan, 1958.

Samuel, Sir Herbert. "The Taxation of the Various Classes of the People," *Journal of the Royal Statistical Society*, 1919.

Samuelson, P. A. "Fiscal Policy and Income Determination," *Quarterly Journal of Economics*, August, 1942.

Sandford, C. T. "Taxing Inheritance and Capital Gains," Hobart Paper 32, Institute of Economic Affairs, London, 1965.

Sandral, D. M. "Taxation of Various Classes of the People," *Journal of the Royal Statistical Society*, Vol. XCIV, Part 1.

Sargan, J. D. "The Distribution of Wealth," *Econometrica*, October, 1957.

Saunders, T. H. *Effects of Taxation on Executives*. Cambridge, Mass.: Harvard Business School, 1950.

Schlatter, R. *Private Property — The History of an Idea*. New Brunswick, N.J.: Rutgers University Press, 1951.

Schouten, D. B. J. "Theory and Practice of Capital Levies in the Netherlands," *Bulletin of the Oxford University Institute of Statistics*, Vol. X, No. 4, April, 1948.

Schwartz, E. L. "The Distorting Effects of Direct Taxation," *American Economic Review*, March, 1951.

———. "Will Your Business Die with You?" *Harvard Business Review*, September-October, 1954.

Seligman, E. R. A. *The Shifting and Incidence of Taxation*. 5th ed. New York: Columbia University Press, 1926.

———. *Essays in Taxation*. 10th ed. New York: Macmillan, 1931.

Seltzer, L. H. *The Nature and Tax Treatment of Capital Gains*. New York: National Bureau of Economic Research, 1951.

Sewill, B. *Treasure on Earth.* London: Conservative Political Centre, 1960.

Shackle, G. L. S. "The Nature of the Inducement to Invest," *Review of Economic Studies,* October, 1940.

Shere, L. "Taxation and Inflation Control," *American Economic Review,* December, 1948.

Shirras, G. F. *Science of Public Finance.* 3rd ed. New York: Macmillan, 1936.

————. "Methods of Estimating the Burden of Taxation," *Journal of the Royal Statistical Society,* Vol. CVI, Part 3, 1943.

Shirras, G. F., and L. Rostas. *The Burden of British Taxation.* New York: Macmillan, 1943.

Shoup, C. S. *Ricardo on Taxation.* London: Oxford University Press, 1960.

Shultz, W. J. *The Taxation of Inheritance.* Boston: Houghton Mifflin, 1926.

Sidgwick, H. *Principles of Political Economy.* 3rd ed. New York: Macmillan, 1901.

Silverman, H. A. *Taxation: Its Incidence and Effects.* New York: Macmillan, 1931.

Simons, H. C. *Personal Income Taxation.* Chicago: University of Chicago Press, 1938.

————. *Federal Tax Reform.* Chicago: University of Chicago Press, 1950.

Simpson, H. D. "Incidence of Real Estate Taxes," *American Economic Review,* June, 1932.

Sims, B. J. "Finance for Estate Duty," *British Tax Review,* December, 1956.

Smith, A. *Wealth of Nations.* 5th ed. London: Methuen, 1904.

Smith, D. Throop. *Effects of Taxation, Corporate Financial Policy.* Cambridge, Mass.: Harvard Graduate School of Business Administration, 1952.

————. "Note on Inflationary Consequences of High Taxation," *Review of Economics and Statistics,* August, 1952.

————. *Federal Tax Reform.* New York: McGraw-Hill, 1961.

Smith, H. "The Economics of Socialism Reconsidered," *Economic Journal,* September, 1955.

Smith, H. E. *Hanson's Death Duties.* 10th ed. London: Sweet and Maxwell, 1956.

Somers, H. M. "Estate Taxes and Business Mergers," *Journal of Finance,* Vol. XII, May, 1958.

Soward, A. W., and W. E. Willan. *The Taxation of Capital.* London: Waterlow and Sons, 1919.

Stamp, Sir J. *Wealth and Taxable Capacity.* London: King and Son, 1922.

————. *Current Problems of Finance and Government.* London: King and Son, 1924.

————. "Inheritance: Practical Proposals," *Statistical Journal,* March, 1926.

————. "Inheritance as an Economic Factor," *Economic Journal,* September, 1926.

————. "Inheritance: A Sample Survey," *Economic Journal,* December, 1930.

————. *Taxation During the War.* London: Oxford University Press, 1932.

Stark, W. *Jeremy Bentham's Economic Writings.* Vol. I. London: Allen and Unwin, 1952.

Statist, The. 1 March, 1963, and 10 April, 1964.

Steindel, J. "Long-Run Changes in the Propensity to Save," *Bulletin of the Oxford University Institute of Statistics,* Vol. VII, Nos. 6 and 7, May, 1945.
———. *Maturity and Stagnation in American Capitalism.* Oxford: Blackwell, 1952.
Stewart, M. "The Wealth Tax," *Bankers' Magazine,* 1963.
Stigler, G. T. *Five Lectures on Economic Problems.* New York: Macmillan, 1950.
Stone, R. "Private Saving in Britain, Past, Present and Future," *The Manchester School of Economic and Social Studies,* Vol. XXXII, No. 2, May, 1964.
Straw, K. H. "Consumers' Net Worth: The 1953 Savings Survey," *Bulletin of the Oxford University Institute of Statistics,* February, 1956.
Streeten, P. P. "The Effect of Taxation on Risk-Taking," *Oxford Economic Papers,* October, 1953.
———. "Some Problems Raised by R. C. on Taxation," *Bulletin of the Oxford University Institute of Statistics,* November, 1955.
———. "A Note on the Kaldor Speculation and Economic Stability," *Review of Economic Studies,* October, 1958.
Strotz, R. H. "How Income Ought to Be Distributed: A Paradox in Distributive Ethics," *Journal of Political Economy,* June, 1958.
Surrey, S. S. "Federal Estate and Gift Taxes," *California Law Review,* March, 1950.
Sweezy, M. Y. "Distribution of Wealth and Income Under the Nazis," *Review of Economic Statistics,* November, 1939.
Swift, T. F. "Changes in Estate Duty Law," *Journal of the Institute of Actuaries,* 1960.
Tait, A. A. "A Comment on Rates of Taxation Varied According to Consanguinity," *Finanzarchiv,* N.F., Band 25, Heft 2, July, 1966.
———. "Death Duties in Britain," *Public Finance,* Vol. XV, Nos. 3-4, 1960.
———. "The Economic and Legal Interpretation of 'Open Market Price,' " *British Tax Review,* June-August, 1965.
Tawney, R. H. *Equality.* 4th ed. London: Allen and Unwin, 1964.
Tayleur, J. "The Valuation of Goodwill," *Accounting Research,* January, 1954.
Taylor, O. H. "Economics and the Idea of Natural Laws," *Quarterly Journal of Economics,* November, 1929.
Tew, B. "Edith," *Three Banks' Review,* June, 1955.
———. *Essays on the Welfare State.* London: Allen and Unwin, 1958.
Tomlinson, A. "Gift Taxes and Tenancies by the Entirety," *The Journal of Accountancy,* September, 1959.
Tribune Pamphlet, Tribune Publications, London, 1951.
Turvey, R. *The Economics of Real Property.* London: Allen and Unwin, 1957.
U.N. Economic Bulletin for Europe. *Changes in the Structure of Taxation in Europe.* Vol. II, No. 3, New York, 1950.
Van Sickle, J. V. "The Fallacy of a Capital Levy," *Journal of Political Economy,* 1926.
———. *Direct Taxation in Austria.* Cambridge, Mass.: Harvard University Press, 1931.

Vickrey, W. "The Rationalization of Succession Taxation," *Econometrica,* July-October, 1944.

———. *Agenda for Progressive Taxation.* New York: Ronald Press, 1947.

Victoria, Queen. *Queen Victoria's Letters.* London: Murray, 1907-30.

Walker, G. B. S. "Valuation of Minority Shareholders in Private Companies for Estate Duty Purposes," *British Tax Review,* March, 1958.

Walker, G. M. *The Things That Are Caesar's.* New York: A. L. Fowle, 1922.

Wallich, H. C. "Taxation of Capital Gains in the Light of Recent Economic Developments," *National Tax Journal,* June, 1965.

Weaver, F. "Taxation and Re-distribution in the U.K.," *Review of Economics and Statistics,* August, 1950.

Wedgewood, J. *The Economics of Inheritance Taxation.* London: Routledge, 1929.

West, M. *The Inheritance Tax.* 2nd ed. New York: Columbia University Press, 1908.

Wheatcroft, G. S. A. "Modern Methods of Minimizing Taxation: Settlements Inter-Vivos," *British Tax Review,* 1957.

———. "Feather-Bedding Death, or Second Thoughts on Section 38," *British Tax Review,* 1958.

———. *The Taxation of Gifts and Settlements.* 3rd ed. London: Pitman, 1958.

———. "Feather-Bedding Death Further Deliberated," *British Tax Review,* 1959.

———. "The Administrative Problems of a Wealth Tax," *British Tax Review,* 1963.

———. "Avoiding Estate Duty on Aunt Eliza's Death," *British Tax Review,* 1964.

———. "Estate and Gift Taxes — A Comparison," *British Tax Review,* September-October, 1964.

Whittle, P., and H. O. A. Wold. "A Model Explaining the Pareto Law of Wealth Distribution," *Econometrica,* October, 1957.

Williams, A. *Public Finance and Budgetary Policy.* London: Allen and Unwin, 1963.

Williams, R. S. "Fiscal Policy and the Propensity to Consume," *Economic Journal,* 1945.

Willis, J. *The Mitigation of the Tax Penalty on Fluctuating or Irregular Incomes.* Toronto: Canadian Tax Foundation, 1951.

Young, A. "Do the Statistics of the Concentration of Wealth in the U.S. Mean What They Are Commonly Assumed to Mean?" *Journal of the American Statistical Association,* March, 1917.

Young, M. D. *The Rise of the Meritocracy.* Baltimore: Penguin, 1963.

GOVERNMENT PUBLICATIONS USED

U.K. *Finance Acts*

   1894 (57 & 58 Vict.) c. 30.
   1910 (10 Edw. VII & 1 Geo. V) c. 8.
   1930 (20 & 21 Geo. V) c. 28.

1947 (10 & 11 Geo. VI) c. 35.
1950 (14 Geo. VI) c. 15.
1954 (2 & 3 Eliz. II) c. 44.
1957 (5 & 6 Eliz. II) c. 49.

U.K. *Inland Revenue*

Estate Duty and Family Business. Report on Statistical Investigation by the Board of Inland Revenue. Cmd. 8295, 1950-51.

U.K. *Inland Revenue*

Reports of the Commissioners:

Report	Year	Cmd.	Vol.
64	1921	1436	XIV
66	1923	1934	XII
68	1924-25	2547	XIV
70	1927	2989	X
72	1929-30	3500	XV
74	1931-32	4027	XI
76	1932-33	4456	XIII
78	1934-35	5015	IX
80	1936-37	5574	XII
82	1938-39	6099	XII
84	1941:1945-46	6770	XIII
86	1943:1945-46	6772	XIII
88	1945:1945-46	6774	XIII
90	1947:1947-48	7362	XII
92	1949:1950	8052	XII
94	1951:1951-52	8436	XV
96	1953:1953-54	9030	XVI
98	1955:1955-56	9667	XXI
100	1957:1957-58	341	XV
102	1959:1959-60	922	XVII
104	1961:1961-62	1598	XVII
105	1962:1961-62	1096	XX
106	1963:1962-63	2283	–
107	1964:1963-64	2573	–

U.K. *Memoranda on the Classification and Incidence of Imperial and Local Taxes.* Cmd. 9258, 1899.

U.K. National Economic Development Council. *Conditions Favourable to Faster Growth.* H.M.S.O., April, 1963.

U.K. *Parliamentary Debates.* Commons 127, 324, 335, 480.

U.K. *Report of Commission on National Debt and Taxation.* The Colwyn Report. Vol. XI. Cmd. 2800, 1927.

U.K. *Colwyn Commission: Appendices.* Cmd. 2800, 1927.

U.K. *Minutes of Evidence to the Committee on the National Debt.* Vols. I and II. 1927.

U.K. *Royal Commission on the Taxation of Profits and Income.* H.M.S.O., Second Report, Cmd. 9474, 1954.

U.S. Advisory Committee to the Treasury Department. *Federal and Estate Gift Taxes.* Washington, D.C.: U.S. Government Printing Office, 1947.

U.S. *Commission on Industrial Relations Final Report and Testimony.* Senate Doc. 415, 64th Cong., 1st Sess., 1916.

U.S. House of Representatives, 708, 72nd Cong., 1st Sess., 1932.

U.S. Joint Committee on the Economic Report. *Federal Tax Policy for Economic Growth and Stability.* Washington, D.C.: U.S. Government Printing Office, 1955.

U.S. Joint Committee, 88th Congress (2nd Sess.). *The Federal Tax System: Facts and Problems 1964.* 1964.

Report to the National Commission on Technology, Automation, and Economic Progress, *Technology and the American Economy.* Vol. I, February, 1966.

Statistics of Income, 1926-1960. U.S. Treasury Department, Internal Revenue Service.

Index

233

97; consanguinity restricts, 101n; and gifts tax, 144
Regressive: wealth tax, 33; price changes are, 37, 56
Rentiers: and automation, 31
Resources: inefficient use, 10
Retirement: size of wealth held, 34
Revoking: a transfer, 157
Risk: and asset holdings, 56; incentive and taxation, 149; definition, 185
Robbins, L.: distributive society, 102, 105
Roosevelt, F. D. R.: on trusts, 165n

Saving: marginal propensity to save, and inequality, 23, 57; and wealth held, 34-37, 113; discretionary, 35; and corporate businesses, 57; and consanguinity rates, 99; Rignano proposals, 106, 108; deferred taxes encourage, 113; and bequeathing power, 118, 119; generations and accruals, 149; incentive and taxation, 149; rejection of wealth tax, 191; and wage earners, 215
Securities: quoted stocks, 38n, 55, 56. See also Assets; Stock
Security: and redistribution, 10; quantified, 20; and size of wealth held, 34; as part of tax base, 147, 150; and completion of transfer, 157; and trusts, 163
Servants: automation and demand for, 32
Shares: speculative, accepted by government, 112-113. See also Assets; Stock
Small businesses: reduced rates, 93
Social choice determination: and wealth, 14-15
Social security: and automation, 30
Solomon Islanders: money, 127
Splitting: an estate, 175
Standard of living: and consanguinity rates, 98
State-owned assets: by high taxation of wealth, 16
Stock: gifts of, as options, 145
Stocks: and net worth taxation, 79

Succession duties, 86
Supreme Court: decision on income tax 1894, 62
Surtax: by a net worth tax, 81
Sweden: value of shares and wealth taxation, 80n; gifts tax, 142n

Talent: and wealth ownership, 11
Tax: on wealth, structure of, 60
Taxable unit: and gifts tax, 133; with marriage and cumulation, 160
Taxation: double, 149
Tax base: erosion, 91
Tax code: legal code upheld by, 99
Taxes: relationship between wealth and other, 60
Tax rates: in excess of 100 per cent, 63; and capital growth, 89; as a function of time, 115; reduced on gifts, 125; and relationship between taxes, 140
Technology: and capital accumulation, 23, 26; and substitutability of labor and capital, 28
Timing: of levy payments, 77; lapse between gift and transfer, 126; of tax liability, 175; of gifts and work effort, 180
Transfer: problem of completion, 156; bilateral, 156; between spouses, 160; between parents and dependents, 160-162
Trust: beneficiary under a, 4
Trusts: in estimates of wealth distribution, 5; and avoidance, 87, 90, 91; and gifts, 132, 135; and accruals tax, 137; tax unit, 161; advantages, 164; avoidance by, 165n; capital taxed, 199. See also Avoidance
Turning points: and asset price changes, 39, 55

Underdeveloped economies: need for tax change, 202
Underwriting: price changes and government, 110
Unemployment: and distribution of wealth, 8; and technology, 29, 30
Union of the Soviet Socialist Republics: theory of property, 3